COMMUNITY AND PUBLIC

Community Development Foundation

Community Development Foundation (CDF) was set up in 1968 to pioneer new forms of community development. CDF strengthens communities by ensuring the effective participation of people in determining the conditions which affect their lives through:

- influencing policy makers
- promoting best practice
- providing support for community initiatives.

As a leading authority on community development in the UK and Europe, CDF is a Home Office sponsored non-departmental public body and receives substantial backing from local and central government, trusts and business.

CDF promotes community development by enabling people to work in partnership with public authorities, government, business and voluntary organisations to regenerate their communities through:

- local action projects
- conferences and seminars
- consultancies and training programmes
- research and evaluation services
- parliamentary and public policy analysis
- information services
- *CDF News*, a bi-monthly newsletter
- publications.

Chairman: Alan Haselhurst, MP
Chief Executive: Alison West

Community Development Foundation
60 Highbury Grove
London N5 2AG
Tel: 071 226 5375
Fax: 071 704 0313

Bradford & Ilkley Community College

Bradford & Ilkley Community College's mission is to promote and underpin the local and national economy and the social fabric of Bradford by providing comprehensive education and training of recognised quality.

Principal: Dr Paul J. Gallagher

Bradford & Ilkley Community College
Great Horton Road
Bradford
West Yorkshire BD7 1AY
Tel: 0274 75 3026

COMMUNITY AND PUBLIC POLICY

Edited by
Hugh Butcher, Andrew Glen,
Paul Henderson and Jerry Smith

Pluto Press

LONDON • BOULDER, COLORADO

in association with

BRADFORD
& ILKLEY
COMMUNITY
COLLEGE

COMMUNITY
DEVELOPMENT
FOUNDATION

First published 1993 by Pluto Press
345 Archway Road, London N6 5AA
and 5500 Central Avenue
Boulder, Colorado 80301, USA
in association with
Community Development Foundation
60 Highbury Grove
London N5 2AG
Registered Charity No. 306130

British Library Cataloguing in Publication Data
A catalogue record for this book is
available from the British Library

ISBN 0 745 30800 7 hb
ISBN 0 745 30801 5 pb

Library of Congress Cataloging in Publication Data
Applied for.

Designed and produced for Pluto Press by
Chase Production Services, Chipping Norton
Typeset from disks by
Stanford Desktop Publishing Services, Milton Keynes
Printed in Finland by WSOY

Contents

Foreword

The relevance of 'community' to public policy is increasingly evident, as is the need to clarify the underlying concepts which inform the decisions of policy makers.

We are particularly pleased that staff from the Community Development Foundation and Bradford & Ilkley Community College have worked together to produce this publication because it has ensured the breadth of approach required by the subject. For an academic or operational organisation to have attempted the project on its own would have resulted in a loss of the mix of ideas and practice which is a distinctive feature of the book.

This has been a North of England initiative, and the end product is proof again that sustained and high quality local and regional work can contribute in major ways to national and international debate. We have no doubt that the questions raised by the contributors will be analysed and discussed in a variety of academic, policy and practice arenas.

There are a number of implications which flow from the book's conclusions. It is gratifying to learn, therefore, that our respective organisations are to play a lead role in taking forward plans for developing training proposals based on the book's ideas. The extent to which these succeed will be one measure of how 'community' can become more central to policy-making processes in the twenty-first century.

We have been fortunate to have had a committed and experienced editorial team to guide and prepare the book. Our thanks go to them as well as to the contributors and support staff.

Alison West
Chief Executive
Community Development
Foundation

Dr Paul J. Gallagher
Principal
Bradford & Ilkley
Community College

Acknowledgements

Publication of this book represents a significant element of an ongoing partnership between Bradford & Ilkley Community College and the Northern Office of the Community Development Foundation. The ideas developed for the book, and the commissioning and editing of the contributions, have thus taken place in a context of exploring the policy, practice and training implications of *Community and Public Policy*. This wider programme of work, developed over a period of more than three years, has been the major building block for the book.

In the course of preparing the publication we arranged two consultations, which were attended by a majority of the authors. This was an indication of their involvement in the book's evolution and our thanks go to them for this as well as for the care they took to write to the book's themes and structure.

Eric Turner, previously a principal lecturer at BICC, was fully involved with the project until his retirement in 1992. His reliability and wisdom were of enormous value and we wish to acknowledge his particular contribution. We were also fortunate to have been able to employ Geoffrey Driver at BICC for a six-month period to help carry out some empirical research into community practice. His handling and analysis of data assisted the book's progress at a key point. Equally essential at BICC was the secretarial support provided by Sue Anderson. She dealt with the flow of manuscripts enthusiastically and efficiently.

CDF's Head of Publications, Catriona May, gave support throughout the book's gestation, and was actively involved in the final editing and production phase. In addition to thanking her, it is also necessary that explicit recognition is given to our respective institutions. BICC and CDF provided encouragement and time to enable us to carry out the work, and we appreciate their foresight in doing this.

Hugh Butcher, Andrew Glen,
Paul Henderson, Jerry Smith

Contributors

Sarah Banks is a Tutor in Community and Youth Work at Durham University. She has worked as a community development officer both in statutory and voluntary settings, and has a particular interest in working with young people and communities in rural areas, and in the ethical and value issues underpinning youth, community and social work.

Hugh Butcher has practised as a social worker and a community worker, and has taught sociology, social policy and community practice at a number of UK colleges and universities. He is currently Head of Department of Community Studies at Bradford & Ilkley Community College, West Yorkshire.

Lola Clinton is an independent researcher on social policy in the arts and community development. She was the researcher for the National Inquiry into Arts and Communities, and has recently completed a report on black organisations and community development. She has published a number of reports and articles on related issues.

Andrew Glen has a practice background in community work and social work and has experience of voluntary sector management. He is currently a Senior Lecturer teaching on community studies and social work courses at Bradford & Ilkley Community College, West Yorkshire.

Mohammed Habeebullah is an experienced community development practitioner who has worked with multi-ethnic communities in Rochdale and Manchester, in paid and voluntary capacities, for over 15 years. He was a member of a community development team at Rochdale Community Project between 1981 and 1991, where he was responsible for several major initiatives in the Asian voluntary sector particularly around employment and training, as well as work on models of participation and involvement which spanned the boundaries between communities. He currently works for Rochdale Metropolitan Borough Council. He is Chair of the Kashmiri Youth Project in Rochdale.

Paul Henderson is Director, North of England and Scotland, of the Community Development Foundation. He has been closely involved with community development for more than 20 years, initially as a practitioner and trainer, and more recently as a consultant and manager. He has written extensively on the theory and practice of community work and community practice.

Jenny Lynn manages the economic programme for Hulme City Challenge, a major urban regeneration partnership in Manchester. Previously, she led an economic development team for Manchester City Council which specialised in community-based economic initiatives, and for many years ran a co-operative development agency in South Wales.

Liz McShane is an independent researcher and consultant in community development and community-based work in health and welfare. From 1989 to 1993 she was the Co-ordinator of the Community Support Programme, a pilot programme in community care in Northern Ireland. She has lectured on social policy and has experience of working with community groups on evaluation and development.

Helen Meekosha is a Senior Lecturer in Community Work at the University of New South Wales, Australia. She worked as a community worker in Manchester and Bradford, before moving to Australia in 1979, where she helped to establish the Illawarra Migrant Resource Centre in Wollongong, near Sydney. She has published research on immigrant access to community services, feminism and disability, access and equity in universities, community conflict and violence, and is currently working on disability, representation and participation.

Maurice Mullard is Principal Lecturer in Economics and Public Policy at Bradford & Ilkley Community College and he is also Visiting Professor at the University of Liberec in the Czech Republic. His most recent publications include *Local Government Under Thatcherism* (1991) with Hugh Butcher, *Understanding Economic Policy* (1992) and *The Politics of Public Expenditure* (1993). He is also at present working on *Policy Challenges for the 1990s*.

Nigel Roome is an academic commentator and practitioner in the area of environmental management and social change. His work has included the relationship between environmental policies and community policy and practice. He has lectured on environmental policy in the UK before taking up his current post as Professor of Business and the Environment at York University, Ontario, Canada. Previously he chaired a Rural Community Council and undertook project evaluation for the Countryside Commission and the Nature Conservancy Council.

David Slater was a member of the team at CDF's Rochdale Community Project between 1981 and 1991. He is currently working on a neighbourhood forum model and community development strategy for the Citizens' Unit at York City Council, with particular emphasis on the experiences of residents from ethnic minorities. He has extensive experience of development work with different communities, and of working with different models of participation, seen from both the community and the local authority point of view. He has published a number of articles on community work issues.

Jerry Smith is Regional Manager, North-East, of the Community Development Foundation. He has worked in community development since the early 1970s, in the Midlands and North of England. He is interested in urban renewal and community regeneration, particularly in applying organisational development and other techniques to the problem of building capacities of communities to respond to increasingly complex policy agendas. He has published widely on community development and related issues.

Mollie Weatheritt was, until early 1993, Assistant Director of the Police Foundation. She is currently on secondment from the Foundation to HM Inspectorate of Constabulary where she advises on methods of inspection. Her review of developments in community policing was published in 1986 as *Innovations in Policing* and she has since written and lectured widely on this and related topics.

Preface

Community and Public Policy explores how the ideas of community and 'community practice' have been incorporated within a wide spectrum of public and social policies during the 1980s and early 1990s. Some approaches (for example community care, community policing and community arts) have become an accepted part of the social landscape, and have provided a focus for public debate and political commentary. Other approaches are more accurately described as emergent. They are all the outcome of a search by decision makers and practitioners for new models of policy making and service delivery that offer forward-looking alternatives to current approaches to public policy.

We call this new kind of policy 'community policy'. It is not an alternative to, or substitute for, 'economic', 'social' or 'law and order' policy; rather, it is an *approach* to policy making and service delivery that can be used *within* each of these and other policy arenas. It represents a new way of 'framing' and thinking about policy goals, and thus represents a significant challenge to conventional ways in which policy makers see and carry out their work.

The idea for the book grew out of a series of meetings between staff of Bradford & Ilkley Community College, and the northern office of the Community Development Foundation. In the course of developing a number of joint initiatives we found we were increasingly identifying some interesting policy anomalies.

We had all lived through a decade in which the word 'community' had not only survived but in some cases thrived in the lexicon of a government committed to the pursuit of possessive individualism.

Further, we noted in common with many others the reductions in funding available to support community initiatives, both in our own locality and nationally; yet our suspicion – which we could not prove but which begins to be vindicated by the results of some preliminary research reported in this book – was that despite this the number of people engaged in community practice has not decreased and might well be increasing.

Again, while all manner of experimentation and organisational advances had been taking place within community practice – from the founding of the Standing Conference on Community Development and developments in accreditation and training to the burgeoning army of trainers and consultants engaging with communities – virtually nothing had been written about 'community intervention' from a social science standpoint or even a practice–theory perspective since the early 1980s.

Finally, we shared the feeling – growing in political, professional and academic circles – that the potential for creative problem solving through established approaches to public policy making was nearing exhaustion. Conventional ways of thinking were failing to address the manifold problems facing late twentieth-century Britain. Market models and state intervention, while continuing to play important roles in structuring collective action to address social problems, either separately or in tandem, can no longer be seen as providing the only options from which policy responses are to be constructed.

Emergent community principles and models seemed to offer a way forward which we felt was well worth exploring in some depth.

There was then, we sensed, a gap which needed to be filled and to edit a book on the subject of the place of 'community' in public policy appeared a good way to begin.

The book is aimed at a varied readership: community practitioners themselves, those responsible for making and implementing community-related policies and strategies at both local and national levels, students, and the managers of community work agencies being perhaps the principle ones.

It is organised to be dipped into as well as read from cover to cover. Part 1 clears the conceptual ground, examining: the meanings of key terms; the roots, trends and main issues surrounding our central concepts of 'community policy' and 'community practice'; the impact of social, cultural, political and economic changes on community practice since the 1960s; and the reasons why 'community' has become such a feature of various public policies in recent years.

Part 2 takes six policy areas – by no means an exhaustive list but one chosen to indicate the range of applications of 'community' in public policy – and critically considers the backgrounds, experiences and prospects of each.

Part 3 reviews the present status and future possibilities for community and public policy from three important political/philosophical perspectives: environmentalism, equality, and democratic citizenship.

The final section (Part 4) summarises some of the major findings from Parts 1 and 2 of the book and provides an opportunity for bringing together the political/philosophical perspectives of Part 3 in a way that establishes a framework for examining community policies and practices for the future.

The contributors are drawn from the ranks of experienced community practitioners – some of whom have moved on to teaching or policy work – and we hope that the book, while representing an important and nowadays rare contribution to theory in this field, nevertheless remains firmly rooted in the experiences of communities and those who work with them.

In summary then, *Community and Public Policy* provides a wide-ranging overview of theoretical and political debates about the relationship between public policy and community values. At the same time we have sought to go beyond reviewing, synthesising, and offering critical commentary on existing thinking and practice; we have edited this book in the hope that it will have a role to play in moving forward public policy planning in a way that will help meet the challenges to be faced by society as it approaches the twenty-first century.

Hugh Butcher
Andrew Glen
Paul Henderson
Jerry Smith

Part 1 Concepts and Context

1 Introduction: Some Examples and Definitions

Hugh Butcher

To explore the relationship between community and public policy would seem, at first sight, to be an unpromising – perhaps even slightly perverse – undertaking. 'Community', as it has been noted on countless occasions, lacks definitional precision. It is one of those 'hoorah' words that seems to encourage warm and positive feelings at the expense of precise and meaningful analysis. Not only that, so-called 'community policies' can easily be seen as something of a rag-bag of programmes and initiatives that have little in common. What, it may be asked, has community care in common with community policing, community architecture with community medicine? Very little, answers the cynic, except perhaps the positive associations that come from deploying the term 'community' itself. The suspicion of lack of substance is reinforced further if it is assumed that community policies must imply the employment of trained community workers, or at least people equipped with some community work skills. The most cursory examination reveals that many community initiatives seem to get by without the employment of those with specialist skills as community practitioners. For all these reasons the conclusion may be drawn that 'community and public policy' is too chimeral and vague a subject to warrant sustained and serious study.

There may be more than a grain of truth in such a conclusion, though it is by no means the whole story. It is certainly true that the subject must be approached with caution; the pitfalls and complexities involved in addressing the theories and arguments explored in this book are ignored at our peril. We must not for example assume that because a policy is called a 'community' policy it differs from other, 'non-community', policies. It is precisely because we acknowledge such traps that we begin with a determined effort to clarify and pin down the key terms to be used throughout this study.

One of the biggest problems to be addressed in any attempt to define terms in a relevant and comprehensive way is the range, number and diversity of such policies and initiatives. In one study Peter Willmott (1989) surveyed five of these in some detail (including local government decentralisation and community policing) and provided briefer portraits of eight others (embracing for example community arts, community education and community social work). In another overview David Donnison (1989) touched on a still wider range of projects and initiatives which he saw as exemplifying the 'community-based approach'. These included initiatives like neighbourhood councils, youth projects, community businesses and housing co-operatives – all either directly funded, or given arms-length support, by public authorities. Additionally, new 'community' initiatives seem to be developed and publicised with alarming rapidity; recent examples include 'community prisons' (Woolf and Tumim, 1991) and 'community pharmacy' (Joint Working Party on the Future of Community Pharmacy, 1992). One of our first tasks, then, is to identify the key characteristics of what *we* mean by community policies and initiatives, specifying with rigour those characteristics that will enable us to sift out contemporary policies that rest on virtually nothing other than the semantic attractiveness embodied in the use of the term 'community' itself.

Community Policies: Five Brief Illustrations

Clarification will be facilitated if the distinctions to be drawn can be immediately related to specific examples. The meaning of community and community values, of public policy and community policy, will become clearer to the extent that their application is made explicit. We begin, therefore, with thumbnail sketches of five community policies. Most of them will receive much fuller treatment later in the book (indeed community care and community government have chapters to themselves in Part 2). All we seek to do at this stage is to introduce them, providing only that detail necessary to enable identification and illustration of their most important, general and defining characteristics. We have, therefore, deliberately chosen examples that illustrate the *range* of policy goals pursued that derive from *both* central and local government policy making and that point up the *diversity* of values attributed to the community approach.

Community Care

This is one of the longest established community policies and is perhaps the one that currently has an impact on more of the population than any other. While its origins can be traced back to the early decades of the present century, it only really became a major element of social welfare policy following the report of the Royal Commission on the Law Relating to Mental Illness and Mental Deficiency in 1957, when the term entered common currency to describe a desirable policy alternative to institutional care. Since then there has been widespread political and professional agreement that it is better to seek to care for mentally ill and mentally handicapped people in their own homes, with domiciliary and other services deployed to underpin the support of family, friends and neighbours, self-help groups and other components of the 'informal' care sector. The definition of community care has progressively broadened during the 30 years since the Royal Commission reported. The idea that care *in* the community was preferable to institutional care was, by the 1980s, augmented by the idea of the importance of care *by* the community; and running in parallel with this shift in approach has gone a general extension of the policy to apply to a wider and wider range of need groups – frail elderly people, people with physical handicaps, and those suffering from chronic illness.

Two features of community care policies deserve to be highlighted here. The first is the underlying assumption that, given back-up support and resources, 'communities' have the capacity and motivation to care for their own vulnerable members. This assumption has been questioned. Neighbourhood networks vary greatly in their ability to 'care' for members. In those cases where such a capacity does seem to exist, closer examination seems to show that the bulk of really effective caring is likely to be undertaken by family members and (with the exception of cases where husbands look after wives) predominantly by women. The second feature relates to the level and kind of public support that is necessary – by the health, social, income support and voluntary welfare services – to make community care a reality. It is widely accepted that a high level of interdepartmental co-ordination, along with active co-operation between the professional workers involved in case management, is vitally necessary. But it is also recognised that interdepartmental rivalries, bureaucratic inertia, separate funding and the sheer complexity of organised welfare provision can undermine effective action. These latter organisational difficulties and deficiencies were increasingly recognised and documented during the 1980s, were thoroughly analysed in the government-sponsored Griffith's Report (1988), and were subsequently addressed in the White Paper *Caring for People* (HMSO, 1989) and subsequent legislation. An important outcome of this governmental review process has been that local authorities are to be given the lead responsibility for co-ordinating the development of community care service plans, with their Social Services Departments given the task of managing and planning (though not delivering) 'packages of care' for individuals in need.

Going Local

Seeking to move 'closer to the people' has been an increasingly popular strategy within elected local government in Britain over the past ten years. Two particular approaches to 'going local' can be usefully distinguished, although it must be noted that there has been an enormous diversity in aims, methods and outcomes within both strands. The most popular approach has involved a move to decentralise local authority services, to ensure that provision – of housing, welfare, environmental health, leisure services, etc – becomes more accessible and responsive to the needs of local communities of users. Large and small authorities, at district and county levels, and of all political complexions, are working towards single- or multi-service forms of decentralisation – though metropolitan boroughs on the political left have generally been in the vanguard of this particular type of reform. The emphasis has been on devolving the *administration* of services and provision to a 'patch' or neighbourhood level, with the goal of reducing the rather remote, centralised and anonymous image of local government.

The second strand has been concerned to devolve an element of decision-making power and influence to the neighbourhoods and communities that comprise a local authority's area. The intention is to improve the democratic accountability of local government, either through an extension of representative democracy or through the introduction of an element of direct democracy (Hoggett and Hambleton, 1987).

A brief look at developments in one local authority – the London Borough of Islington – will put flesh on this rather generalised account of devolution within local government. Islington, a relatively poor inner-city borough, has been a pioneer in this field since the early 1980s, when a new Labour council took office and began to give practical effect to the manifesto commitments it had made concerning service decentralisation. By the mid 1980s 24 neighbourhood offices, many of them purpose built, had been opened, each one providing improved public access to a range of services (housing, social services, environmental health, etc), with some discretion for neighbourhood teams to plan and deliver their services in line with perceived local needs. New staff have been appointed, but many staff (e.g. home helps, gardeners, welfare rights workers) formally operating from central offices have been relocated to the neighbourhood level with the aim of achieving a more co-ordinated approach to serving the needs of the residents in their area. Alongside this administrative decentralisation Islington has also embarked upon an ambitious programme of political devolution; there are to be 24 neighbourhood forums run in accordance with locally determined constitutions, and with an ability to spend a proportion of Islington's 'partnership' budget on local environmental improvements, estate security, social activities and so forth. In common with many 'going local' schemes significant devolution of political decision making have been somewhat less easy to achieve than the parallel move to administrative decentralisation.

Third Sector Enterprise

This is the term coined (Murgatroyd and Smith, 1984) to describe a variety of contemporary approaches to local economic development. This relatively new and growing sector, existing alongside the public and private sectors, often has a community dimension, and approaches economic regeneration through a variety of organisational mechanisms – community businesses, local enterprise trusts, workers' co-operatives, community co-operatives and mutual aid groups. Community development workers are sometimes, but by no means always, involved in supporting such initiatives, and when they are their role and remit takes a great variety of forms. In *Building Bridges into Work*, Paquita McMichael et al (1990) explore the role of the community worker in promoting and developing such initiatives; educational and purposefully interventionist approaches, as well as more traditional facilitative and non-directive methods, are all illustrated in the detailed case study accounts reproduced in the book. The authors' accounts also point up the diversity of ways that public bodies have supported these kinds of community initiative as an integral part of their policy approach to economic development.

In a case study of the Park Lane Garden Centre in South Aston, Birmingham, we are provided with an interesting account of how the residents' association in this multi-racial, inner-city area of tower blocks and terraced 'town houses' sought to find an economically productive use for a piece of waste ground adjoining the primary school, the site of a recently demolished factory. The establishment of an adventure playground was followed by the development of a garden centre which, after delays and setbacks, sought and won support from a number of public bodies. The local council gave approval for use of the site as a garden centre and allocated about £90,000 towards capital costs; the council's economic initiatives unit offered specialist advice. An employment training (ET) scheme was started, with the council's economic development unit fulfilling the role of managing agency. This scheme provided 17 ET places (to augment the small handful of jobs created to manage the centre) in horticultural training, catering, and a print workshop. The garden centre staff worked hard to make the venture self-financing, but its aims were always broader than commercial viability. The community worker helped to define these wider aims, conceptualising her own role in educational terms. For example she sought to ensure the active involvement of local people in the determination of what to produce and sell, encouraged skill sharing and collective learning, and suggested and stimulated ideas for new developments (a plant doctor service, garden clubs, clean-up campaigns, etc). Local people ran the centre management committee and the worker took a fairly directive role in ensuring that the three segments of the community – Asians, Afro-Caribbeans and whites – were all well represented. Ideas were pooled, plant labels were translated into Asian languages, and the centre was opened up to school visits; in an area that boasted few shops (other than general grocery stores) the centre served to increase community identity and encourage widespread resident participation in the project by young and old and by people from all cultural and ethnic backgrounds.

Community Health Initiatives

These are, according to one authority, 'an established and expanding area of social and health care in Britain' (McNaught,

1987). He suggests that such initiatives generally fall into one, or a combination of, the following categories:

- neighbourhood-based community health projects, which use a community development approach to working with groups who are oppressed, assisting them to identify their own health needs and concerns, and to take appropriate action (e.g. form a support group, mount a campaign)
- community-based initiatives run by health professionals (e.g. health education projects organised at the community level by community nurses or health education officers, to raise knowledge and modify attitudes around a particular issue)
- single-issue projects and organisations like the Sickle Cell Society or Bradford Against Dysentery
- advocacy projects – often aimed at securing more appropriate and sensitive services from particular health organisations and professional groups (e.g. Hackney Multi-Ethnic Women's Project)
- self-help support groups and networks, set up to provide mutual support around a particular health issue (e.g. women's health groups) (McNaught, 1987).

As this list illustrates, such initiatives may concern themselves with the needs of geographical or interest communities, and may have a national or a purely local focus. They receive support (including funding) from a variety of sources, including the National Health Service, local health authorities and other public bodies, and many raise funds through charitable giving.

In general terms, the strategies of such organisations are woven from three strands:

- provision of support and mutual aid (including counselling, etc) to their 'constituency'
- campaigning for change in the policies and practices of formal health organisations including a greater emphasis on preventive as opposed to curative medicine
- encouraging and enabling people to take more control of their own health (often through informal community education that aims to demystify and spread health knowledge and skills).

This latter strategy – of enhancing people's control via raising levels of awareness and understanding – has been given particular emphasis by the Sickle Cell Society, which has targeted ethnic minority communities and their health professionals since its inception in 1979. Founded by a group of parents, patients and health professionals concerned with sickle cell disease, the organisation has raised considerable financial resources, including grant aid from the DHSS and other public authorities, which it has used to mount publicity campaigns and underpin the development of a number of local support groups. Its educational activities have included the organisation of film and slide shows, speaking at conferences and seminars, and the production of leaflets and books. Like many such community initiatives the informal educational work of the society rests on the belief that the hegemony of professional definitions and understandings can and should be challenged, and the development of community problem-solving measures encouraged.

Community Development

This has been taken on board by a number of local authorities as an integral part of their strategy to secure the overall social development of their areas. A study by Broady and Hedley (1989) suggests that about one-quarter of all local councils are pursuing a coherent and substantive programme of community development, though the research also shows that such community development programmes vary widely in their aims and objectives (including encouraging the self-management of community facilities, co-option of the 'community' in the provision of services, and general support for the voluntary sector. We seek to give precision to the term 'community development' in the chapter that follows). In an interesting case study of community development in the town of Swindon the authors chart how such strategies have evolved over time. The post-war experience of that town was one of steady economic expansion and population growth, and the local Thameside council has used various community work strategies to help ensure that its social objectives are met. In the early 1950s Swindon was designated an 'Expanding Town' under the 1952 Town Development Act (and thus shared many of the same social priorities as the post-war 'New Towns') and this prompted it to adopt two main community development policies: small multi-purpose halls with ancillary meeting rooms were built on each new housing estate, and neighbourhood workers were appointed to help accelerate the establishment of stable, functioning and integrated communities among the newcomers. This latter objective was pursued via a dual strategy of grassroots locality development, while ensuring that information about progress and problems was fed back to council in order to inform adjustments and changes in policy.

During the 1960s the role of community development was broadened: it lost its exclusive focus on the new estates, and it was no longer targeted solely on assisting with the settlement and facilitating the development of social participation and neighbourhood networks among newcomers. Since the 1970s the council has further endorsed community development, confirming its aims as 'developing conditions for a full social, cultural, working and recreation life for the people of the area, comprising a participatory, just and caring community' (Broady and Hedley, 1989, p. 99). These comprehensive aims have been matched with a distinctive decision-making and delivery structure. A separate committee of council – the community planning committee – determines the policy and oversees the work of the community development division which comprises 27 officers and forms a major part of the authority's economic and social development group. The community planning committee is a very active and politically important committee in Thameside; it oversees the work of a number of subcommittees (race relations, community centres, etc) and has positively welcomed lay involvement in its decision making, and in the various working parties it has set up to address particular concerns (e.g. 'women's issues', 'youth in a multi-cultural society', etc). The professional workers help local people with the management of the social halls; disperse grants to voluntary organisations; act as a resource to local residents and community groups, councillors and others; and compile detailed community profiles as a resource to both local elected members and local action groups in the town.

In broad terms the council sees the benefit of pursuing a social development policy that encourages the continued development of a lively and healthy voluntary sector, one in which local organisations and community groups can organise to 'have a say', provide a service, or meet a need.

Defining Community

With these illustrations of community initiatives in mind, we can now attempt to unpack and define some of the key concepts to be used throughout this book, most notably the ideas of 'community', 'public policy' and 'community policy'.

First of all we turn to what is probably the most important and most frequently used concept of all in this book – community – which, as we have already noted, has proven an extraordinarily difficult word to pin down. Our desire to use the term with some precision is not made any easier, however, by virtue of the fact that we will need to differentiate and deploy three distinct, though interrelated, senses of the term. We call these the 'descriptive', 'value' and 'active' senses of community.

Descriptive Community

Here we are deploying the social scientists' use of the concept, to refer to a group or network of people who share something in common. We used 'community' in this sense when, in our illustration of community initiatives, we reported that Islington's neighbourhood offices have been set up to serve more adequately the needs of their local communities, and when we suggested that the Birmingham Garden Centre sought to recruit a management committee that reflected the variety of cultural and ethnic communities in South Aston. 'Community', in this sense, refers to a network of people who share a sense of belonging to, or membership of, that network. Etymological explanations of the origin of the word point to 'having something in common' as its root, and that 'something in common' generally refers either to a characteristic of the network itself (e.g. that a particular type or level of interaction exists between members) or to the people who make it up (common culture, or religion, or ethnicity, etc). Very often, of course, the two go hand in hand: shared culture may promote greater social interaction which, in turn, can reinforce a sense of cultural identity. The social scientists' use of 'community' thus has both social and psychological referents. Members of communities *interrelate* as part of a social network and they *recognise* themselves to be part of that network. Peter Willmott (1989) advocates using the idea of the 'attachment' community, a useful concept in that it conveys the twin notions of 'being part of' in a sociological sense and 'identifying with' in a psychological sense.

Conventionally, social scientists draw a distinction between two types of community, and our pen pictures of community initiatives help us to illustrate this distinction too. On the one hand it is common practice to refer to 'territorial' communities. Here what people have in common, what helps to determine who they relate to and what they psychologically identify with, is their geographical location – their neighbourhood, village, town, or 'place'. Territorial communities are to be differentiated from interest communities, which are based on characteristics *other* than physical proximity – ethnicity, occupation, religion, sexual propensity, etc. Thus when we talk of the Jewish community, the black community or the lesbian community we are again referring to social networks to which people have a social/psychological attachment, but this time the social base for such attachment may have nothing to do with geography. Of course, some communities may be rooted in both shared locality *and* common interest, with important consequences for an understanding of their dynamics. Some occupational communities, e.g. many mining communities, come into this category, and the overlapping attachment to a 'single industry' pit village and to a hazardous occupation (in which personal safety can rest on action taken by workmates) helps to account for the camaraderie and solidarity often evident in such communities. As we have seen, both territorial and interest communities provide a foundation for community initiatives and policies, though there are probably more that are locality than interest based. While our Birmingham case illustrated work with the unemployed, and Swindon's community development division had focused some of its efforts on work with women, ethnic minorities and young people, all of the five types of policy examined were grounded in area- (territorial) based work.

Two caveats need to be entered with respect to this discussion of the descriptive use of community in public policy, both of which stem from our desire to sharpen up the precision with which terminology is used in this book. The first is to note that commentators, policy makers, and others are apt to assume that *because* a certain population segment live in the same area or have some other characteristic in common they *therefore* can be referred to as a 'community'. We shall avoid doing this as far as possible, because it confuses a necessary condition for the development of community (some sort of common social base) with the defining or constitutive characteristic of community itself (the fact that community membership demonstrates some kind of attachment to a group or social network). Thus neighbourhood work on the new Swindon housing estates of the 1950s was undertaken (partly) to 'develop' community. The fact that scores of people live cheek by jowl in a particular area does not give us licence to conclude (or talk as if) such people constitute a 'community'.

Equally, and this brings us to the second caveat, we will always try to distinguish between 'community' and the social action consequences (desirable or undesirable) that seem to arise from it. It may well be, for example, that strong occupational communities engender feelings of solidarity, and that such feelings may, in turn, influence patterns of industrial relations at the workplace. However, we believe that it is important to regard such observations as contingent rather than necessary; in other words, whether and how far particular types of community produce particular levels and types of solidarity should be investigated as an empirical question rather than be assumed *a priori*. This issue is of more than purely academic importance with respect to questions of community policy. For example, policies for community care, as we noted above, characteristically rest on an assumption that strong community attachments imply that the people in a locality community will have both the capacity and motivation to provide certain levels of 'care' to their more vulnerable members. Such a leap may or may not be valid, and will depend on a host of factors other than the existence of 'community' ties between the people in the network concerned. The point is that such a link must be demonstrated, not assumed.

Community as Value

When reference is made to community policies and initiatives it is possible that 'community' is being used in its descriptive sense only, to refer to the territorial site or social location of the initiative. 'Community nursing' may, in some instances, mean little more than the application of standard nursing procedures 'in the community', rather than 'in the hospital'. Similarly 'community care' may mean no more and no less than organising support services for people in their own homes, rather than in an institution.

However, many of the policies and practices that carry the 'community' tag embody an aspiration to do something *qualitatively* different. It is far from easy to pin down what this is, exactly, although a number of authors have attempted to distil what is distinctive about 'community' interventions (Willmott, 1989; Donnison, 1989).

Our approach is to suggest that what defines community initiatives and policies is their attempt to embrace, and find a practical expression for, particular community values. We will stress three in particular, identifying them as the principle of solidarity, participation and coherence. Such values, we suggest, inform different policies in different combinations; and we have to note immediately the further complication that, like so many value terms, each is prone to receive a variable interpretation according to the ideological stance of the user. The ideas of solidarity, participation and coherence are, in other words, 'contested' concepts (Plant, 1974) just as the meaning of community is itself.

In their strongest form such community values are to be seen as grounded in a particular philosophical perspective – communitarianism – which advances a distinctive view about the nature of the individual and of society. From such a view communitarians develop a perspective on what marks out right conduct for the individual and on what constitutes desirable social arrangements in society (Kymlicka, 1990). At its simplest, communitarians hold that individuals are, in a very profound and comprehensive sense, 'constituted' by society; their personality, values and identity, indeed, their very being, is realised in, and manifested through, association with others in society. Men and women are, according to this view, irredeemably social beings. What we are, and what we can become, is profoundly affected by our inherent disposition and need to associate with, and to live a life with others in society. The concept of a pre- or a- social human being is at best a hypothetical abstraction, at worst a nonsense.

Such a view stands opposed to those theories of philosophical individualism which place the 'unencumbered' and pre-social person as, in some sense, a reality that can be sensibly conceptualised in isolation from society. In the most influential version of individualistic theory, men (sic) are regarded as having created collective life through the formation of a social contract – and a long line of contract theorists ground the claims of their particular political and social principles in this view of the individual as an autonomous and calculating being who *chooses* to live with others in society. It matters not whether such a view has historical support: its plausibility turns on philosophical argument, not empirical evidence. Communitarians reject the idea that the 'individual' can be conceived of as an entity outside of their association with others in society or, indeed, that it is plausible to see human beings as the narrowly autonomous, instrumental and calculating decision makers of the individualist model.

The communitarian tradition, with its stress on the centrality of society and 'associativeness' to human beings, has led its key thinkers to advance, in their turn, a number of principles concerning individual behaviour and social organisation. It is these principles which, for us, provide the distinctive *value* base of community initiatives and policies.

Relationships of *solidarity* sustain community members at an emotional level. In a community it is legitimate to talk of relations of fraternity, trust, selflessness, 'sisterhood' and loyalty; social solidarity is expressed through mutuality and co-operation in relationships, it is what inspires affection, even loyalty, of an individual member towards the group.

This positive affirmation of solidarity as a community value underlies the communitarian critique of key aspects of modern life: much contemporary experience, it is argued, is isolating and individualistic. Modern society seems to be overwhelmed by self-centred egoism, possessive individualism, and a competitive 'me and mine' mentality. Mutual aid, co-operative relationships and welfare values are played down; we become strangers to each other, isolated in our selfish pursuit of individual interests.

Many community initiatives, then, emphasise and build upon the community value of solidarity. Community care emphasises neighbourhood support and informal care; mutual aid groups and certain types of community development are predicated on the belief that people can move beyond a purely self-centred concern with strictly individual, private concerns and preoccupations.

Community also provides members with opportunities for shared, *participative* activity with others. The individual benefits from a sense of involvement in realising common goals, of playing a part in, and contributing to, the collective life and aspirations of the group. People gain a sense of recognition and significance through 'public' activity and involvement. The value placed on participation by communitarianism implies a further critique of contemporary society and social relations: the 'privatism' of modern life is regretted, and the manner in which social relations and institutions (particularly power structures) serve to exclude people is deprecated. The operative on the production line can be seen as an extreme metaphor for this general tendency; an appendage to the machine, minutely controlled by others and disconnected from workmates, the worker on the track is effectively denied the sustenance of authentic participation.

Again, community initiatives and policies seek to work in opposition to such tendencies; the garden centre project in Aston sought to involve local people in debating and deciding on what it should produce and how it should work. Islington's neighbourhood forums, and Thameside's commitment to resident involvement in its committees and working parties, provide examples of attempts to enhance opportunities for public involvement in decision making.

Lastly, it is through community that individuals come to embrace a framework of *meanings* and *values* that provide some overall sense of their world, and their relations and activities with others in it. Again community 'connects-up' the individual to something wider, in this case a more *coherent* appreciation and comprehension of self and situation. Cultural, religious and ethnic communities operate particularly powerfully in offering 'meaning' to their members' lives, but all communities provide some sense of coherence that would not otherwise be available.

The attenuation of community in modern society can help to account, according to the communitarian critique, for the sense of meaninglessness, pointlessness and alienation that is said to be so characteristic of the modern condition. In our exemplars of community initiatives we saw how community development often works, implicitly or explicitly, to increase community members' understanding of the interrelatedness of social, economic and political factors, and the relationships between such 'systems' and personal experience. Similarly, community health initiatives like those of the Sickle Cell Society often put particular emphasis on awareness raising and informal education programmes that help people to understand better their bodies and how the health of their bodies is affected by wider social conditions and circumstances. Greater awareness can lead, in turn, to a more proactive and 'participative' approach to health matters.

Active Community

Finally, we turn to the third meaning of community, that of the 'active' community. This is the idea of community that public policy makers often have in mind when they seek to promote initiatives that draw upon, or seek to develop, community strengths and capacities. Their image is that of a neighbourhood alive with activity and cross-cut with networks of relationships, providing a locus for informal support and mutual aid as well as acting as a base for social and political action in wider arenas. Through participation in such activity community members enjoy a sense of rootedness, belonging and identity, and perhaps develop a greater awareness of themselves and their social world. This meaning of community *subsumes and builds upon* the 'descriptive' and 'value' meanings already discussed above; community 'action' (in the broadest sense) refers to collective action by members of locality or interest communities, and it is action that embraces and expresses one or more communal values of solidarity, participation and coherence.

Of course, communities, as such, don't 'act'. It is their members who take action, through the vehicle of groups, networks and organisations. We recognise an 'active' community, therefore, through evidence of the diversity and vitality of the groups and organisations that play a role within it, the extent to which those groups and organisations are engaged in purposive action, and the extent to which community members are seen to be committed to their goals and activities, roles and functions.

Community policies are designed to *develop*, *maintain*, or *draw upon* 'active community', and our earlier examples illustrate all three intentions. Early post-war community development in Swindon was concerned to 'develop' active community. The provision of local meeting places, and the efforts of the neighbourhood community workers, were directed towards helping people who were strangers to each other to extend their contacts and begin to form a basic community infrastructure of networks and groups. In South Aston and Islington, and again in Swindon, the provision of grants and other supports to the voluntary sector was one of the means through which public policy makers sought to 'maintain' the vitality of community groups and organisations.

Finally, many community care and community enterprise schemes seek to 'draw upon' and use existing community networks and support structures as part of their social welfare and employment generation schemes.

Public Policy

In so far as 'community' strategies have been deployed as part of the policy armoury of public bodies during the past quarter-century, this has not generally been undertaken in a conscious, systematic and thought-through way. Community initiatives have generally been used as part of, or as an adjunct to, wider policy strategies – 'wheeled-in' to the policy arena to address particular policy problems at particular times. The resulting picture is one of muddle and contradiction. Adaption of a typology devised by Webb and Wistow (1982) to analyse policy developments within the personal social services provides a useful framework for reducing such confusion to some kind of order. Community strategies and initiatives have been, it can be argued, drawn upon as an adjunct and support to five types of government policy:

- service policies – these are policies which embrace ideas concerning the most appropriate methods of meeting needs, identification of priority groups, along with preferred ways of designing services for effective delivery (the shift from residential provision toward policies of community care is an example of a change in service policies)
- governance policies – these are policies concerning the proper role and function of the state and include those policies that seek to regulate the relationships between governmental and non-governmental bodies and the public (devolving some decision-making power to neighbourhood forums, or seeking to resource the voluntary sector as a 'partner' to local government in service provision, are examples of shifts in governance policy)
- resource policies – these are concerned with desirable levels, and appropriate functions, of public expenditure; levels and types of taxes to be levied, etc (an example of a shift in resource policy would be a local authority decision to devolve certain expenditure decisions to neighbourhood or community councils)
- economic policies – these are policies concerned with levels of employment, aggregate output, infrastructural development, economic planning and so on (support by some local authorities for third-sector enterprise is an example here)
- public order policies – these are policies concerned with law and the maintenance of public order, social control, counter insurgency, etc (an example of a shift in public policy would be the introduction of 'community policing' to remedy some of the deficiencies of conventional reactive or 'fire-brigade' policing).

Our contention is that community strategies have been utilised to support all of these types of policy over the past quarter-century. Sometimes local government has taken the lead ('going local' as an aspect of governance policy); sometimes central government has taken the initiative ('community care' strategies as an element of service and resource policies). Part 2 of this study uses this fivefold classification of public policy arenas as its organising framework; separate chapters explore how different community initiatives and strategies have been incorporated into the fields of service, governance and economic policy making.

Community Policy

We are now in a position to provide a definition of 'community' policy. We put it forward as having general applicability, although it has been specifically developed to underpin and frame the analysis that is the focus of this study.

In the first place, and as we have seen, community policy is not to be viewed as a separate and discrete type of policy; rather, it is a mode of policy making and implementation that may be, and has been, utilised within a range of substantive policy areas. In this study we choose to focus on its place within governance, service, resource, public order and economic policy spheres.

Secondly, its utilisation within any one of these policy fields is, we have suggested, differentiated from other policy approaches in three distinctive aspects: it involves understanding, and relating to, the beneficiaries or recipients of the policy as *members of a community* (territorial or interest); it implies that the policy will embrace one or more distinctive community values (solidarity, participation, coherence); and it requires that policy implementation involves working in partnership with groups and organisations *active at the community level*.

Thirdly, and most significantly, community policies tend to be oriented to the needs of disadvantaged, oppressed or marginalised groups in society. This characteristic is amply illustrated within the case study material presented earlier in this chapter. Community care and community health initiatives are concerned with providing support to socially vulnerable groups, 'going local' initiatives have been most in evidence in local authority areas with higher than average indices of material and social need, many 'third-sector' enterprises have been pioneered in areas with sustained and high levels of unemployment, and most community development is committed to work with poor and powerless people. The tendency for such initiatives and policies to be biased towards the less advantaged in society (in terms of power, income and social resources) is sufficiently marked for this to constitute a key feature of our working definition. One further point must, however, be made clear: this characteristic should be seen, in part at any rate, as stemming from a commitment to community values themselves. Thus, for example, a commitment to the value of 'participation' will almost inevitably direct the policy maker and practitioner to favour initiatives that give priority to the needs of the powerless, excluded or marginalised. A bias to the disadvantaged and oppressed is, in other words, to some extent a consequence of those features of community policy already identified, rather than constituting a wholly new and independent variable to be added to our definition.

With this and all our other preceding qualifications in mind we are now in a position to summarise our understanding of community policy in diagrammatic form. Figure 1.1 represents the defining characteristics of those policies to be discussed, analysed and appraised in this book and, indeed, is offered to the reader as a general definition of the field in question.

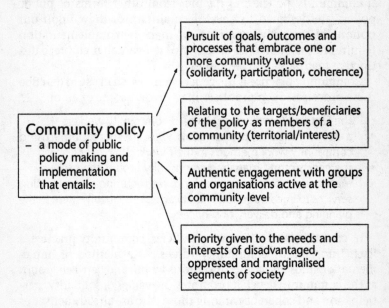

Figure 1.1: Community Policy – the Key Elements

2 Methods and Themes in Community Practice

Andrew Glen

Introduction

If community policies, as distinct from other forms of public policy, are designed to develop, maintain or draw upon our notions of the active community, then their implementation requires forms of practice and service delivery that embrace distinctive methods and techniques.

Community practice is the generic term we shall use to describe these processes. Such processes may involve some or all of:

- the sustained involvement of paid community workers
- a broad range of professionals who are increasingly using community work methods in their work
- the efforts of self-managed community groups themselves
- managerial attempts at reviewing, restructuring and relocating services to encourage community access and involvement in the planning and delivery of services.

In common with community policies, community practice is itself informed by community values. As a method of implementation it fosters partnership efforts within and between groups at the community level; it promotes the values of solidarity, participation and coherence among those who are already active, or becoming so, in communities; and, since the particular focus for community policy is the concern to challenge oppression and injustice, in practice this means directly working with and on behalf of those individuals and groups marginalised by or excluded from mainstream economic, political and social structures. A community practice approach to service delivery may also constitute a vehicle for questioning the substance and form of

public policy itself. Thus, following Willmott's (1989) conceptu-
alisation of community initiatives, a community practice approach
may emanate from 'top down' initiatives promoted by central and
local government and indeed voluntary organisations, as well as
from 'bottom up' organising within communities.

Three Approaches in Community Practice

In our review of community practice as a method both derived
from and aiming to promote community policies, we distinguish
between three approaches:

- community development
- community action
- community services approach.

In so doing, we acknowledge our debt to various practitioners
and writers who have, over the years, constructed a variety of
typologies, frameworks and models for analysing and developing
guidelines for practice (e.g. Leissner, 1975; Rothman, 1987;
Thomas, 1983). We recognise that in themselves each of these terms
has been extensively and variously used in the past. 'Community
development', for example, has been used to refer to post-colonial
efforts of international aid agencies to promote social and economic
progress in developing countries uniting voluntary effort with that
of governmental authorities. More recently, as we have noted, it
has been used to refer to approaches made by local authorities to
make their own services more community oriented, encourage
the voluntary sector and promote social development. 'Community
action' has been used in a broad sense to describe any kind of
activity by community groups and, more narrowly, to describe
community groups and organisations who are prepared to deploy
conflict tactics in pursuing their campaigns. The term 'community
service' is often associated with both benevolent and compulsory
forms of 'voluntary assistance' to people in need; more generally
community services may refer to the multiplicity of locally based
statutory and voluntary services.

For our purposes we are using the terms community development, community action, and community services approach to
refer to distinctive models and methods of community practice.
Both community development and community action operate at
the grassroots level, with community development being
concerned to promote self-help, and community action actively

embracing campaigns. A community services approach is more concerned with promoting, developing and maintaining community oriented organisations primarily within the statutory and voluntary sectors.

Within the literature these terms are sometimes used interchangeably, and different practitioners may describe the same processes in different ways. We shall endeavour to use the terms as distinguished here consistently throughout this book. In this chapter we use these methodological distinctions in order to illustrate a variety of examples of community practice in the UK, to highlight some central issues and, in response to Salmon's (1991) plea, indicate some lessons drawn from past experiences.

Community Development

In a frequently quoted passage describing community development as a programme for social and economic progress in developing countries, the United Nations refer to:

> the participation of the people themselves in efforts to improve their level of living with as much reliance as possible on their own initiative, and the provision of technical and other services in ways which encourage initiative, self help and mutual help and make them more effective. (In Roberts 1979, p. 179)

Along with other practice theorists (Batten, 1965, 1967; Biddle and Biddle, 1968; Goetschius, 1969; Milson, 1974) we see community development as an attempt to translate the paternalistic style of promoting local self-determination and self-help within developing countries into positively democratic ways of working 'where people are at' within communities in urban industrial multi-cultural societies. As such, a community development approach entails three main elements in that:

1. the aim is for a community to define its own needs and make provision for them
2. the processes involve fostering creative and co-operative networks of people and groups in communities
3. there would be a community practitioner involved with community development skills operating in a non-directive way.

Communities Define and Meet their Needs

The goal of the community development approach is to develop self-help and hence establish a sense of community principally, though not exclusively, on a neighbourhood basis. Community Matters (previously the National Federation of Community Associations) was founded in 1945 and has been one of the main grassroots proponents of neighbourhood communities. For example, in its early days, the promotion and setting up of community associations within areas that had been severely affected by the depression of the interwar period and further impoverished by the absence of any church and community facilities was an effort to rekindle community spirit. People had moved from the poorer housing of the urban slums to the new municipal housing estates on the outskirts of cities and to new towns, and while these localities were environmentally healthier, they often lacked social, leisure and recreational facilities (Broady, 1979). Securing the provision of locally based community centres similar to village halls in rural communities, run and locally managed by community associations, came to be seen as a necessary response to both the absence of facilities in new urban areas and the need to foster social relationships with strangers.

The development of neighbourhood care schemes, play projects, advice services or youth clubs provides opportunities for people to identify their needs and express their views, develop confidence, learn new skills and work collaboratively with others in providing and running local services. As Butcher et al (1980) have noted, the successful establishment of a self-help group may lead to provision of a service that goes beyond merely *complementing* existing established services. Greater choice and a real *alternative* source of support may become available for those whose needs have hitherto been ignored, hidden or unrecognised. Self-help groups may even provide a *substitute* to existing services in their focus and in their management. Their very existence may be a fundamental challenge to existing services, e.g. the health and preventive orientation of Well Woman Centres contrasts strongly with the illness and curative preoccupations of the NHS.

However, a reliance on 'starting where the community is at' or a 'felt needs' approach may neglect those needs of which communities are unaware or prefer to ignore. For example, as Scott (1991) notes, relation to HIV/AIDS crisis community practitioners must recognise their responsibility in challenging and persuading people to change their sexual practices. Also, by

relying upon local communities to meet their own needs there
may be less pressure upon public authorities to invest in local
services, e.g. play groups are an easy option to state-run nurseries.

Yet in many of the areas where community development work
takes place it is simply not realistic to rely on local resources.
Funding has to be sought from elsewhere. However, such funding
may be short term, conditional upon certain activities being
developed, requiring funders' representation on management
committees and thus potentially undermining a group's local
accountability and credibility. Funding is often insecure. Where
external funds are being targeted to 'organised' neighbourhoods
this may well deplete the injection of resources into other areas
where self-help activities have not yet begun.

Communities as Creative and Co-operative

The view that communities are potentially creative and co-
operative reflects a social idealism concerning positive collaborative
effort and communal identity. The National Federation of
Community Associations' model constitution for community
associations required that membership of an association was
open to individuals and organisations 'without distinction of sex
or of political, religious or other opinion', in order to associate
local authorities, voluntary organisations and inhabitants in a
common effort (Broady, 1979). Theoretically, everyone was
welcome at the community centre.

While conflicts do exist within and between communities
which may also reflect deeper divisions in society, community
workers have argued that these can be reduced in order that
people can work together in a co-operative way. In some cases
this co-operative working might result in a divided community
engaging in collective action on a common problem. Through
enabling a community to achieve results on issues that are not
divisive it may be possible at a later stage to develop collaborative efforts to take on more contentious and oppressive experiences.

Thus in reaching out, listening and working within an inner-
city community in Camden in London, two white community
workers became aware of a large number of attacks and abuses
on the Bengali community by white young people. Contact had
been made with the Bengali community through a female Bengali-
speaking community worker but until then members of the
Bengali community had not been involved in local community
groups. The local tenants' association took up the incidents in the
context of increasing violence on the estate and set about

organising a range of activities to respond to the harassment. These included discussions with the police about the inadequacies of their response, the establishing of a local support network for victims of harassment, pressuring the council to improve safety for the whole of the estate, organising a successful women's self-defence course and maintaining close involvement with young people through youth work (Buckingham and Martin, 1989).

Being Non-directive

It is suggested that the community practitioner's role in working within a community development approach is one of enabling, encouraging and educating. According to Batten, a non-directive approach is preferable to a directive approach because: 'people are more likely to act on what they themselves have freely decided to do than on what a worker has tried to convince them they ought to do' (Batten, 1967, p. v). Community development workers value the social and educational processes of people getting involved as much as the practical services provided. In order to generate these processes they need to spend time tuning into the needs of a neighbourhood and gaining acceptance. Some may choose to live in their patch and experience 'life on the estate'. Others carry out community surveys, making contacts with residents via local councillors, shopkeepers, doorknocking, etc in order to assess needs, identify issues and seek out potential leaders. In this approach community practitioners have no particular agenda of their own. Workers stimulate people through a non-directive approach to think about their needs, feeding in information about possible ways of meeting them and encouraging people to decide for themselves what they will do in order to meet them. Practitioners should, theoretically, be responsive to the needs of all potential groups in the community and act as a bridge between them. Their primary concern, as Ilys Booker (in Mitton and Morrison, 1972) expressed, is with groups' own development to the extent that community practitioners' continued involvement is not necessary. In time they should be able to withdraw.

In reality it is doubtful whether even the most charismatic community development worker can be all things to all people and sustain the impartiality and objectivity that Batten assumes is possible. To ignore the political auspices under which community development workers are employed is to ignore their dual account-ability to employers and the community. Most paid community practitioners are employed to achieve predesigned results and are themselves not value free. As Salmon notes:

Because we are engaged in community development we do
not have to behave as though we have no beliefs or ideas.
The important thing is to be sensitive to how people are
responding to what we have to say. (Salmon, 1991, p. 2)

Community practitioners may need to take on a more proactive
role particularly where individuals or groups lack the confidence
to organise community projects. They also may, for the sake of
expedience, take on official roles in groups, e.g. convene and chair
meetings at an early stage of a group's development or when
factions jeopardise the potential of subgroups from meeting each
other. The concern to 'withdraw' may reflect the agendas of
funders, 'hit and run' professionals or workers employed on fixed-
term contracts eager to demonstrate short-term results rather
than respond to the intractable and persistent nature of many of
the problems facing communities. Dependable long-term support
by community development workers may be a more realistic
option.

Community Action

In marked contrast to the community development approach,
community action involves communities in making demands of
policy makers to acknowledge their interests and be responsive
to their demands. The community action approach can be seen
as part of the UK's long tradition of social and political protest
that has included the slave trade abolitionists, urban social
movements, the votes for women campaign, and campaigns
against racial discrimination and other forms of oppression.
Specific examples of community campaigns that have occurred
in the twentieth century include the Govan women's organised
rent strike on Clydeside in 1915 against proposed rent increases;
the mass trespasses of Kinder Scout in 1932 to campaign for the
'freedom to roam' for walkers on open moorland; the spontaneous
squat of empty army bases following demobilisation after World
War Two; the Greenham Common and other peace camps at
military installations during the 1970s and 1980s; women's
support committees for striking miners during the 1983–4 coal
strike; the Birmingham Six, Bradford Twelve and Broadwater
Farm Three campaigns against criminal injustices and investiga-
tion procedures; and, in 1990, the anti poll tax campaign.

At the local level it was in the 1960s and 1970s that evidence of a 'strong political life' beyond party political organisations became apparent in the emergence of 'thousands of tenants' associations, residents' groups and independent community action groups throughout the country' with many and varied demands (Craig, 1989). For some writers this heralded a new and radical trend (Calouste Gulbenkian, 1973; Baldock, 1981). For others it reflected a failure of representative democracy to reflect the wishes of the electorate, and a failure of the welfare state to ameliorate the excesses of power and inequality within capitalist society (Hain, 1975; Mayo, 1982; Wilson, 1984). However, for communities, in many cases organising for the first time, it was about collective empowerment. As Bryant has noted, community action is an approach:

> in which the political impotence or powerlessness of these groups is defined as a central problem and strategies are employed which seek to mobilise them for the representation and promotion of their collective interests. (Bryant, in Henderson and Thomas, 1980, p. 83)

It is a distinctive approach for community practice in so far as:

1. the goals involve organising for power around concrete issues
2. it employs conflict oriented strategies and tactics
3. organisers are generally activists or paid professional organisers.

Organising for Power

Community action has usually been concerned with a single issue or specific grievance over which collective action is taken by people who are themselves directly affected. It is not about advocacy by others, though alliances may be formed with those who are sympathetic. The issue or grievance may be particular to people who live in a locality or may be a result of common experiences. More often than not the goals of community action are modest, reformist, reactive and defensive. Groups have organised to oppose the closure of local schools or hospitals, or to protect their areas from environmental damage caused by industrial toxic waste. Individuals have come together to protect and promote their legal rights, e.g. the initiative and leadership of black people to scrap the 'sus laws' which, it was argued, were being used by the police to harass black people (Clarke and Huggins, 1982). People joined groups to campaign for and protect their expression of individuality and sexuality in the face of restrictive legislation (e.g. Clause 28, Local Government Act 1988). In response to victimisation and abuse, both physical and psychological, people have combined to protect themselves against racial attacks, and women have organised to publicise their experience of domestic violence, and to campaign for and run refuges, rape crisis lines and support groups. People have joined forces in community action groups to challenge negative images that others hold of them. For example, people with disabilities have campaigned for 'rights not charity' to help reassert their position as citizens as well as to shrug off the all too pervasive negative notions of dependency. As Donnison notes, community action can help ensure that:

> those who suffer injustice, pain or humiliation gain a voice within the wider society and thus find ways of conveying their own experience to that society and making effective demands on groups that dominate it. (Donnison, in Bulmer et al, 1990a, p. 218)

While membership of community action groups may involve individuals for a limited period of time only, it has brought into collective action a wide number of people who are often excluded and alienated from any form of political, economic or social activity. The common experience of organising for power promotes collective solidarity – the gains from successful community action campaigns need not have a merely parochial value; they can set precedents for other neighbourhoods and can be an inspiration for other people to take action.

Conflict Tactics and Strategy

Community action groups frequently organise through simple structures with a caucus leadership which enables them to make fast decisions and mobilise through networks for mass action. Frequently they involve people who have limited experience of political organising yet they need rapidly to become credible and politically adept in identifying and pressurising actual sources of power. The use of 'influence', real or perceived, is a crucial determinant of a group's effectiveness. The selection of tactics depends on how the targets (individual decision makers, organisations) of a group's actions are seen in terms of their legitimacy in making decisions and determining policy priorities, and their likelihood of so doing in the group's favour. Where the target is seen as having a right to make policy and resource allocation decisions, and is predisposed to be responsive, *collaborative* tactics might be employed (e.g. presentation of information, deputations). The less the target is seen either to have the right to make decisions or to be responsive, the more likely a group will need to engage in *campaign* tactics (e.g. petitions, mass letter writing, rallies) or *coercive* tactics involving (often) creative and direct confrontation methods. Rent strikes on an organised basis by tenants opposed to the Housing Finance Act in the 1970s and non-payment of poll tax in 1990 were designed to hinder the implementation of legislation and signal the hardship of those families on low incomes. The 'shock' tactics of Act Up (Aids Coalition to Unleash Power) in organising 'kiss ins' and 'die ins' were designed to maximise media publicity in the face of complacency over the HIV/AIDS epidemic. These were organised alongside more general campaigns to stop discrimination of gays, lesbians and people affected by HIV/AIDS by life insurance companies, workplaces, religious institutions, etc.

The very abrasiveness of some of the tactics employed in community action can lead to reprisals and recriminations. In the 1940s squatters were described as 'communist' inspired, and denounced for jumping housing queues and conspiring to trespass (Anarchy, 1963). While left groups have indeed been actively involved in co-ordinating community political protests, they have not done so exclusively. Within these struggles, much community action has emerged spontaneously. Some neighbourhoods and campaigns have successfully become involved in alliances with other areas. But then, they have had to balance their need for political representation with the servicing of local member groups – the membership of a community action group is often its most precious resource. There is a danger that the energy of a community action group may become dissipated once involvement in wider national and political campaigns occurs.

Activists and Organisers

The leadership of community action groups is usually taken up by individuals who are personally or politically affected by, and committed to, the issues of the group. As a result of learning through action, individuals may experience a fundamental change in their personal and political perspectives of the world. Women, for example, may face opposition from their families and others to their committtment to becoming involved with community groups. Yet women historically have been extensively involved in organising and leading community action groups. Hence community action can be a vehicle for challenging patronising and sexist assumptions about women and an important arena for activism by women.

Community practitioners may be employed by groups as external organisers, mobilisers and agitators, or by agencies committed to community-based work. A dilemma for activists/organisers is that they may well be politically further ahead than the community being organised and unless organisers are prepared to spend time and effort informing, educating and persuading people to become involved they will experience personal frustration. In turn they may fail to develop local leadership. In addition, leading activists need to avoid being personally 'bought off' by those people the campaign is trying to influence. Even though many campaigns are relatively short term the energy required to sustain a creative momentum means that organisers are liable to 'burn out', and activists need to find ways to support their own political and personal energies.

Community practitioners employed by public authorities face very real dilemmas if the groups they are supporting become involved with community action campaigns. For example, in his study of paid community work in Leicester, Cliffe (1985) reported the clash of loyalties experienced by community workers:

> Some employers explicitly, or sometimes less directly, prohibited workers from adopting certain approaches. In particular this applied to the community organisation and community action approaches especially where the policies of the employer were the target of the community group. (Cliffe, 1985, p. 187)

This type of dilemma was clearly apparent in relation to the poll tax. Banks and Noonan (1990) reported limited direct involvement, particularly by local authority community workers, on an issue which was clearly 'adversely affecting people in areas where community workers tend to be based'. In their brief survey of 25 community workers during 1990 they found only one community worker actually advising and supporting the meetings of an anti poll tax group. Other community workers had chosen to separate their personal and professional roles and to become active in anti poll tax campaigns during their own time, or to help organise welfare rights projects for those finding difficulty with payment of the tax. A large number of the workers contacted had not been involved in any activity regarding the poll tax though one worker, not wishing to push his own values, was providing support to a pro poll tax group. Most of the community workers were keeping their heads down or engaging in action only in the 'nooks and crannies' (Rigby, 1982). And yet it is through such campaigns that policies come under public scrutiny, may be made more responsive, are challenged and changed.

Community Services Approaches

By community services approaches we mean those methods and strategies that are employed to develop and maintain community oriented service delivery and planning organisations. This very much reflects Briscoe's (1977) view of service delivery oriented work as distinct from community-based work with community groups, in that its concern is with:

> the planning, organisation and delivery of services; that is they concentrate on improving and developing agency outputs to client groups both to improve existing services and to provide new services to enhance the quality of life. (Briscoe, in Specht and Vickery, 1977, p. 184)

Both Thomas (1983) and Barr (1991) have remarked that such an approach has generally been neglected by British community workers. Yet within the voluntary sector, councils for voluntary services or equivalent bodies have been active for most of the century in developing and supporting voluntary organisations relevant to local needs. Race equality councils (RECs) provide local co-ordinated forums for ethnic organisations to be involved in planning services and as a platform for challenging racism. Within the statutory sector, community health councils are a vehicle for the patient's voice to be heard by health authorities. Crime prevention panels and domestic violence forums implement, monitor and review policies for community safety. Equal opportunity units in local authorities have encouraged an emphasis on priority targeting strategies to widen participation for specific groups such as women, people with disabilities, young and older people, and ethnic minorities. As public services have become more 'consumer conscious', attempts have also been made to democratise services and encourage a view of clients and public as co-participants in the determination of important aspects of service provision. And, finally, partly within the context of 'contract culture', partnerships between commercial, voluntary and statutory organisations are increasingly being forged to facilitate the delivery of community-based services. Whether this is the result of legislation, e.g. charging local social services departments with the responsibility of implementing community care jointly with health and housing authorities, or the result of a recognition of the importance of engaging local groups in defining and meeting needs as they perceive them, 'partnerships' is a key element within community services approaches.

More often than not a community services approach has been developed by community practitioners operating at middle and senior management positions within voluntary and statutory organisations. The approach challenges the traditional method of services allocated and provided according to professional assessments of need, the fostering of dependency on service personnel, and reliance on functionally distinct forms of provision. As Butcher (1986) notes, importance is attached to the restructuring of transactions between front-line workers and users of a service; thus professional skills will need to become redefined as these methods of working are developed.

As a particular form of community practice, community services approaches are concerned to:

1. develop services and organisations that are responsive to community needs
2. maximise opportunities for community involvement
3. promote inter-agency collaboration to further community interests.

Developing Responsive Organisations

Drawing from Kotler's (1982) classification of organisations into four levels of responsiveness, exemplars can be suggested for the ways in which voluntary, statutory and indeed commercial agencies can become more community oriented.

At one end of the spectrum is the *'unresponsive organisation'* typically characterised by an impersonal bureaucratic mentality giving more regard to the command structure of the organisation than to its responsiveness in meeting needs. The organisation knows what people need, therefore there is no sense in consulting them. Reception staff are often officious and unwelcoming;

appointment systems are rigidly adhered to; waiting areas are dreary and unstimulating; and the person you want to see is often 'busy'. Users are compliant or apathetic or alternatively may become frustrated and angry.

A *'casually responsive organisation'* is one that encourages members of the community to submit complaints, opinions and suggestions, and that occasionally surveys consumer views. The Skeffington Report (1969) for example recommended that local planning authorities convene meetings and set up community forums to discuss planning and other issues of importance to an area. It also recommended publicity to enable those wishing to participate to do so, and the employment of community development officers to secure the involvement of those not readily joining organisations. While the recommendations implied a serious commitment to public participation, the practice has often been cosmetic; organised economic and political interests have a major influence upon planning decisions. If participation carries with it no real opportunity for those taking part to affect decisions, then those who may already be disaffected, alienated and ignored will not be inclined to participate in legitimising an authority's plans.

At the other end of Kotler's scale of responsiveness are those organisations that can be categorised as *'highly'* or *'fully responsive'* in their service delivery relationship with users. A community responsive service vigorously attempts to break down 'we–they' distinctions. Barriers to communication are reduced through the commitment of the organisation to outreach work and to the development of information channels, interpretive services and self-advocacy schemes that enable targeted user groups to gain access as freely as possible. Such an organisation embraces equal opportunity policies in recruitment and selection, publicises its anti-oppressive stance, and monitors its methods and achievements in positive action initiatives. Creative possibilities for community consultation are tried, tested and then reworked. Transport, crèches, signers, preferred diets are all considered as a matter of course in planning and organising community events.

Such organisations make deliberate attempts to develop their knowledge of local community needs, resources and networks. In their study of community work and the Probation Service, Henderson and del Tufo (1991) note that this can take time. It was often the most experienced probation officers with local and personal roots acquired over a number of years who had slowly built up contacts. Such officers, they suggested, took it for granted that their contacts and local knowledge result in being well placed to help their clients. This was invaluable in opening up links for clients with other community groups and organisations.

The need to get to know 'one's' community is not a new concept for community workers and can be taken on more systematically by other professionals. If community practitioners are to be credible in a social planning role they will need to demonstrate the soundness of their knowledge of their localities, interest groups and services.

Maximising Community Involvement

Those local authorities which began to experiment with decentralised approaches to service delivery in order to encourage the participation of service users have already been referred to in Chapter 1. Statutory and voluntary agencies engage in a range of methods to promote community involvement, including community provision, consultations, co-option, self-management and community control (Broady and Hedley, 1989).

Community provision involves local authorities as direct providers and managers of local social and community facilities. Community consultations, as we have seen, include those efforts, albeit in a limited way, to test out public opinion on local councils' plans and proposals. Neighbourhood care groups mobilising volunteers to do ancillary work with social services, or conservation groups working in collaboration with community recreation departments, are examples of community co-option. The degree of power of a group either to manage or to be self-accountable for its own resourcing, finance and staffing determines whether or not the level of community involvement reflects community management or community control. While an authority might be committed to funding community and voluntary initiatives it should not itself be carried away by its own community euphoria. The development of the expertise to manage even small-scale projects is important. Community groups often need assistance in developing management structures and take time to acquire the confidence to run their own organisation. That assistance needs to be provided in a manner that is neither patronising nor covertly controlling.

Fostering a collective way of working within organisations may also be a way of promoting community involvement and diffusing power more widely. This does not mean that groups and organisations should be structureless, as this may lead to control by cliques and personalised hegemony. A community services approach should attempt to create relationships which try to help every individual to maximise their contribution rather than reproduce more hierarchically oppressive structures (Dixon et al, 1982).

An awareness of cultural and personal diversity and the consequent variety in terms of definition of need can be reflected in flexible structures that enable needs to be expressed. The commitment to meeting the needs of oppressed groups should enable creative approaches to develop pathways for community involvement. It is important to recognise the importance of indigenous community resources in the promotion of services designed to meet needs. Thus, Yusuf and Kettleborough's (1990) account usefully describes their experience of setting out to enable black women's voices to be heard through a local authority's structure. With the local authority's commitment to positive action, erstwhile isolated black women employees were able to form a support group involving other women, e.g. friends, neighbours, and women from local black organisations. This group met as a matter of course at different venues and in places that were unthreatening and least daunting to them. Meetings with each of the major local authority departments explored issues of concern to both black women and the wider community – health, employment, racism – and led to specific discussions, e.g. with the social services departments concerning transracial fostering, and with the libraries and art department concerning the contribution of black women to literature. The group became an important vehicle for the exchange of ideas and information between the women and the council.

In prioritising and targeting specific groups, it is necessary to recognise that there may be fundamental differences within and between them. Thus Yusuf and Kettleborough drew attention to the fact that the area in which they worked contained three distinctive Asian communities. For some groups and communities it is important that they are responsible for managing their own services, while for others it may be preferable to build development opportunities into mainstream programmes rather than to offer one-off workshops or day events.

Interagency Work

The fostering of links between organisations is an important part of community service approaches as a strategy for promoting co-ordination and social planning. Whether within economic and social regeneration initiatives or arts and recreational development programmes, partnerships between agencies, both formally and informally contracted, are increasingly evident in the UK. Organisations may not, however, always be willing to collaborate. At an abstract level Reid (1969) identified three forms of organisational coexistence: independence, interdependence and conflict.

An '*independent*' organisation pursues its own goals in isolation and has no need to use another's resources because it has security and control over its finances, staff and premises.

An '*interdependent*' organisation actively requires the assistance of another organisation in the pursuit of its goals. Partnerships and exchanges between charitable and commercial organisations via sponsorship, community awards schemes and loaning of staff are mutually beneficial. When local authorities and community groups combine to run a community centre, legal, administrative and building maintenance expertise can be provided by the local authority, with the community group providing the contacts and encouragement for users to attend. Organisations can avoid duplication of effort by working together. Their services can be more widely promoted and, by joining a consortium, their interests may be better represented. They also may gain political and social prestige from being seen to be associated with certain community initiatives. However, where one organisation is power dependent upon another (e.g. for funds) it may run the risk of being manipulated, dominated and legally directed.

Organisations that are in '*conflict*' with each other are often in contest either over their competition for resources (e.g. for funding, availability of premises, staffing and volunteers) or over their legitimacy. Community practitioners who wish to promote liaison, co-ordination or collaboration will be dismayed if they assume that community-based organisations are by nature co-operative in interest. In combining with other organisations to meet community needs, organisations will inevitably have to give up some of their autonomy. Whether they aim to pool resources, e.g. through shared use of premises, centralisation of equipment and transport, or set up innovative community projects, combination with other organisations will take time and energy and will require agencies to operate to the deadlines of others.

Community practitioners therefore need to have expertise not only in facilitating but also in inducing agencies to co-operate. Where they have appreciable financial resources, possess political, ideological or professional credibility, are able to gain access and entry to influence other organisations and are knowledgeable about community networks, they will be more influential in promoting interagency collaboration.

Community Practice and Community Policies

In reality, the three approaches we have described (summarised in Table 2.1) are not as methodologically distinct as might be thought from our consideration of each approach separately. As we have described it community practice is a method both derived from and aiming to promote community policies. Community practitioners, we would argue, need not be captive to any one of these methods over and above the others.

Table 2.1: Three Forms of Community Practice

'Distinctive methods and practices concerned with promoting, fostering and implementing community policies.'

	Community development	Community action	Community services approach
Aims	Promoting community self-help	Campaigning for community interests and community policies	Developing community oriented organisations and services
Participants	Community defining and meeting own needs	Structurally oppressed groups organising for power	Organisations/ service users as partners
Methods	Creative and co-operative processes	Campaign tactics on concrete issues	Maximising community/user involvement and interagency links
Roles	Professionals working in a non-directive way	Activists/ organisers mobilising for political action	Service managers restructuring transactions with users

Although the *community development* approach has been criticised as non-political (Craig et al, 1982; Dixon et al, 1982) in that it seeks to ameliorate rather than challenge social divisions, inequality and oppression, its strengths lie in the attention given to personal and group development. If that attention can lead to the formation of groups that are genuinely structured to enable participation, without being dominated by cliques or being patriarchally organised, and enable people excluded from mainstream activities to regain some control over services they need, that is positive. Organising for self-help is not necessarily a reactionary step.

The commitment in *community action* to grassroots active involvement is a significant contribution in the struggle towards greater equality and justice. Involvement in protest about the adverse impact of public policies on both people and localities has led to public policies being reappraised by those whose political futures are dependent on periodic electorate mandates. Community action can be successful in engaging those who are economically weak, socially oppressed and frequently excluded from political channels in direct political action and can help to re-establish their dignity, individuality and claims for citizenship.

The *community services approach* explicitly requires staff, professionals and policy makers to rethink their policies, procedures and priorities. As an approach to community practice it requires the development of methods concerned with establishing community responsive services which depend upon agencies getting to know their communities. To maximise community involvement it is important to encourage wider participation and ensure that opportunities for participation exist; its form and content can only be determined through dialogue. Furthermore, agencies can be persuaded to collaborate in partnership approaches in responding to community needs.

If public policy structures and services are open and responsive, the initiative for the promotion of community involvement might come from within them. Where this is not the case, community groups and community practitioners will need to campaign for community policies and practices.

3 Social Change and the Active Community

Jerry Smith

Introduction

Few would deny that British society has undergone fundamental change over the past quarter-century – change that has had a dramatic impact upon communities whether based on locality or interest. While there is scope for debate about the source of the impetus for change – social, economic, political and cultural – it is not difficult to draw a list of the key ways in which society has changed: deindustrialisation, the resurgence of market ideology and economics, new social movements, the break with the consensus values of the post-war settlement, a populace which is more mobile, ageing, ethnically and culturally diverse, the permeation of new technologies. These and a host of other changes have had a profound effect on community life and, therefore, on the potential for 'active community' which, as we have seen, is a key defining component of community policy.

This chapter will survey how the social landscape is changing, emphasising the implications of particular trends and changes for community life in general and community practice in particular. If community policy is to rest on the motivation, skills, organisation and commitment, time and concern of people to engage with public affairs at a community level as suggested in Chapter 1, then it is important to be clear about the present and likely future health of community life.

This chapter will, in short, examine how community life has been affected by various key themes during the past quarter-century, through an examination of four themes:

- political change
- demographic change

- the economy: poverty, inequality and the labour movement
- the changing institutional environment.

Political Change

The post-war period up to the mid 1960s appears, in retrospect, to have been an era of extraordinary stability during which academic interest in 'community' concentrated on community as description and as value (Bell and Newby, 1971; Young and Wilmott, 1957; Jackson, 1968). The instances of community activity which concerned these and other writers were more commonly of a social and recreational nature rather than attempts to present alternatives to welfare state service provision or campaigns to defend homes, jobs and lifestyles. 'Community' was of sociological, but not political, interest. It was also, almost without exception in the examples studied, white, working class, male dominated (though woman operated) and, while by no means cosy, generally free of deep internal conflicts. It was a community of shared basic values which might have a socialist political expression but which was, in the small 'c' sense, conservative.

All of this was beginning to change during the second half of the 1960s. At around this time a cluster of diverse, though sometimes connected, social trends simultaneously reached a critical mass. Much of this breakdown of stability was a consequence of increasing affluence itself, sometimes referred to at the time as the 'revolution of rising expectations'. The increased spending power of young people, which fuelled various aspects of an emergent 'youth culture', was now accompanied by a massive expansion of higher education. 'Youth culture' moved from being merely rebellious to a concern, however naive, to create an alternative society in which the values of community were often central. And for every thoroughgoing hippie there were others, also influenced by such ideas, who sought to express themselves through more worldly, if unconventional, political means, ranging from student protests to shop-floor entryism and agitation, to mobilising campaigns and protests in the community. The ideas of the 'new left', fomenting in journals for a decade, had reached the streets and the factories.

The role of the state in the late 1960s and early 1970s in relation to community practice was to assume the position of impartial arbiter between two unequal combatants–communities and commercial development interests. It did this principally through the planning profession which, under a cloak of technical progress, was able to preside over the destruction of communities in co-operation with, and largely for the benefit of, industrial and commercial interests (Davies, 1972; Goodman, 1972). It is ironic that these same planners came to be as vilified by the Thatcherite right in the 1980s as they had been by the activists of the new left in the 1960s and 1970s. Ironic, but not surprising, however, since both movements shared a distaste for statism which the planning profession represented *par excellence*.

In between these eras there lay a period during which the crisis of the state came to be seen as a crisis of government and governability, a theme taken up in Chapter 4; in relation to community policy the response during the 1970s was to embark upon a series of social experiments and pilot projects: area management, the urban programme, and the community development projects are some examples (Lawless, 1979). Some of these prefigured, to an extent, the new institutions which are now a more familiar part of the political landscape, a point returned to later in the chapter.

Cockburn (1977) argues that the decline of working-class political activity through the Labour Party at this time created a political vacuum which had to be filled by creating artificial neighbourhood organisations and participation schemes, while O'Malley (1977) draws different conclusions from a similar starting point. For her, the political vacuum was filled by a new, community-based radicalism notably involving previously marginalised groups such as black people and private tenants. Both of these accounts derive from the particular ideologies and experiences of the writers, and each contains a partial truth, as does Gyford's (1985) account of community activity of the period as the breeding ground for a cadre which re-emerged in the Labour Party of the early 1980s as the 'new urban left'. In fact, all of these things were happening, in different relationships to one another, in different places.

Unrest and civil disobedience are also aspects of the political process. In its earliest days some forms of community practice were closely associated with civil disobedience, notably the squatting movement. Even 'safe' issues such as campaigns for play facilities or pedestrian crossings were not averse to using peaceful direct action tactics, while it was the stock in trade of anti-motorway campaigners. Indeed American research indicated that 'poor people's movements' tended to gain most when using such tactics rather than 'working the system' (Piven and Cloward, 1977), though no comparable study seems to have been carried out in the UK. More recent examples, however, such as the inner-city riots of the early 1980s or the disturbances over the poll tax and on peripheral estates appear to be spontaneous responses to police or other action: unorganised, lacking in solid leadership and lacking in any long-term or medium-term aims (Benyon and Solomos, 1990), though some local anecdotal evidence suggests otherwise.

Where the political vacuum was not filled by radical community activity the 1970s provided fertile ground for racism. As the British sense of national competence and power continued to decline the attention of those who needed to believe in a 'great' Britain turned increasingly towards blaming, victimising and abusing black and Asian people for their part in the breakdown of the old society. It is possible that the impact of the National Front and other racist organisations might have gone much further had the wind not been taken out of their sails to a large extent by the rise of the new right, whose broader and more politically respectable ideology nevertheless contained a significant racist element.

However, the distinguishing feature of the Thatcher decade was perhaps not racism or any other specific policy it endorsed but its general sense of authority and certainty, combined with the simplicity of its central messages of individualism, competition and the acquisition of personal wealth; all values which are counterposed to those of community. This theme is explored in Chapter 13.

In terms of community activity women have always been central and, in purely numerical terms, as much as or more involved than men. There is plenty of case study material to suggest a tendency for men to take on the high-status, high-visibility positions in community organisations, even to the extent of usurping women's positions once a campaign 'takes off' and begins to be noticed by politicians and the local media (Presley, 1985; Curno, 1978). As the second-wave feminist movement gathered momentum from the early 1970s onwards the self-image of working-class women active in communities began to change. They began to perceive their separate interests as women as well as being part of 'the community'.

In the 1960s and 1970s it was widely believed that community organisations represented a significant, if largely potential, political force. This made them the focus of much attention – some of it friendly, some of it wary or hostile. Many local victories were chalked up but somehow the whole seemed less than the sum of its parts. Far from being a potent new political force, 'community' eventually proved generally unable to defend itself, whether against the ravages of inner-city developers in the 1960s and early 1970s or the cuts in public services of the period since then. But to understand the reasons for the political weakness of 'community' we need to look at other factors.

Demographic Change

The last quarter-century has seen the end of primary immigration; an absolute and a relative increase in black and ethnic minority populations; a falling birthrate but increasing lifespan creating a more ageing population; a growth in the number of households, especially small households, with one household in four consisting of a single person and only one household in three now including a child; a growth in the rate of divorce and in the numbers of single-parent families. The most deprived neighbourhoods are no longer the inner cities but the peripheral council estates (MacLennan et al, 1990).

In terms of its impact on community, one of the most significant aspects of demographic change concerns housing tenure. Council housing has changed from a tenure which catered for a wide range of household types and income levels to one catering mainly for those on low incomes and for those who require 'special needs' housing not readily found in other sectors. Less than half of council tenants now live with a partner, one-quarter are aged 60, and women predominate (a reflection both of growing numbers of older women living alone and of younger single parents) (MacLennan et al, 1990). The great majority are in receipt of housing and other benefits.

Owner-occupation has more than doubled since 1961 to 66 per cent in 1989 (*Social Trends 20*, 1990) and may be at or near a ceiling level. A further expression of the growth of affluence was the extension of owner-occupation into the working class. Though this had still some way to go before reaching its present extent, it was already in the late 1960s at a level which had implications for the concerns of this chapter.

Ethnic diversity, class fragmentation and multi-culturalism have had a powerful effect on community activity. The impact of this set of changes has undoubtedly made it more difficult to develop broad neighbourhood representative organisations. There are exceptions to this trend, principally the peripheral council housing estates which remain, for the present at least, largely white monocultures. But in a growing number of neighbourhoods there is little basis for solidarity among the diverse groups which populate them. This has helped to turn community practice away from the construction of long-term, democratic representative organisations and towards the development and support of more limited and instrumental organisations.

Changes in household structure have also affected community activity. Two-parent nuclear families are a small and declining proportion of households. Kinship ties, at least in so far as they relate to neighbourhood, are growing weaker. Even the assumed importance of the extended family in Muslim cultures is proving to be to some extent an oversimplification created by economic and housing conditions.

The breakdown of local kinship networks has both cultural and practical implications for community practice. On the cultural level it is arguable that neighbourhood means less than it once did. People are likely to be less committed to a place which does not include their closest family and perhaps other friendship ties. Generally greater mobility exacerbates this effect. On a practical level, lack of support networks makes it harder for people, especially women, and most especially single parents, to participate in community life. Running counter to this trend, in the poorest neighbourhoods with which community practice is most concerned, the lack of mobility of people and their dependence on neighbourhood institutions such as local shops and schools creates an increased commitment to neighbourhood, but at the cost of a sense of isolation and entrapment. Such people are less concerned with abstract notions of community than they are with immediate practical issues such as getting a local chemist. The main implication here for community practice is to further the trend towards more short-term, instrumental goals rather than the grand plans for community-led regeneration hoped for by the community workers of yesterday and many of the public policy makers of today.

The absolute and relative growth in the elderly population also has implications which community practice must take account of. Positively, there is a growing pool of 'third agers' with experience, abilities and time on their hands who are likely to play a fuller part in society; negatively, those who are no longer active represent a further drain on the time and resources of younger members of the community, again especially women, as community care policies take root as a potentially cheap and oppressive alternative to what is becoming prohibitively expensive state provision.

Severance of the traditional links between residence and occupation was well under way in the 1960s and is now all but complete. One effect of this change on community action has been to weaken the formal links between community and labour movement organisation, considered below, though these links were perhaps never strong in the first place. A more significant effect has been that members of community organisations are unlikely to meet at work or to share a common work experience. Thus a further basis for solidarity is weakened. The largely (but by no means exclusively) male solidarity of the workplace as a basis for community organising has been replaced by the typically female solidarity of the shared experience of caring.

We have seen that the period from the mid 1960s has been characterised by what sociologists refer to as 'fractionalisation', and part of the result of this has been a reduction in the power and meaning of class labels, especially among younger age groups. Related to this is the debate about the nature – or indeed the existence – of something referred to as 'the underclass'. Different writers attach different meanings to the term, so that it is, for the present at least, probably not a helpful one (Gans, 1990) though for most commentators who use it, the term appears to relate more to behaviour than poverty (Ricketts and Sawhill, 1988). From the literature and experience of community practice, however, it is hard to escape the feeling that the combination of the trends towards fractionalisation, alienation from the political system and long-term, hopeless poverty is resulting in the creation of neighbourhoods where internal conflict is endemic and people can no longer perceive their real interests or enemies (Miller, 1989).

In the light of this it is worth commenting on the notion that Britain is becoming a 'classless society'. As already noted, this was an idea in common currency in the late 1960s, though there were attempts by Marxist sociologists to re-emphasise (and redefine) class during the 1970s – attempts which in part have led on to the present debate about the 'underclass'. If a 'classless society' is taken to mean an equal, or more equal, society then clearly nothing of the sort is happening or is in prospect – rather the reverse. But if it means that the old division of society into a few giant blocs sharing common interests has been replaced by a more differentiated, fractionalised and competitive social structure, then the notion clearly has validity.

The consequence for community life and community practice of these changes has been that difference is emphasised: unifying features of community practice as a potential social movement, as it had been seen in its early years, are played down in favour of the alignment of community organisations with 'parents' outside the community setting; or, more accurately, the small-scale locality concept of community is replaced by the broader interest-based sense of community as defined by being a woman, a Muslim, a person with a particular disability, or a carer, for example. In the fragmented and often competitive politics of identity there is a danger that the voice of 'community' will not easily be heard (see Chapter 11).

The Economy: Poverty, Inequality and the Labour Movement

The late 1960s were a time of rising real living standards for almost everyone and a period of full employment. The general expectation was that living standards would continue to rise and that inequalities of income and wealth would diminish, albeit gradually. The phenomenon of 'the affluent worker' was being commented upon (Goldthorpe et al, 1968), and the income differentials between this working-class elite and much of the middle classes had been substantially eroded, even if differentials of wealth and property as well as substantial differences in expectations and prospects, working conditions, culture and lifestyle, remained.

The last decade has seen the deepening of income inequality to levels many people thought had been consigned to history. Real disposable income per head almost doubled between 1971 and 1989, but the income of the highest decile of male full-time employees rose from 162 per cent to 180 per cent of the median wage during this period while that of the lowest decile fell from 65 per cent to 59 per cent (*Social Trends 20*, 1990). Most of these changes occurred during the 1980s. At first sight, wealth inequalities appear to have lessened but this is due to the increase in owner-occupied housing; when this is excluded wealth inequalities, too, have increased (*Social Trends 21*, 1991). The political management of the breakdown of consensus has been achieved through the economic empowerment of the majority of the population at the expense of a substantial minority who have paid the price for the restructuring of the economy since 1979.

Poverty is not just about lack of money but lack of power and social exclusion. The two go hand in hand; effective participation means being able to influence people. This requires the means to travel, to look good and to be able not only to sit in meetings but to socialise before or afterwards. Community practice is mainly concerned with the disadvantaged, the poor, the disenfranchised, the underclass or whatever name is given to the approximately one-third of the population who have not shared in the benefits of economic growth. Community practitioners cannot simply start by creating organisations; they are increasingly required to work at the level of the individuals, building personal skills and self-confidence to offset in some small way the enormous handicaps placed on them by enforced non-participation in society. Another tentative hypothesis, then, might be that this also helps to account for the trend in community practice away from organisation building and towards personal growth and development.

In the early 1970s it was widely assumed that once unemployment passed the magic figure of one million it would result in social unrest, yet it has reached more than three million during the early 1980s and early 1990s with little more than an annual round of urban riots as its political price. Once a touchstone of economic policy, full employment is now regarded by all but the economic fringe as an unattainable dream in an era in which political economy is dominated by issues of money supply, interest rates and the public sector borrowing requirement. The present UK government's attitude to unemployment, beyond a little hand wringing, is essentially that it is a phenomenon which occurs when workers 'price themselves out of jobs'.

Full employment, then, may be a thing of the past. But more than that, the whole structure of employment has changed. The days when a father could guarantee his son a job in the pit or the docks, or a mother her daughter a job in the biscuit factory or textile mill, have disappeared, lost in the shake-out of the traditional manufacturing sector and the curbing of trade union power in the 1980s. The creation of 'community enterprises' has often served as a policy fig-leaf intended to mitigate the effects of the wholesale closure of 'smokestack industries'.

Alongside rising unemployment is the increased participation of women in the labour market. The two phenomena are unified by the overall process of casualisation of labour, with women typically occupying part-time, low-paid and often insecure jobs. The implications for 'community' (and for women themselves) are largely negative. Women are spending less time in the neighbourhood, have less leisure time than men – though they are still 50 per cent more likely to be engaged in community activity (*Social Trends 20*, 1990) – and are under increasing pressures to act as both breadwinners and carers. In even the poorest communities there is noticeably less street life than 15 or 20 years ago, which in turn has implications for issues ranging from crime to the viability of local shops.

The creeping casualisation of the labour market has accompanied the shift from manufacturing to service sector employment. While the latter sector was largely insulated from the recession of the early 1980s this is not so in the present recession. This labour market shift has not only meant the end of 'jobs for life' but has had two further important consequences for the purposes of this book.

Even well into the 1970s it was common to find that the leading lights of community organisations were also active in the trade union movement. Such figures are now rare. In so far as they were typically white and male with a trade unionist's tendency towards a bureaucratic model of organisation, their passing may not be entirely regrettable. Nonetheless, they did bring to community action a range of skills and political contacts which it arguably now lacks. A background in labour movement activity was one of the key success factors for community activists identified by Donnison (1988). Beyond this, it may be argued that many of the members of today's community organisations have little or no experience of 'real' (i.e. paid, full-time, secure) work and the discipline which goes with it, and that this lack of experience had a negative effect on the capacity of community groups to organise. Certainly some effective criticisms have been launched on the failure of the libertarian left in particular and of community practitioners in general to create and sustain effective organisations (Landry et al, 1985; Pitt and Keane, 1984).

The situation in the early 1990s is one of almost complete separation between the concerns and activities of community organisations and those of trade unions. Those unions which have best survived the wintry climate of the last 15 years have been white-collar unions which have had the lowest level of common interest with the disadvantaged groups community practice seeks to empower. The concerns of community action have, moreover, moved into areas which are not the labour movement's strong suits, notably equality of opportunity in its various forms. It is also true that community organisations have, perforce, espoused some of the tenets of Thatcherite economic and social policy in ways which are unlikely to make them new friends in the labour movement. Contract tendering and tenant-managed housing are examples.

Finally, it would be a mistake to presume that deindustrialisation of itself works against community. As Abrams and Brown (1984) point out, sociologists at one time associated industrialisation with the loss of community and are now in danger of making the opposite mistake. Deindustrialisation is likely to transform rather than destroy community, posing new challenges and presenting new opportunities.

The Changing Institutional Environment

Community practice has been, and remains, most directly concerned with local rather than central government. But it is increasingly central rather than local government that creates the climate in which community practice takes place and determines the limits on the local authorities which have always been the primary target of community activity.

We have seen how the diversification of community practice has in any case moved its concerns beyond the remit of local government to include such issues as health or policing. At the same time the role of local government has contracted and a range of new, or sometimes revamped, organisations has been brought into play.

The quango – an unelected publicly funded body acting as an instrument of policy – is one such form of new institution. Examples include task forces, housing associations, city challenge organisations and urban development corporations. All of these bodies are supposed to involve local communities and to be responsive to their needs and demands. In practice, their performance on this criterion has been poor (CDF, 1992a; MacFarlane, 1993) but that is not the point at issue here. The point is that even a government ideologically committed to radical individualism has had to recognise the continuing importance of the collective in British political life.

The trend towards contracting out of public services to suppliers other than local government and health authorities is now well established. This, too, is intended to empower communities and to give better value to individual consumers by providing new opportunities to choose suppliers and to organise to provide services directly (Gutch et al, 1990). In practice, because of the specialisation and organisation of contracts, the lack of guidance and models, short-term and insecure funding arrangements and the lack of resources to help communities to organise in response to these opportunities, the effects have been limited (Beardon, 1993).

There have been changes in local government that have taken place from within, in addition to those imposed by central government. In relation to the question of activating communities they have been less far reaching and positive than has sometimes been claimed (Seabrook, 1984; Blunkett and Jackson, 1987). Indeed, the early changes were almost wholly negative in the sense of creating larger and generally more remote units of local government. Local authorities became more concerned with the management than the delivery of services (Stewart, 1983).

In many ways the changes that have since occurred in the political culture of local government may be seen as an attempt to regain what was lost in 1974, albeit in a more modern form. There is certainly a heightened concern with the delivery of services and with 'consumer satisfaction' and performance indicators, much of it prompted by the threats to local authority direct service organisations posed by legislation requiring a growing list of services to be subject to compulsory competitive tendering (NCC, 1988).

Perhaps the most relevant reform in relation to community practice is decentralisation. This is a subject which is taken up in Chapter 9.

These moves have had little impact on local political behaviour as evidenced by voting patterns. Radical reforming local parties such as Labour in Basildon or the Conservatives in Bradford have remained as vulnerable to swings in national voting patterns as they ever were. There is more to political participation than voting, of course, and the evidence suggests the domination of other forms of political activity – membership of pressure groups, contact with councillors, members of ward parties – by white men from skilled working-class and middle-class backgrounds (MORI, 1987). Community activists and community practitioners alike tend to have little direct contact with the political system (Barr, 1991).

The inescapable conclusion is that community practice, the election of various 'new urban left' Labour councillors notwith-standing, has made little impact upon the political process. It is ironic indeed that local politicians' memories are so long that some of them continue to treat community action in the 1990s as though it were still the unreconstructed, rebellious child of the 60s.

Conclusion: the 'Active Community'?

Communities will always generate action. Collective grievances will continue to result in protest meetings and the formation of action groups as long as there are local politicians to lobby and local papers to report their activities. But such groups are rarely sustained without outside help, whether this comes from political activists or paid community practitioners. If community action is to play a continuing part in the democratic process, as politi-cians of all shades claim to want it to, the support of community practice must be an integral part of public policy. Nevertheless, wider social changes will impact, for better or worse, on the viability and sustainability of community organisations, and this concluding section will try to summarise the implications for the 'active community' of the social changes discussed above.

It is ironic, though entirely explicable, that political interest in 'community' began with the end of the period of community stability and coherence. 'Community' as a sociopolitical construct has come to the fore over the last quarter-century precisely because it was perceived to be fragmenting. Demographic diversification, the breakdown of class allegiances and mass political parties, the fracturing of links between workplace and residence (and the destruction of large-scale manufacturing industry as a basis for solidarity) and the new forms of poverty which in an individu-

alised, competitive and mobile society mean social exclusion –
all of these trends have threatened 'community'.

Politicians have, then, sought to revive 'community', initially
through fear of an anticipated wider social breakdown that could
result from the melting of the social glue provided by 'community',
more recently as a legitimation for policies that seek to supersede
statist welfare in favour of empowering the individual as consumer.

Clearly, then, it would be wrong to suggest that community is
less relevant now. But it is an altered vision of community with
which we have to grapple: one which is more diverse, more
instrumental and in a closer relationship to governmental and
other institutional structures. In terms of the values of solidarity,
participation and coherence elaborated in the previous chapter,
that of participation appears to enjoy higher status in public
policy terms than either solidarity or coherence.

The principal public policy function of 'community' in the 1990s
is to replace local government and to render the partial disman-
tling of the welfare state socially acceptable. 'Community' is
counterpoised to 'bureaucracy'; the one sensitive, local, small-scale,
caring and flexible, the other unfeeling, remote, large-scale, self-
serving and rigid. We should not rush to condemn this rather naive
reconstruction of the concept of community, though. Perhaps we
ought, rather, to be persuading its advocates (who come from
almost all parts of the political spectrum) that their vision of
community simply does not exist and needs to be created – not
by planners and politicians, but by people themselves with appropriate resources and help, and enough space and time in which
to do it.

As ever, the contradictions are there for those with the wit and
the will to exploit them. In particular, the 'Thatcher decade'
during which government seemed possessed of boundless
authority, confidence and competence is past, and questions
about the credibility and authority of institutions once again
dominate the political agenda. The environment of community
action and community practice involves opportunities as well as
threats. It would be a brave commentator who would predict which
will become dominant as we move into the next century.

4 Why Community Policy? Some Explanations for Recent Trends

Hugh Butcher

Earlier chapters give rise to a paradox: on the one hand a wide range of post-war policy initiatives explicitly embrace a 'community' dimension, indeed commentators now talk of a growing trend towards the adoption of policies that build on the attractiveness of community values. On the other hand it is clear that many social and political changes over the past 25 years – e.g. accelerating geographical and social mobility, increasing centralisation of state power, the celebration of individualism in social and economic life – have posed a significant challenge to both locality communities and the values that underpin 'community' more broadly. If the social base of community seems to be systematically eroded, how can we account for the arrival of 'community' as a concept in good currency within public policy practice? What, in other words, lies behind governmental support for programmes like community care and community policing? How do we account for the movement by a small but growing number of local authorities towards the adoption of community development as an integral part of their longer term planning? And how do we explain the movement by a variety of 'human service' professionals (in fields as diverse as health, recreation and education) to adopt a community dimension to their work?

Later chapters will reflect further on these questions, in the context of their particular concerns with specific policy initiatives. This chapter seeks to provide a more general and historically grounded account of the forces and influences that lie behind the growing interest in community policy. It constitutes the fourth and final contextualising element in this part of the book but it will, hopefully, offer something more than mere historical background; in deploying and further exemplifying the concepts already introduced in previous chapters it will develop a theoretical framework for the concluding analysis taken up in the final part of the book.

Attempts to account for the growth of community in public policy have been undertaken, we suggest, at three distinct levels of analysis:

1. First, 'community' is embraced if and when it offers a possible solution to pressing problems facing the policy maker. Here the movement to community is not value driven; it may not even be a 'trend' at all, in the sense of drawing sustenance from a common, underlying, source of ideas and sentiments. Its manifestations, in this view, are best seen as the outcome of pragmatic, short-term and practical responses to policy makers' needs to find workable alternatives to existing patterns of decision making, provisions and practices.

2. The second level of analysis digs a little deeper than the first and connects contemporary policy interests in community to a series of state crises – 'performance', 'legitimation', 'fiscal' – that have confronted British governments in the quarter-century since the mid 1970s' break with the policy assumptions of the post-war consensus. Questions about whether a single identifiable community trend can, or cannot, be identified is misplaced. Community approaches are best seen as having been incorporated into public policy thinking in at least three or four distinct ways, and once their role is seen in this way similarities as well as notable differences can be detected and analysed.

3. The third level of analysis digs deeper still, uncovering the forces that link 'community' policies with those wider tendencies towards the evolution of a 'post-modernist' social order. The centralised and bureaucratised nature of much government activity in which, for example, welfare rights are dispersed along standardised and universalistic lines is seen as mirroring many of the characteristics of the so-called 'Fordist' organisation of modertn industrial society. However, new technologies and new social movements throw up new post-modern social forms, giving rise to cultural and political pluralism, the consumerist ethic, dispersal of power, individual responsibility, and a new 'localism'. 'Community' politics and

policies, it is suggested, find themselves the beneficiaries of such trends.

'Community Policy' as Practical Problem Solving

Accounts by both David Donnison and Peter Willmott exemplify the first of the three types of explanation. David Donnison offers the insight that it has been within the most centralised and pro-fessionalised public services that we see the most concerted search for the new community-based models of practice (Donnison, 1989). This is because, he suggests, such services have come under the greatest pressure to substitute 'traditional' models of organi-sation and service delivery with those which more thoroughly engage with the public at large, or some specific 'client group' in particular. Officials and professionals find that they can no longer meet their organisational objectives using the old methods. Thus the experience of housing authorities in seeking both to rehouse people in purpose-built estates and to improve older housing has been frustrated by hostile and obstructive public reaction: fierce opposition from those who were to have their homes modernised was paralleled by increasing vacancies, vandalism and lost rents in new build housing. New methods of housing and estate management, community ownership schemes, housing co-operatives, and partnerships with voluntary sector housing associations have been some of the 'community' responses to these challenges.

But as Donnison points out housing is only one example, albeit an early one, of public authorities taking on an element of the community approach. Lord Scarman's investigations into how and why the police were driven from the streets of Brixton during the 1981 disturbances crystallised and gave extra impetus to those schemes for liaison groups, community relations, and community policing methods already under development elsewhere in the British Isles. In similar vein, Donnison suggests that the medical authorities – confronted with numbers of health problems to which, like AIDS, they can offer no remedy – have tried to find ways of encouraging and assisting ordinary people to take more responsibility for the care of their own health.

As he points out, the search for community-based approaches within housing, police and health bureaucracies 'was not an invention of starry eyed enthusiasts. It has been developed, sometimes as an act of desperation, in order to solve problems which defeated conventional services operating in conventional ways' (Donnison, 1989, p. 202).

Peter Willmott takes a similar line:

> to some extent local government politicians and managers turned to de-centralisation to help deal with the excessive scale of local authorities and the public criticism of much public housing management . . . The Home Office and senior police officers saw community policing as a way out of a set of new problems . . . and . . . some thoughtful architects, recognising the low reputation of their profession after the high-rise disasters of the post-war years, tried to find an acceptable new role for themselves. (Willmott, 1989, p. 30)

Of course, to suggest that community oriented programmes offer solutions to problems 'which defeated conventional services operating in conventional ways' only prompts a further question: what accounts for the apparent exhaustion of conventional practices? Both authors offer some clues.

Willmott suggests that from the mid 1960s onwards there was a general movement away from a faith in centralism and professional expertise towards a belief in ordinary people, complemented by a growing recognition of the importance of 'intermediate' institutions to people's lives.

Donnison identified a rather different set of factors, pointing to an important general shift in public attitudes. The wartime generation that constructed the top-down, centralised, professionally dominated structure of the post-war welfare state could see its institutions – of social assistance office and housing department, of planning system and economic intervention – as reliable and relatively benign buffers to the vagaries and injustices of private markets, private landlords and an unregulated economy. But by the 1970s a new generation had grown up; institutionalised welfare rights could be taken for granted, but the machinery that made those rights a reality was increasingly experienced as inflexible, interfering and oppressive.

Reactions and outcomes varied – hostility, resignation, alienation – and gave rise to a raft of policy problems that provoked a search for new approaches to decision making and service delivery. Which brings us to a consideration of the second 'level' of explanation identified above: community approaches as a response to 'crises' in the welfare state.

Welfare State Crises and the Incorporation of Community Policy

Chapter 1 offered a particular approach to thinking about public policy, an approach that will be used here to take further our search for explanations of the growing popularity of the community approach. It was suggested there that policy questions could on occasion be helpfully analysed by thinking about *types* of policy under the following heads:

- service policies
- governance policies
- resource policies
- social control policies.

The main argument to be developed here is that community strategies have been utilised to support all of these types of policy over the past quarter-century – in particular as specific difficulties or 'crises' have developed within that sphere of policy. The subsidiary argument is that when such patterns of governmental incorporation of community strategies are examined over time three broad phases are discernible, the shifts in emphasis from one to the other being explicable in terms of contemporary historical developments and the way in which they helped to structure the political and policy agendas of the day. We will look at each phase in turn.

From the Late 1960s to the Mid 1970s: Community Strategies for Service Delivery

During this period community interventions were characteristically deployed by the state as innovatory adjuncts to professionally led reforms introduced to tackle residual pockets of poverty and deprivation. In retrospect this period has been seen as the 'tail end' of the long post-war boom, a period characterised by a bipartisan belief in Beveridge-inspired state welfare along with positive administration of the economy via Keynsian demand management techniques. However by the mid 1960s the post-war consensus, with its supporting beliefs in socially engineered progress towards a new post-capitalist social system (Mishra, 1984), was wearing thin. This was particularly evident on the welfare state front. Evidence was revealing significant 'holes' in the net of welfare state provision. It was evident to Labour Party leaders and their advisers that poverty had not been abolished, and that significant inequalities remained. The analogy of 'holes' was apt – the enfolding garment of the welfare state protected most, but left others out in the cold, unprotected. Centralised welfare statism – the delivery of services according to need by professional experts – was still appropriate, but it was no longer seen as a panacea for all social ills. 'More of the same' would not do, and we witnessed the search for alternatives. 'Community' approaches offered one way forward and three examples of service-delivery approaches in this period may be given here.

The Community Development Project

The CDPs were set up from 1969 onwards, explicitly charged with finding new approaches to vanquishing social deprivation resistant to the ministrations of mainstream welfare services (see Loney, 1983). The projects were established on an assumption that need was geographically concentrated, and that there was maybe something pathological about the culture of people who lived in multiply deprived areas, something that prevented them from taking up the services provided by the welfare state. After all, the rest of British society had 'never had it so good' and the majority of people had been able to grasp the opportunities provided by full employment and steady (if relatively slow) economic growth, and a beneficent welfare state. It was not of course only the people's own culture that held them back, that ensured their entrapment in a cycle of deprivation; the service-delivery apparatus of the welfare state also required attention, with need for an 'integrated' approach. But, above all, there was an assumption that a community work approach would help to enable, or encourage, people to help themselves, to grasp the opportunities presented to them.

The Seebohm Report

Chapter 16 of this key report (*Report of the Committee on Local Authority and Allied Personal Social Services*, 1968) on the future development of the personal social services also looked for ways of involving clients and their communities in meeting social need. Here the emphasis was on finding new, preventive methods of social work help. Family casework could provide a valuable form of social treatment for some people, but the community could and should also be a focus of intervention, making a contribution at the level of social problem prevention, and at the level of social care rehabilitation. Community work, some argued, represented a way of modernising social work.

Intermediate Treatment (IT)

The Children and Young Persons Act 1969 echoed and crystallised a similar line of thinking in the juvenile justice field. Juvenile delinquency constituted a major political and media concern throughout the 1960s. At the same time professional understandings had been changing, in that the child who got into trouble was increasingly seen as 'deprived' rather than 'depraved' – a victim of a disabling social environment, rather than a destroyer of it. From the Ingleby Committee Report of 1960 onwards a number of official documents and statutes had called for treatment of delinquency by promoting the welfare of children through helping them and their families in the community. The 1969 Act provided a statutory framework for 'intermediate' treatment of young offenders in the community.

The argument here, then, is that up to the late 1960s a broadly bi-partisan approach to welfare could be discerned. There were beginnings of a radical critique of the welfare state, but by and large there was a confidence in the basic structure of welfare institutions. Intellectuals and politicians were optimistic that 'technical' solutions to social problems could be found and the Community Development Project, Seebohm Report, and Intermediate Treatment can be seen as early examples of the ways in which community work was incorporated as part of state-led and 'professionalised' approaches to service reform.

These are, of course, very broad-brush generalisations and it is true that 'resource' questions also informed government perception of how small-area deprivation should be addressed, and social work and social services reformed. The size and growth of public expenditure, particularly in the social welfare field, was already becoming a concern; and the desire to rein in public expenditure created a favourable climate for selectivity and 'priority', for small-scale, experimental, demonstration projects, and for approaches which sought to encourage lay, community involvement in meeting needs as a partial substitute for expensive professional forms of provision. However, the next major 'phase' in government involvement in community initiatives was *not* primarily concerned with resource questions, but with issues of governance.

Through the 1970s: the Community Work 'Boom' and the Problem of Governance

The first half of the 1970s witnessed the biggest expansion of community work seen to date (Baldock, 1977; Waddington, 1979). This expansion was partly attributable, as we have seen, to the growing emphasis given to the 'service-delivery' capabilities of community work initiatives but Baldock identifies a further set of factors, and introduces the central feature characterising the state's involvement in community practice in the early and middle 1970s. He writes:

> With the continuing growth of the welfare state, there were rising expectations that met head-long the increasing inability of the government to cope. The initiatives of 1968–9 took place against a background that included rent strikes in almost every major city as council rents went up, and rebate schemes became more and more common in the run up to the 1972 Housing Finance Act. Coincidentally, the slum clearance programmes of many cities, having run through the worst older housing, came up against areas where older housing was often owner occupied and suitable for improvement. To the amazement, even downright incredulity, of many Labour councillors people began to protest against proposed demolitions. The issues relating to housing found parallels elsewhere. There was a new attitude abroad of assertively claiming the 'charity' of the state that led to the formation of claimants' unions and other groups concerned, partly or entirely with state benefits that were organised not by concerned professionals (as the Child Poverty Action Group had largely been) but by claimants themselves. (Baldock, 1977, p. 263)

Baldock characterises this as a 'new rebellion'; Marxist political scientist Ralph Miliband wrote of 'desubordination' (1982). With the increasing break-up of the post-war consensus came a breakdown in old patterns of deference, a new willingness to question, challenge, and on occasions take direct action against duly constituted authority.

As Baldock points out this new rebelliousness was important to community work in a number of ways, not least because it created a problem that the authorities needed to manage.

Community work interventions provided one means of managing this problem of governance, of desubordination. Chris Jones in the *Bulletin of Social Policy* (1983) provides a particular view of the nature of this governance problem. He, like Baldock, suggests that the early to mid 1970s saw 'Western political leaders anxiously debating the problem of governability'. He quotes extensively from reports produced by the Trilateral Commission – a standing organisation of leading politicians and capitalists, which met to examine the deepening crisis of western industrialism. Social scientists, he notes, were appointed to examine issues of 'disintegrating civil order, the breakdown in social discipline, the debility of leaders and the alienation of citizens'. They duly identified the 'overloading of the state' as an important factor.

> The role of the state had greatly expanded with an accompanying tendency for more and more people and groups to look to the state to solve their problems. (Jones, 1983, p. 72)

The state lost credibility as it:

> Patently failed to satisfy expectations adequately on the one hand, and generated more and more political conflict on the other . . . as it became enmeshed in ever widening areas of social activity. (Jones, 1983, p. 72)

To summarise, then, the state was increasingly overloaded; expectations were being raised which state agencies could not meet; and government agencies had become embroiled in more and more political conflict as they became enmeshed in ever widening areas of responsibility.

A number of solutions presented themselves. Most radical were those which involved 'rolling back the state', either through privatisation of state provision or through some system of state/voluntary-sector partnership via a move towards welfare pluralism. The other alternative, and the one that gained most immediate support during the 1970s, involved an attempt to 'relegitimate' large-scale state activity and involvement by government in the lives of the citizen. A particular strategy here, that of 'public participation', provided an impetus for the further deployment of community practitioners and community work strategies. Strategies for citizen participation enhanced the credibility of representative democratic government by grafting on an element of direct democracy. Although the institutions of electoral democracy may well be able to regulate the activities of the minimum 'night watchman' state, it was seen that they needed to be augmented with newer, more direct, forms of popular involvement as educational levels rise, the administration of state services become more complex, and the expectation of involvement in decision making grows. Public participation, in planning, transport, housing management, neighbourhood government, the National Health Service, school government and so forth, became an 'idea in good currency' in the 1970s (Boaden et al, 1982; Richardson, 1984). Community practitioners were either drawn in directly to help administer such processes or were otherwise employed to help 'organise' voluntary associations and community action groups in a way that would secure their proper articulation with the organs of government (Smith, 1981).

The 1980s: Enabling and Containment

Governmental overload has also stemmed from what O'Connor (1976) and others have called the fiscal crisis of the state. In order to finance increasing social provision, taxation had been raised to levels that began to threaten profitability and capital accumulation within the wealth-generating private sectors of the economy. This problem had been aggravated by the way in which public-sector dynamics work to foster departmental budget maximisation rather than the efficient meeting of consumer needs. The two solutions to these problems, which became hallmarks of the Thatcher years, but which pre-date 1979, have involved extending the scope of market forces (through privatisation, or the creation of 'internal markets' within the state sector) (Ascher, 1987) or, alternatively, rebalancing the contribution of non-commercial provision in favour of voluntary- and community-sector involvement. Malcolm Johnston (1984) and others have documented the relative increase in funding of the voluntary sector during the 1980s, and the ways in which the self-help ethic and the attack on the 'dependency culture' has transferred the burden of care from state agencies to (particularly female members of) families. Both of these strategies involve a redefinition of the role of the state, but it is with respect to the second – the movement to the so-called 'enabling' state, within a mixed economy of welfare – that provides us with some prime examples of the incorporation of community initiatives in the service of 'resource' policies. As Martin Loney has pointed out, from the mid 1970s we have seen central government give an increasing emphasis to the virtues of community care and the 'do it yourself' ethic. Loney shows that from this time onwards there has been an increasing all-party commitment to self-help, 'to encouraging the helpless to help themselves', a reflection, as he says, of a growing concern over the rising costs of state welfare provision. With the 1976 economic crisis, the issue of public spending was brought dramatically to the fore and in his 'letter of intent' to the International Monetary Fund, the Chancellor, Dennis Healey, committed the government to a continued reduction in public spending.

Since then there has been a consistent effort to reduce public expenditure and from 1979 this has been reinforced by an ideo-logical attack on state welfare expenditure. Calls for informal community care, an enlarged voluntary sector, advocacy of welfare pluralism, and support for things like the patch system in social services are all, according to Loney, understandable against the backdrop of these wider expenditure policies. Indeed, he goes further and suggests that such concepts are used fairly cynically, as a smokescreen behind which real attacks on the welfare state can be exploited.

To summarise, then, community practice in this phase has been deployed to support developing policies for community care, voluntary initiative, and self-help. At the same time long-term unemployment has given rise to the use of community strategies as unwitting props to 'special measures' and schemes to employ people on limited-term contracts funded by short-term monies.

But this is not all: the 1980s also illustrate how community ini-tiatives have been utilised as an arm of public order policies. An example of a 'community' approach within the juvenile justice system has already been noted, within the earlier discussion of service policies. This was appropriate, as 'intermediate treatment' had its origins in a belief that 'deviant' youth was also 'disad-vantaged' youth and as such required a social service intervention as much as, or more than, a social control response. The 1980s, however, witnessed the growth of community approaches within the explicitly public order context of policing and law enforce-ment.

Economic recession and record levels of unemployment, de-teriorating public services and benefit levels, the widened disparities in material circumstances and life chances of sections of British society have all served to amplify alienation and disaffection amongst those who have failed to benefit from the 'enterprise culture'. This has manifested itself in various ways: inner-city tensions, sometimes boiling over into riots; racial distrust, scape-goating and harassment; escalating rates of crime, hooliganism and vandalism. The government has, of course, made law and order one of its foremost policy priorities. Nevertheless it has become clear that something more than a mere increase in conventional policing methods (or investment in hi-tech, fast reaction techniques) would be necessary if the anti-social reactions of young people, black people, inner-city residents and other 'marginal' groups were to be contained. Community policing, as a rationalised and all-embracing successor to earlier juvenile liaison schemes, community relations projects and schools link work, has developed apace over the last decade (Willmott, 1989), providing a significant increase in police forces' capacity for sur-veillance and intelligence gathering, preventive action, and mobilisation of consent (Gordon, 1984).

Community Policy – a Post-modern Trend?

This final section is concerned with a third, even deeper and more generalised set of trends, trends that are best described as 'emergent', as yet only partly identified and comprehended. Such trends flow from fundamental changes in the social structure, and particularly the sociotechnical organisation, of work and production, in late twentieth-century society.

The development and application of new technologies (par-ticularly in information handling and control), along with other social changes, are seen to be opening up radically new approaches to organising, controlling and managing industrial and other non-industrial forms of production. The new technologies, for example, facilitate a movement away from standardised products, mass assembly line technologies, and 'Taylorist' models of scientific management supervision and organisational control. Arms-length, computer assisted planning and control promotes more decen-tralised decision making and 'flatter' management hierarchies, the diversification of products, and some job enlargement for the employee. Older, 'producer driven' thinking – 'you can have any colour motor car so long as it's black' – gives way to a more consumer led and responsive approach. Diversified markets can be handled, and an increasingly 'pluralist' society accommodated.

Such trends are 'deeper' than those explored earlier in this chapter, and are most appropriately described in 'structural' and long-range historical terms. Such trends will rarely be invoked to justify or rationalise the decisions and actions of those seeking to make policy and ensure service delivery; they operate at a level once removed from the concrete day-to-day agendas, plans and action of those working on public policy problems. But they are nonetheless important context-providing realities. Moreover, they are also more general in the sense that their impact is felt far beyond the specific concerns of this book. They are increasingly affecting the way that large corporations, as well as intermediate size firms, are organising and managing their affairs, which is in turn reflected in new management thinking and organisational theory. Their consequences are, similarly, sparking off new thinking about the structure and purposes of government, at both central and local levels. While their long-term outcomes and consequences are not yet clear, this final section is concerned to explore how such imperatives have moulded current thinking about community policy. The debate is thus broadened, and 'community' approaches and policies are examined within a more generalised understanding of the way that societies are changing.

A variety of attempts have been made to review the implications of such trends and thinking for the public sector (Aucoin, 1990; Cochrane, 1991; Stoker, 1989), with questions of control of organisations and work, and the new management systems that arise as a consequence, providing a fruitful focus for analysis (Hoggett, 1991). A new way of thinking has emerged, that of the 'new public management', the concerns of which contrast with, and offer a significant challenge to, the preoccupations and vocabulary of the older 'public administration' school of thinking. In Hoggett's analysis 'bureaucratic' and 'post-bureaucratic' models of organisational control are contrasted as a way of pinning down the radical change in perspective that lies behind the new thinking, the new organisational practices, and the new management approaches.

In outline form, the argument is as follows: bureaucratic control, exemplified in and through the operations of large public- and private-sector organisations during the three or so decades following World War Two (e.g. in the National Health Service, British

Aerospace), was characterised by a range of features: a centralised command structure along with highly standardised systems of co-ordination and control, and excessive attention to formalised procedures (Aucoin, 1990, p. 198). Other defining features included functional specialisation and organisational segmentalism ('departmentalism', 'divisionalism'), the vertical integration of production, with 'delegation upwards'. Bureaucratic organisation allowed for mass production of goods and services, but also led to giant, slow-moving organisations that suffered from all manner of bureaucratic 'dysfunctions'. These included a tendency to emphasise attention to procedures at the expense of outcomes, departmental competition rather than corporate co-operation, and the growth of informal structures that subverted formal procedures. The 'solution' to such problems was often even more bureaucracy. Significant changes in the mass manufacture of motor cars has come to symbolise the debate about new methods of organisational control and management. Gyford summarises the debate as follows:

> The basic proposition is that we have been witnessing the decline of old style assembly-line mass production methods aimed at satisfying a mass consumer market, of the sort pioneered by Henry Ford: under this system of production work was highly routinised, closely supervised and organised under tight hierarchical control along the lines of 'scientific management' as pioneered by Frederick Taylor. Post-Fordism argues that new technologies are drastically altering production, stocking and retailing methods, leading to a new pattern of small batch production of customised products and employing a more versatile work force with a greater degree of autonomy on the job. In the latter context post-Fordism also implies a post-Taylorism and thereby has a wider significance for systems of management beyond manufacturing industry. (Gyford, 1991, p. 29)

The exact outlines of the new post-Fordist model are much contested. However it does seem clear that new post-bureaucratic models are developing, made possible by new social conditions and new technologies that have come to the fore since the late 1970s and early 1980s. Revolutionary methods of handling information have rendered redundant old techniques of bureaucratic control, and offer new ways of planning, supervising and co-ordinating organisational work. Alongside the information technology revolution private-sector corporations have had to adapt to a more turbulent market environment. Not only is more product diversity the order of the day ('any colour so long as it's black' will no longer secure market share) but the rate of product development and change is far more rapid. The new technology comes in again here too – small batch production, with products and services customised to meet the demands of a particular market segment, can be more quickly produced in response to sophisticated and up to the minute analyses of consumer preferences.

The point for us here, of course, is that these trends have their parallel within the public sector. This is partly a consequence of private-sector 'new wave' management thinking – symbolised in the rejection of old-style management assumptions in discussions like Peters and Waterman's *In Search of Excellence* (1982) – permeating public-sector thinking. But it is also because similar environmental pressures have been at work. British society has become more diverse and fragmented. Allison, for example, has seen the 1980s as:

> a period during which many kinds of social division have magnified. The sense of affiliation to a social class declines constantly, but the perceptions of other distinctions intensify: north against south, city and suburbs, rich and poor, employed and unemployed, black and white, right and left, and so on . . . The picture suggested is of a society literally and slowly falling apart . . . This is the age of social fragmentation. (Allison, 1986)

Alongside this growing pluralism has gone an increasing assertiveness – a greater willingness on the part of these diverse publics to demand, contest and assert their needs and demands – partly as a consequence of an increased confidence arising from mass education and the exposure to exemplars in the mass media. Political thinking from the new right constitutes a further influence. Partly as a response to fiscal pressure and monetarist prescriptions a move to devolved management and cost-centre budgeting in the health, education and social service fields has given a further impetus to new forms of operational decentralisation within a system of centralised strategic command.

In his analysis of 'post-bureaucratic' control within public services, Hoggett identifies two ways in which the new paradigm achieves operational decentralisation – internal decentralisation (devolved service units) and external decentralisation (operations devolved to units outside the organisation altogether). We see here how the particular initiatives discussed in the second section of this chapter can be seen as a reflection of these deeper processes. Devolved service units – decentralisation in local government, estate management, social services – create opportunities for greater responsiveness to local conditions and needs, but also opens the door for a greater devolution of policy making. Hoggett writes:

> Devolution will only permit greater responsiveness if DSUs (Devolved Service Units) either have the ability to create locally-specific policies or to interpret and adapt corporate policies to local requirements. For example, this would imply that devolved units have the power to target services towards the needs of particular groups (e.g. elderly people, children with special learning difficulties, etc.) or to introduce entirely new kinds of services to a particular area (e.g. a community education initiative attached to a local library, a support unit for survivors of psychiatric services) or to deliver existing services in radically new ways. (Hoggett, 1991, p. 253)

'External decentralisation' also encourages a measure of pluralism and provides opportunities for community-level initiatives and involvement. In another publication we have distinguished between 'competitive pluralism' and 'cultural pluralism' (Butcher et al, 1990). The first involves government agencies contracting tasks to voluntary and community organisations; less 'monolithic' and more responsive and cost-effective services are seen as the result. The second strand rests on an explicit recognition of diversity in local culture, lifestyle and needs, and seeks to promote indigenous control over local services:

> Diverse service users and client groups, sectional and community-wide interests, may all be supported through grant-in-aid and community development approaches in an effort to augment representative democracy with a measure of participatory or 'direct' democracy. (Butcher et al, 1990, p. 149)

These models clearly represent new right and new left versions of 'post-bureaucratic' public service provision and democratic accountability; and they both entail new relationships between state and community. Finally, as Hoggett notes, they potentially:

Open up space for new political roles at the grass roots level and for much greater user involvement at the point of service delivery. Without managerial devolution there really was very little point in users becoming involved in service delivery matters except as complainants and antagonists, but once real power over decisions and resources has been located at the point of delivery user-based forms of local democracy become a more tangible possibility. (Hoggett, 1991, p. 254)

It should by now be clear that the three 'levels' of explanation explored in this chapter are complementary rather than alternatives. They must all be taken on board if we wish to achieve a rounded account of where community policy is 'coming from'. The understandings of the policy actors who grapple with day-to-day policy issues must be embraced, but so too must an understanding of the deeper social currents that structure the context of their work and choices. Only through such a comprehensive account will we be able accurately to understand contemporary developments and promote appropriate change.

Part 2 Community Policy in Practice

In selecting community policy fields for inclusion in Part Two, reference was made to the five types of government policy identified in Chapter 1: service, governance, resource, economic and public order policies. We aimed to include community initiatives and strategies across the range of these policy types in order to explore their incorporation, or otherwise, in public policy. The community policies subsequently selected were:

- community youth work
- community arts
- community enterprise
- community policing
- community government
- community care.

The fivefold policy framework was primarily used as an organising framework for selection. The resulting matrix (see Table 1) suggested to us that community policies have different degrees of emphasis according to public policy type.

Sara Banks's chapter opens Part Two with an overview of community youth work as it has developed in the UK within local authority and voluntary organisation contexts. She provides an extensive range of examples from locality-based youth work initiatives, illustrates projects that have struggled to find ways to challenge inequalities and discrimination facing young people and outlines a community practice approach that supports and involves young people in taking action themselves. Within the context of the diminishing role of local authorities as direct service providers she argues that a community youth work approach needs to address the collective needs of young people and that the processes of encouraging empowerment and participation should be key performance indicators for good practice.

Table 1: Community Policies and Public Policy

Community setting	Dimensions of Public Policy				
	Service	Governance	Resource	Economic	Public order
Community youth work	***				**
Community arts	**		**	*	
Community enterprise	*		**	***	
Community policing		**			***
Community government	**	***	*		
Community care	***		**		

Emphasis of community policy: ***   High
                                    **   Moderate
                                      *   Low

In a similar vein, Lola Clinton and Andrew Glen in their chapter on community arts show how the development of community-based arts activities requires access to artistic resources. Community arts emphasise active involvement, collective creative expression, identity, and help to communicate a variety of social, political and economic concerns. Thus, the challenge for public policy is to sustain the spontaneity and diversity of artistic and cultural expression within communities without imposing predefined and excluding notions of artistic excellence. Accordingly, within a national strategy for supporting community-based arts, they argue for a flexible and accessible policy-making framework that will enable the developmental role of the provider to be strengthened, funding to be guaranteed, networks and alliances to be encouraged and good practice to be documented.

Jenny Lynn's chapter on community enterprise initially identifies the different forms of community enterprise that have emerged in the UK historically and in more recent times. She suggests, in light of this experience, a number of practical steps for their successful establishment. On the grounds of their potential for partnerships between public policy makers and local communities and their role in promoting 'corporate responsibility' she argues for their continued incorporation in mainstream economic regeneration programmes and the need to exploit European funding sources to help realise cross-cultural partnerships.

Molly Weatheritt's chapter critically appraises the policy and practice of community policing specifically in relation to the increased use of foot patrol and local area responsibility, partnerships in crime prevention and community consultation.

With its emphasis drawn from community values, she argues that at the presentational and political level community policing reflects all that is 'best in British policing', though in practice its development has been somewhat piecemeal. She concludes by pointing to the very complexity of the conflicts within and between communities to which the police are called upon to intervene. She argues that it is in dealing with such conflicts, derived as they so often are from social and economic divisions, that the police are challenged to seek out and apply consensual bases for action as implied by community policing.

Within the context of recent debates about the role of local government, and in the light of the current restructuring to incorporate market mechanisms and consumer preferencing, Mohammed Habeebullah and David Slater's chapter appraises different models of community government in practice. However, irrespective of ideologies, they argue that political parties in the UK have shown a significant reluctance to engage in dispersing power and promoting local community involvement. Accordingly, for community government to be more vigorously implemented significant changes are required in the political culture across political parties, in the assistance given to the voluntary sector and in the encouragement given to community groups.

In the final chapter in Part Two Liz McShane illustrates the importance of developing local networks to support the implementation of community care policies. Drawing from experiences in Northern Ireland she demonstrates how community practice methods were employed to encourage, resource and support local community and user groups in the support of vulnerable and dependent people. While the example reflects a markedly different approach to community care than the highly structured management-led approaches, it is not 'care on the cheap'; a community practice approach, she argues, requires appropriate resourcing in order to enable service users, their carers and advocates to play their part.

75

5 Community Youth Work

Sarah Banks

Current Trends in Youth Work and the Youth Service

Youth work as part of a publicly funded service – the Youth Service – is in the midst of a period of change. In this sense it is no different from any other public welfare service in the early 1990s in being subject both to central government scrutiny to demonstrate its effectiveness and efficiency, and to local authority expenditure cuts and restructuring. As with many local authority services its very existence hangs in the balance as local authority powers and resources diminish and the contract culture takes hold.

At the same time, the social and economic conditions of a significant minority of young people are worsening. The ineligibility of 16 and 17 year olds for income support, changes in housing benefit, the board and lodgings regulations and the lack of rented housing coupled with high unemployment have created what some commentators have termed an 'underclass' of young people effectively excluded from the mainstream of society. While street disturbances in the early 1990s (Hobbs, 1992; Conway, 1992) have brought some of the issues to the forefront of public discussion, this has focused more on policing levels, car security and punishment than on the development of youth provision (Community and Youth Workers' Union, 1992, p. 4). However, there is evidence that in bidding for additional central government funds (for example through the City Challenge competition introduced in 1991) local authorities are including youth work projects with a focus on youth unemployment and training based in the inner- and outer-city housing estates. This is just one example of a general trend towards work targeted either at areas of deprivation or at particular groups of young people thought to be at risk or in trouble. It marks a move away from the idea of

77

universal youth provision open to all which has been part of Youth Service philosophy since its inception within local education authorities in the 1940s. It also signifies a shift in the balance of the Youth Service's public policy aims from service (provision of leisure-time activities) towards control (keeping young people off the streets and from committing crimes). For youth workers this means more specialisation, more short-term project work, increasing employment in the voluntary as opposed to statutory sector, the development of skills to undertake short-term, outcome-focused work and the ability to manage increasing tension and conflict within the aims and values of their work.

The last decade has also seen a growing concern for equality of opportunity and practice that is participative and empowering. At a ministerial conference in England in 1990 participants drew up a statement of purpose which declared that:

> The purpose of youth work is to redress all forms of inequality, to ensure equality of opportunity for all young people to fulfil their potential as empowered individuals and members of groups and communities; and to support young people during the transition to adulthood. (National Youth Agency (NYA), 1991, p. 3)

While there is no doubt that these principles inform much youth work practice, 'participation' and 'empowerment', rather like 'community', have a variety of meanings ranging from token consultation to genuine power sharing; and from personal development to collective action for social change. The contradictions in youth work practice (between controlling and empowering, for example) and the gap between what workers think they are doing and the actual practice will be discussed later in this chapter.

Youth Work as Informal Education

Before moving on to discuss various manifestations of community youth work it may be helpful to clarify briefly what is meant by the term 'youth work'; recent definitions have tended to characterise it as informal educational work with young people aged roughly between 11 and 25 with the aim of promoting their personal and social development (see Smith, 1988, pp. 124–39; National Youth Bureau (NYB), 1990). This distinguishes it from other types of work with young people such as purely leisure or social activities (where the primary purpose is not educational); from formal schooling and training; and from youth social work (the main aim of which might be control or treatment). These categories are, however, by no means watertight; individual workers and projects may be working simultaneously within more than one, and the views of workers, users, employers and funders frequently differ in their definition of the purpose of the work. This chapter will focus largely on what might be termed 'professional' youth work, that is, youth work that is organised and funded through local authorities and/or voluntary organisations that form what might loosely be described as the Youth Service.

Community Youth Work: Three Manifestations

In this section we will explore three different senses of 'community youth work' – locality-based youth work; work with young people who constitute a community of interest; and a 'community practice' approach to youth work.

1. Locality-based Youth Work

Centre Based
Most youth work organised through the Youth Service consists of decentralised provision in a locality, the most typical example being clubs held in youth and community centres. Even relatively small villages may have their own youth club once or twice a week in a village hall or community centre. Often they may rely on local volunteers and may be run by voluntary management committees. So in this sense it could be said that youth work is generally community based. Yet although such youth provision is located in the area where its potential users live, in some cases little work takes place outside the clubs or centres.

Area Based
Within the last decade there has been a move towards 'area-based' work (as opposed to centre-based work) which has the potential to encourage workers to consider the needs of the people living in an area, rather than just the users of a centre. The redeployment of Youth and Community Service staff into area teams is proceeding at an accelerating pace across England and Wales

and has often been accompanied by a restructuring of Adult Education and Youth and Community Services into a Community Education Service – a structure already well established in Scotland (Smith, 1989, p. 8). There are several explanations for this trend towards area-based work. One reason commonly given by local authority officers is that it improves the effectiveness and responsiveness of the service, enabling resources to be directed to real needs or priorities, rather than being attached to particular buildings or projects, often for historical reasons. It usually means a rationalisation of funding and staff, however, and may also be used as a way of saving money. Newcastle City Council, which had previously been planning to turn its Youth and Community Service into a Youth Service, very rapidly switched to a Community Education Service model in 1992 as a way of saving one million pounds. An area team structure is often accompanied by the devolving of budgets to areas, so that area workers and local councillors have more say in how resources are distributed.

Detached Work

As part of the same move away from the club-is-the-youth-service approach, the number of detached youth work projects has increased in recent years. The problem of the 'unclubbable' or 'unattached' youth was noted in the Albemarle Report in 1960, reinforced by the Fairbairn-Milson Report (1969), and during the 1960s and 1970s several youth work projects with 'unattached youth' were established and literature began to emerge (Goetschius and Tash, 1967; Marks, 1977; MacDonald, 1980). By the time of the Thompson Report in 1982 it was noted that most local authorities employed some detached workers, but that the work was not well understood. Throughout the 1980s, however, the amount of detached work has increased, and this trend appears to be accelerating in the 1990s.

The role of the detached youth worker is to meet young people on their own territory, and to work from their expressed needs. The detached worker is based in a locality in the very real sense of working in the streets, bus shelters, or wherever young people congregate. The reasons for the growth of detached youth work are various. First, projects may have developed out of an egalitarian concern that traditional club-based youth work was meeting the needs of only a minority of young people in an area. So work outside centres and clubs on young people's own territory developed to reach those who might have even greater need of youth work but who would not attend a centre (National Youth Bureau, 1983). A second reason is connected with the needs and concerns of adults and the authorities to control alienated groups of young people in particularly deprived areas. The Detached Youth Work Project on the Meadow Well estate in North Shields, for example, was established in 1984 with Inner Areas Partnership funding as a result of concern about severe vandalism at the newly opened Metro Station. Other measures, including a strong police presence, heavy fines and imprisonment had failed. The first annual report of the workers at the project (Barrigan and Manktelow, 1985) describes a variety of sensitive and bold interventions with groups of young people on the estate. The workers speak of the pressure to produce 'seen' results, and ask whether such a project can benefit the community. They acknowledge that they cannot solve many of the issues they are dealing with (the involvement of the young people in crime and anti-social behaviour) but suggest they can help young people to confront and cope with these issues. They suggest that:

> Learning some of the basic social education skills may enable young people to get on better, which in turn, may create more opportunities and results, for themselves and the community. (Barrigan and Manktelow, 1985, p. 18)

A third reason for the more recent growth of interest in detached work may simply be cost. With many buildings in a dilapidated state and no funds to repair, it is cheaper to employ detached youth workers working from a small office base. They can also move easily around a patch to 'trouble spots' or areas of need. With falling numbers of young people, and the general unattractiveness of youth centres compared with other leisure facilities, it is a way of targeting resources more effectively (Smith, 1991, p. 15).

Peripatetic and Mobile Work
As might be expected, detached work has been given highest priority in Metropolitan and London Boroughs (Smith, 1989, p. 44). Peripatetic work and mobile projects have been a response in recent years particularly to the needs of young people in rural areas where small settlements cannot support a full-time youth worker or youth centre. Rural areas began to gain attention in the late 1970s as rural deprivation, including the plight of relatively isolated young people, was 'discovered' and publicised. During the 1980s innovative projects designed to cater for such young

people began to be developed (Fabes and Banks, 1991; Fabes and Knowles, 1991; National Advisory Council for the Youth Service (NACYS), 1988b). For example, until its recent reorganisation, County Durham's Youth and Community Service had two peripatetic workers in Weardale and Teesdale, the most sparsely populated and rural parts of the county. These workers would support and develop youth provision in the various small villages and hamlets, including the establishment of a mobile community bus in Teesdale (Costigan, 1991). The peripatetic youth worker in Teesdale adopts a community development approach where possible, supporting and enabling local adults and young people to set up and run their own youth clubs and activities. Inadequate facilities in some villages, difficulties with transport, and the reluctance of local people in some communities to work with young people, led to the establishment of a community bus in 1987. The bus serves as a multi-purpose, mobile resource, offering transport between villages, space for youth activities and group work on board, and advice and information sessions. It can be parked in a village and used, in effect, as a youth centre. It can change locations according to need and demand, and be used to stimulate further interest or provision which might then lead to the setting up of a youth club in a village hall. As with detached work, mobile projects can go to where young people are and in addition attract young people on board out of curiosity.

Targeted and Preventive Work
Recently there has been a growing trend towards establishing specialist youth projects to work with young people in the community around drugs, homelessness, HIV/AIDS and car crime, or to work in neighbourhoods or estates identified as having a high level of deprivation, especially unemployment, among young people. Very often the style of work adopted may be detached and outreach work, or counselling and advice projects. The move towards such projects is partly pragmatic – other solutions to the problems of youth crime or drug taking have not worked, as was the case with the Meadow Well Detached project. A recently published handbook on youth crime prevention describes twelve youth projects in this field (Findlay et al, 1990). They range from outdoor adventure activities to drug prevention and a youth enquiry service resource unit. The latter, for example, is a unit which aims to set up a network of local youth enquiry services (YES) projects in areas with high crime rates, poor youth

facilities or high unemployment. Such projects provide free information, advice and support for young people aged 16–25 and involve them in managing the YES projects (Findlay et al, 1990, p. 37).

Care and Control in the Community
Perhaps the most noticeable move towards community-based provision is within youth social work and the field of juvenile justice. Although the main emphasis of this chapter is youth work, rather than youth social work, it is important to mention developments in this field as they impinge on youth work, and the boundaries are becoming increasingly blurred (Teasdale and Powell, 1987). With the introduction of the DHSS Intermediate Treatment Initiative in 1983, the number of projects offering alternatives to custody for young people has mushroomed. Very often these are run by voluntary organisations staffed largely by social workers, but increasingly staff trained in youth work are becoming involved too. This can obviously be seen as part of the wider trend towards community care and preventive work developed to save money by diverting young people from residential institutions and as a result of changing views on the most effective methods of crime prevention. The extent to which alternative-to-custody projects also reflect changing views on the causes of crime and social problems – a movement from individual pathology approaches to consideration of social, cultural and environmental factors – is debatable, however (Pitts, 1992). Most projects focus on changing young offenders' attitudes and individual circumstances, rather than raising collective issues or campaigning for change in the neighbourhood as a whole.

Simonside Lodge in South Tyneside is a good example of an alternative-to-custody project set up in the mid 1980s by a voluntary organisation (Barnardos) in co-operation with Social Services through the DHSS initiative. The centre undertakes community assessments, the aim of which is to prevent young people being sent from the borough for assessment; reintegration into mainstream education for young people regularly absent from school; and an alternative-to-custody programme for young people facing custodial sentences. The alternative-to-custody programme is geared to each individual. It entails individual counselling and peer group work, it examines the reasons for offending and the effects on the victims, and its aims are to help the young people to make informed and appropriate decisions in the future and to encourage greater self-esteem so that pressures from others to engage in criminal activities in the future can be resisted (Simonside Lodge Report, 1990).

2. Work with Communities of Interest

Young People as an Interest Group

As Franklin and Franklin (1990) argue, prejudice and discrimination against both young and old people are ingrained in the cultural, political and economic structures of our society. Young people have little economic or political power – since they either do not work or are poorly paid, and cannot vote until aged 18. They tend to be perceived either as dependent and in need of protection or as threatening and in need of control. Young people over 16 have recently suffered a decline in the level of state benefit entitlements, which has severely curtailed their capacity for independence and increased levels of poverty and homelessness (Kirk et al, 1991; Killeen, 1992). There is no doubt, therefore, that young people could be regarded as an interest group. Yet despite the rhetoric of the Youth Service, it would be misleading to imply that most publicly funded youth work exists in order to encourage young people collectively to demand and achieve more economic and political power. The purpose of youth work is more about encouraging the 'active citizenship' or 'social and political education' of individuals, which really means giving young people some help during the so-called turbulent transition from childhood to adulthood, so that they can fit into existing societal structures.

Of course, youth organisation councils do exist in many boroughs, and young people may sit on decision-making bodies connected with the Youth Service, but often this amounts to no more than token participation, albeit resulting in a great deal of personal development and confidence building on the part of the individuals involved. The main campaigning work done in the area of young people's rights is at a national level, often outside a youth work context, for example the Youth Rights Campaign or the National Association of Young People in Care.

Specific Interest Groups

Given the complexities and regional variations in the Youth Service it is hard to obtain even a rough picture of the extent to which work with communities of interest on their own specific needs and issues has been or is taking place. However, it is certainly the case that the Thompson Report (1982) gave some legitimacy to this type of work, stating that separate provision may be appropriate and that youth work should reflect the values and attitudes of neighbourhoods from which young people come. It is also clear that during the 1980s youth work with girls and young women, black people, people with disabilities, and gay and lesbian young people was developed, partly because of the demonstrable failure of the traditional Youth Service to attract and therefore to meet the needs of many groups of young people (Cross, 1977; NACYS, 1989; HMI, 1991; Kent-Baguley, 1990). In the sections that follow we will look at just three areas of specialist work in more detail.

Work with Girls and Young Women. Even the most widespread of these areas of work – work with girls and young women – is not as common or as accepted as many youth workers, particularly feminist workers, feel it should be (Spence, 1990). This is partly because of continued male dominance and control in youth work (Sawbridge and Spence, 1991) and also because young women generally are not perceived as threatening and in need of control in the way young men are (Nava, 1984). Nevertheless, largely through the pressures and persistence of women youth workers, there has been some Youth Service response to the demands of girls and young women which has allowed for the creation of regular girls' nights, girls' clubs or young women's groups where issues around gender roles, stereotyping and femininity can be explored along with other activities (Spence, 1990, p. 84). The National Association of Youth Clubs Girls' Work Unit, established in the early 1980s, was a major source of support and stimulus to women workers in developing girls' and women's work. It published a national newsletter and organised national conferences and networks, and its closure in 1987 was a major blow to women workers. However, girls' and women's work has continued, and in many local authorities there are specialist workers whose brief is to develop the work. In 1988 it featured as a priority area of work in 80 per cent of the local authorities surveyed by Douglas Smith (1989). How much of this work will survive in the new local authority structures remains to be seen.

Work with Young Lesbians and Gays. Although the 1970s and 1980s saw some raising of awareness of the needs of young lesbians and gays and the establishment of several campaigning groups (such as the London Gay Teenage Group in 1976), according to Kent-Baguley 'the struggle in the Youth Service, from a national point of view, remains very much in its infancy' (Kent-Baguley, 1990, p. 116). The Thompson Report of 1982 made no mention of the needs of gay and lesbian young people, and despite cogent arguments on the part of committed workers and groups such as the Gay Youth Workers Group (founded in 1976) and the National Joint Council for Gay Teenagers (formed in 1979 to facilitate the development of lesbian and gay youth groups throughout the country) there is still very little specialist provision. What does exist tends to be in the larger cities, particularly London, and often takes the form of helplines or counselling services (Heathfield, 1988). With the abolition of the Inner London Education Authority (which had funded specialist work with lesbians and gays) and the introduction of Clause 28 into the Local Government Act in the late 1980s (which prohibited local authorities from 'promoting homosexuality') much progress in this area of work was inhibited. At present a significant proportion of the work that is being done tends to be in the voluntary sector and is still at the campaigning and awareness-raising stage.

Work with Young Black People. In 1980 the Commission for Racial Equality (CRE) published figures showing the low take-up of youth provision by black people and called for a radical review of the service. The CRE itself subsequently funded a special initiative to set up Afro-Caribbean and Asian youth clubs. As already mentioned, the Thompson Report (1982) expressed concern and recommended separate provision if appropriate. While the number of black clubs and projects and black workers has increased in recent years (Popple, 1990) their distribution is still patchy, and many black workers feel that the case for separate provision, and the type of provision, has to be constantly argued for. Williams argues that black youth workers must increasingly emphasise the political role of their clubs and projects (Williams, 1989, p. 137). At a recent conference of black community and youth workers the arguments for separate provision were put very strongly: to help black young people cope with racism and oppression; to enable them to experience the positive aspects of their lives as competent, caring people; and to provide the opportunity for black workers to develop their skills (National Black Workers and Trainers, 1990, pp. 32–7). Many local authority Youth Services have appointed specialist workers to work with black communities or 'ethnic minorities', although often these may be funded through special central government funds, such as that provided through section 11 of the Local Government Act 1966.

There is obviously a never-ending list of potential 'interest groups' with which the Youth Service has, or might have, dealings – young people with disabilities, young people in care, Jewish young people, Muslim young people, and so on. And special projects and organisations exist for all these groups at both local and national levels. Given the variety of interest groups it is simply not possible for the Youth Service as presently constituted to meet the demands of these groups for separate provision at the same time as offering a neighbourhood-based service open to all young people and responding to the latest moral panic about car crime, drug abuse or teenage pregnancy.

3. A Community Practice Approach to Youth Work

So far we have covered the descriptive meanings of 'community' (as locality and community of interest) in our discussion of the extent to which youth work is becoming more 'community based'. And at this relatively superficial level we have argued that community-based work has always existed and that in many respects it has been developing in recent years. But this is not the only meaning of 'community'. As Butcher has demonstrated in Chapter 1, it also has an evaluative meaning connected with notions of solidarity, participation and coherence. And these communal values are expressed by members of an *active* community in taking collective action to meet their needs or express their views. To what extent do the types of youth work discussed above reflect these other senses of 'community'? To answer this question we have to look deeper into youth work practice, not only at the stated aims and purposes of the work, but at the methods used, the levels of user participation, the focus of control and power.

While 'participation' has become a key word in youth work, it can be interpreted in several different ways ranging from consulting young people about decisions, to involving them in decision making, to empowering them to have the control and power to make and act on their own decisions (NACYS, 1988a). Just because a youth project is community based and has a policy statement about participation this does not mean that participation occurs in the strong sense. Quite often youth work is about offering provision or delivering a service, the decision about which has been taken elsewhere. This need not necessarily undermine the sense of solidarity (mutual aid and co-operation) or coherence (meaning given to an individual in relation to others) that a specific activity or piece of work may engender or build on. Outdoor pursuits, competitive games or international exchanges organised by workers can still do that. But it may not be quite what we mean by a community practice approach. Participation in decision making and planning does seem essential. A community practice approach to youth work means not only working within a community (as locality) or community of interest, but working in a way that enables the people involved *collectively* to work together to grow and change according to their *own needs and priorities*.

The Top End Youth Action Group based in Ferguslie Park in Paisley is an interesting example of a community practice approach to locality-based preventive youth work. It is one of the projects described in the *Youth Crime Prevention Handbook* (Findlay et al, 1990, pp. 13–16) in which crime reduction is listed as one of its major achievements. Yet within this framework of 'social control' the project could be said to have operated according to principles of empowerment and participation. It was started by an inter-agency group of voluntary and statutory organisations and local people concerned about the 'anti-social and criminal activities of local youth'. Four youth workers were drafted in to tackle the problem. They decided to adopt a 'social action' rather than a service delivery approach – that is, rather than developing youth clubs or activity groups they made contact with the young people, built up relationships, and found out their views on the problems of the area and their ideas for possible solutions. With support from the youth workers some young people formed the Top End Youth Action Group and began to meet with local community activists, police, councillors, officials and other young people. Eventually they gained support and funding from various sources to convert local shop premises into a Youth Action Centre and to employ two youth workers. The centre and workers are managed by a committee of eight young people elected from the Youth Action Group. Crime figures, youth referrals to social services and complaints from local residents have all apparently declined since the project started. This is a good example of an initiative targeted by welfare agencies at an area of high crime, but where the approach adopted was to support collective action for change, and to encourage individual and group empowerment. It started by looking at the needs of the area from young people's point of view, it involved local adults and professionals from a variety of agencies, and it supported the young people in taking action themselves and in controlling and managing their own project.

Work with communities of interest also tends quite often to develop the active community and participants' feelings of solidarity and coherence. Williams's (1989) comments about the political nature of work with black young people emphasise this, and the same could be said of work with young lesbians and gays and women, although this is not always the case.

Future Developments in Youth Work

As mentioned earlier, local authority organised and funded youth work (the Youth Service) is beginning to undergo quite far-reaching changes in the structures and systems of delivery. These have been stimulated partly by financial pressures. Out of 59 authorities responding to a survey undertaken in March 1991 nearly two-thirds recorded a decline in income for the Youth Service from 1990/91 to 1991/92 (NYA, 1992a, p. 5). According to the same survey, a majority of authorities said they were increasingly prioritising work with particular groups of young people, developing project work and non-building-based work. Some responses apparently emphasised that the reasons for the changes were to improve the quality of service offered to young people, but others stated they were due to declining resources (NYA, 1992a, p. 14). Further changes reported include the devolution of budgets to local level (either areas or individual units), service agreements or contracts for grant-aided staff, and programme funding rather than core funding for the voluntary sector (NYA, 1992a, p. 15). More recent research on delivering local youth services (NYA, 1992b and 1992c) shows evidence in several local authorities (e.g. Warwickshire) of moves to contract out the Youth Service, or parts of it.

As local authority Youth Services change roles from service providers to enablers the tendency will be for the policy aims for youth work (which may be determined as much by central government as local government) to veer away from universal *service* provision to problem oriented, targeted prevention and *control*. That is, projects with top priority for limited funding may well be those doing generalist work in deprived or problematic neighbourhoods or those doing specialist work with a target group (such as young offenders or homeless people). The trend towards these kinds of project is already apparent. Yet while the public policy aim may be moving towards the control end of the spectrum, on a micro-level the philosophy and methods adopted by some of these projects and the workers in them may be based on principles of participation and empowerment as articulated in the recommendations from the second ministerial conference and demonstrated in the case example from Paisley described earlier. The projects will be community based – located where the young people they wish to make contact with are living (in a way that 1960s' youth centres rarely can be now). So in this sense they could be described as 'community youth work'. But in many cases the needs and problems of the young people will not have been self-defined, and the empowerment will be at an individual rather than a collective level. The confidence and self-esteem building work done by a youth project may help individuals to cease offending, or drug taking, and to become useful members of society. But will it also collectively empower a group of young people to campaign for jobs or for benefit changes? It is vitally important that we distinguish between individual and collective empowerment, although, of course, the former often leads to the latter.

While the location of special youth projects in areas of deprivation, for example to prevent and divert offenders, demonstrates to some extent a recognition of the links between social deprivation and crime, and the methods adopted to tackle it may be based in the community where it can be 'nipped in the bud', many of the projects still focus on diverting or changing the *individual* young people rather than changing the social and economic conditions in which they live. The boundaries between youth work and youth social work will become ever more blurred, as the control agenda in youth work, which has always been present, although often hidden or implicit, becomes more up-front. Governmental pressures to specify outcomes for youth work are already leading policy makers and youth workers to define very specific and product-oriented outcomes such as reductions in youth crime, which are easier to measure and easier to use in order to convince funders of efficiency and effectiveness than more nebulous outcomes such as increased confidence and self-esteem.

However, even within the broad policy aims of control, there is room for manoeuvre by local policy makers and by youth workers. The move from centre-based to detached and outreach work provides the ideal opportunity for the promotion and implementation of a community practice approach. There is evidence that some policy makers recognise that community-based approaches to preventing social problems have some effect and are relatively cheap. The next stage is for them to reappraise their use of concepts such as performance indicators and learning outcomes and to ensure that the processes of the work are evaluated as well as the more tangible outputs. Within this framework, youth workers can use and develop a community practice approach by taking account of young people's views and needs, and by encouraging them collectively to take control of parts of their lives and to work towards small changes. Being realistic, this is all that can be expected within state-controlled and funded youth work.

6 Community Arts

Lola Clinton and Andrew Glen

Introduction

Communities display variety in terms of artistic expression, and diversity in terms of culture, and they contain within themselves great potential creativity. This variety, diversity and creativity is vital for the expression of personal identity as well as a basis for communities' social and economic development. Without it there is a very real possibility that many parts of the country would become cultural wastelands. It is in recognition of this that over recent years a variety of different interests have argued for a review of arts development policy, particularly as: 'National policies for the arts in the UK have tended to undervalue the importance of providing adequate resources and explicit encouragement for the development of education and wider participation in the arts' (Hutchison and Forrester, 1987, p. 133).

The community arts movement of the 1960s challenged the right of the Arts Council to spend public money solely on art forms and venues accessible to the privileged few. Increasing demand by minority groups for access to venues and funding has demonstrated potential gaps in the national heritage. The voices of people with disabilities pointed to the inaccessibility of many arts venues and to their exclusion from artistic expression. Through these and other challenges to public policies to the arts, the community arts movement has drawn attention to the wealth of popular arts and creative activities that are taking place in communities, activities which in themselves foster, sustain and support the aspirations of active communities with particular reference to oppressed and minority interests. In this chapter we affirm the case for an active role for public policy in promoting community arts and suggest some guidelines for good practice within the context of current discussions concerning a national arts and media strategy.

Community Arts is...

Arts based in communities are uninhibited. Art forms, styles, tools and instruments reflect a variety of cultures – they are liberated from narrow definitions of form and style and generally free from commercial considerations. As such, community art, variously known as local arts or participatory arts (CDF, 1992b), is distinct from traditionally funded 'high art' in that the activity is more than likely to have a purpose beyond its aesthetic value. It is not an art form in itself but involves arts created out of the imaginations and experiences of communities.

As with other forms of community practice, arts activities in communities may be generated with the support of paid workers but the purposes, context and often the art forms used are determined by individuals and groups in the community. Involvement, therefore, in the processes of artistic creation and production is crucial, as is the gaining of access to artistic and community resources. Under ideal conditions community arts enables people collectively to create something which expresses their identity, interests and concerns.

In relation to locality and to interest communities we distinguish community arts activities into four main types:

1. amateur and cultural arts
2. access to arts
3. professional arts activities
4. arts as a sociopolitical tool.

Amateur and cultural arts include any form of art activity produced by individuals or groups within their leisure time for private pleasure or public presentation. On a collective level they include amateur dramatics, folk, jazz and country music clubs, photographic and painting groups and a variety of culturally distinctive activities such as local carnivals, Asian dance groups, orature, east European choral groups, men's and women's morris dance sides, the gospel music movement – all of which represent a richness reflective of global diversity. Involvement in amateur and cultural arts is extensive (Hutchison and Feist, 1991) and highly participative in that it involves many people in a variety of voluntary support activities, e.g. in organising events and performances, costume design and stage work, fundraising, committee membership, etc. With an emphasis on a particular art form or art forms that cut across the traditional divides of theatre, music, dance, literature, etc, such involvement is indicative of the extent to which a community is indeed an 'active community'.

As a means of promoting *access to arts*, community arts reflects a range of intervention attempts at making arts more available to a wide spectrum of people both as producers (performers, musicians, writers) and as consumers (audiences). The strategic location of multi-media arts venues and centres to complement centres of artistic excellence (e.g. London's South Bank) can be a means of overcoming regional disparities in provision as well as being a base from which to develop community-based arts provision. Venues and centres themselves may also be made more accessible: 'passport to leisure' and subsidised ticket schemes with targeted times for particular groups, flexible daytime and evening adult education arts and craft courses, crèche provision and the organisation of community transport and escort schemes can all contribute to ensuring that venues can be made 'community accessible'. Through arts development, workers attached to galleries, touring companies or museums, gaining access to people through outreach work, can promote appreciation and active involvement in arts work through taster workshops and training programmes.

Consequently community arts may be seen as an area of *professional arts activity* where artists' expressed purpose is to involve others in creative arts work within community settings. Often individual artists and arts organisations are based in art and community centres or are attached to specific settings through 'residencies'. The activities they engage in range from drama, music, painting, dance and mime, kite making, circus skills and festival planning to more modern creative media such as video, computer graphics, moving sculptures and tactile arts. They work in conjunction with local authority departments (e.g. social services, the education service, planning, leisure and recreation departments) and also with other agencies such as the prison and probation services, adult and further education, and within the health service. The concern is to produce art forms *with* people – the process is important – rather than a finished product. This engagement of artists with people as 'animateurs' challenges the view that art and artists are separate from, and somehow 'above', society. Professional community artists must not only relate their work to specific social and cultural contexts but must also engage in co-authorship work with people in communities.

As a *sociopolitical tool* community arts can be a vehicle for promoting dialogue concerning local environmental, regenerative or other planning schemes. Exhibitions, plans and models prepared by professionals and/or members of communities can help portray alternative scenarios. At a more conflictual level, and often usefully linking in with community action campaigns, community arts may be used by community activists and groups to help in the presentation of demands. In communicating positive images of particular groups or communities, their feelings and experiences of injustice, the arts are being employed as part of wider social, political and economic struggles, creativity and radical struggle going hand in hand: badges, T-shirts and banners can all display symbols demonstrating solidarity; clearly designed posters and leaflets help to bring people to meetings and rallies.

We can summarise the objectives of community arts as an approach in community practice embracing a range of artistic and cultural activities that:

- emphasise active involvement
- generate collective creative expression, discovery and release of latent talents and skills
- positively reinforce and communicate collective identity, culture and a sense of community
- help vocalise social, political and economic concerns of communities.

Such activities may encourage an appreciation of and wider access to the arts but they are also a challenge to those who might presume to impose a cultural hegemony on others. They can help promote cultural awareness, tolerance and respect for others. They should foster celebration and enjoyment.

How far, then, have these objectives been shared by those involved in formulating and implementing public policies?

UK Public Policy and Community Arts

The agencies and institutions involved in the support and funding of community-based arts are the same as those for other forms of art. The Arts Council of Great Britain and the ten Regional Arts

Boards, together with local government, are the main funders for local arts organisations and national and performing companies and institutions.

Arts Council and Regional Arts Boards

The Arts Council emerged from the wartime 'Council for the Encouragement of Music and the Arts' which had promoted amateur music, drama and painting as well as professional touring companies. Its main purpose has been the support and development of major national arts institutions such as the Royal Opera House, the Royal Shakespeare Company and the National Theatre Company, including the support and encouragement of the types of artistic talent required by these flagship companies. In 1993–4, the government allocated £225.6 million to the Arts Council to fund the arts.

The focus for expenditure on the arts continues to be biased towards national prestigious performing companies, mainly London based, which attract tourists. This suggests that the government's concern for the arts is primarily about their economic importance. It also raises questions about the political significance of London as a leading world centre of high culture and as the embodiment of British cultural identity.

Regional disparities in arts and cultural provision have long been recognised by the Arts Council. Indeed, in 1945 on the occasion of becoming the first Chair of the Arts Council, Lord Keynes stated:

> We of the Arts Council are greatly concerned to decentralise and disperse the dramatic and musical and artistic life of this country, to build up provincial centres and to promote corporate life in these matters in every town and county. (Arts Council of Great Britain (ACGB), 1984, p. iii)

Though laudable in intent, this view did little to recognise the important contribution of community-based arts creativity; rather, the concern was for more audiences to receive the arts than for more people to become involved in their definition and creation. It was not until the 1970s when, in response to the Association of Community Artists' challenge that the Arts Council was exclusively preoccupied with the 'high' arts, that a working party was set up (ACGB, 1974) to determine whether or not it should be involved in funding community arts. The report recommended that it should, and that community arts should be treated as a new and separate category for funding. The then Regional Arts Associations appointed community arts officers and panels to respond to applications for funding.

The involvement of the Arts Council in the funding of community arts produced dilemmas. In the course of the process to get community arts recognised for funding purposes, its form, content and indeed criteria for excellence had been left rather vague (Kelly, 1984, pp. 21–2). It was therefore up to those who had hitherto been responsible for the funding of other art forms to devise criteria for evaluating the quality of community arts funding applications. There were few, if any, additional resources. Key questions concerned: the value that should be given to the processes of generating creative expression as opposed to the quality of the end product; the priority that should be given to community arts as an area of professional arts activity; and, following the publication of the jointly sponsored CRC/Arts Council/Calouste Gulbenkian Report *'The Arts Britain Ignores'* (Khan, 1976), the attention that should be given to 'ethnic minority arts'.

Following our earlier discussion, community arts clearly involves more than simply encouraging people to attend galleries, theatres and concert halls. Community arts workers themselves place greater emphasis on the processes of participation, creative production, expression of identity, social action and celebration through artistic and cultural activities (Clinton in Community Development Foundation (CDF), 1992b, pp. 106–8).

The very appointment of specialist 'community arts' officers and panels implied that community arts, including ethnic minority arts, could be treated as a separate and distinct art form. There are, however, dangers in the practice of lumping together a variety of culturally distinctive artistic activities under the one umbrella 'minority arts', particularly in relation to funding issues. It does little to acknowledge the very diversity of 'ethnic' categories; nor does it really acknowledge the historical or contemporary roles, for example, of black artists in contributing to and fostering artistic expression within British and European culture. Black artists should not be ascribed to narrow, culturally defined roles. To some extent the more recent practice of Regional Arts Boards to set up joint arrangements between specialist panels or 'combined arts' panels reflects a positive structural reponse to the multi-media and cultural content of many community arts funding applications. Co-options to panels have attempted to include new interests in community-based arts, though, as we note below, there is a demand for greater representation in wider policy-making arenas.

By making community arts financially accountable to established institutions, it has been argued (Kelly, 1984) that some of the challenge and political content of community arts will be dissipated. As a sociopolitical tool community arts needs an element of independence; it must avoid becoming over-dependent upon any one funding source if it is to retain its ability to help excluded groups to articulate their interests. Rather than 'incorporation' with its negative connotations of loss of control and identity, community arts requires encouragement to sustain its creative sponteneity.

The Regional Arts Boards have begun to take responsibility in partnership with local authorities and voluntary arts interests for placing local arts development more centre stage. However, re-organisation has imposed upon the boards greater financial and developmental responsibilities for strategically located major arts organisations which could be set against support for community-based arts. Thus, there are concerns that the orthodox thinking and policies of the Arts Council, as being concerned with traditional ideas of excellence, may still predominate in the regions (Clinton, 1993). The relatively recent association of community-based arts with the Arts Council has demonstrated that it is essential that: 'Criteria of excellence of participation and access are established alongside excellence of content and presentation in arts work' (CDF, 1992, p. 95).

Local Government

Local government has played, and continues to play, a strategic role in supporting arts in communities, yet it does this in the absence of a statutory requirement to do so. Expenditure on the arts is compulsory in only two areas, both concerned with education, i.e. art as a national curriculum foundation subject, and through mandatory grants for some students attending arts degree courses. Both come from central government monies. The legislative power for local authorities to engage in expenditure on arts-based activities derives largely from the permissive clauses of the Local Government Act 1972. Since the abolition of the GLC and metropolitan counties, arts expenditure in these localities has been possible as a result of a discretionary measure, section 48, in the Local Government Act 1985. In Scotland locally based arts have been supported as a result of a series of directives from 1963 by the Secretary of State for Scotland that urge local authorities to pool resources with voluntary organisations in efforts to develop local arts activities and centres.

In 1989–90 gross arts related spending by local authorities totalled £480 million (ACGB, 1993), which, given an approximate 50 per cent return on income generated from arts and cultural events (Audit Commission, 1991), means a net expenditure similar to that of the Arts Council. Local authority municipal or 'civic' culture includes the running of 260 theatres, 100 concert halls and 50 arts centres, and in 1991–2 £45 million was allocated through grants to artists, performers and arts organisations. As various reports have argued (Myerscough, 1982; ACGB, 1982; Audit Commission, 1991), an active and stimulating arts environment can be attractive to potential business interests and in itself augment the local economy. Like the Arts Council, such spending combines support for the arts having both national and local significance. Thus the largest spender, the City of Birmingham, supports the City of Birmingham Symphony Orchestra which has a major international reputation. Bradford, another large spender, has a long track record of support for multi-cultural arts; it is also the base for the National Museum of Photography, Film and Television with which the local authority is in partnership, for example, in funding and staffing the education unit.

Arts development in communities has been most hampered where local authorities are not committed to the idea of the arts having a legitimate place in the lives of all people. Consequently, the average net expenditure per head is variable. Whereas local boroughs in London were spending an average of £4 per head per year, expenditure in the metropolitan and shire districts was approximately half of this, and in county council areas it was significantly less (Audit Commission, 1991). As local authority spending on the arts generally is not compulsory it is an easy target for cuts and political manipulation. Bearing in mind that nearly half of all local authorities in England and Wales have net revenue expenditure of under £100,000 on arts and cultural activities, the potential for the allocation of the whole arts budget to 'preferred' art schemes is high – leading to the exclusion of any other arts interests.

Where arts policies have been well developed local authorities have attempted to embrace a variety of approaches to ensure that opportunities for access and participation are available to as many individuals and interest groups as they can reach. Looking back at the activities of the GLC, it is interesting to see how, first, the GLC's community arts and ethnic arts work in the early 1980s was begun by the politicians who engaged in open discussion with arts activists; secondly, social groups in need of funding were positively prioritised; thirdly, creative ways of ensuring that traditional art forms remained funded were sought; fourthly, the funding criteria used required evidence of 'participation' (thus, theatre and dance companies would be expected to run workshops as well as performances) and, fifthly, efforts were made to attempt to evaluate the take-up and involvement of the targeted community in the planned activities. Lessons from the GLC experience point to the adeptness of professional and organised groups in securing funding at the expense of less well-organised interests; indeed, it has been noted that perhaps more attention could have been given to preliminary outreach and strategic work prior to the start of funding cycles, as 'otherwise the already marginalised social groups once again get crushed in the rush' (Mulgan and Worple, 1986, p. 76).

The recent CDF report, *Arts and Communities* (1992b), offers examples of a range of support given by local authorities to community-based arts initiatives in metropolitan and rural areas. In Kirklees, West Yorkshire, these included the development of a cultural strategy bridging economic and community regeneration which explicitly drew from wide consultations within all sections of Kirklees communities including the voluntary arts sector. In St Helens, Merseyside, a 'remarkable flowering of the arts' followed the setting up of a Community Leisure Department and the Arts Council/DES-funded Community Arts St Helens. Performance indicators to help evaluate, document and demonstrate delivery in terms of value for money, equal opportunities, innovations, audience building and response were developed. In Walsall, in the West Midlands, an arts audit identified the need for affordable, accessible central bases around which to focus arts activities. Through further public discussion, priority groups were identified for attention by the new Arts and Cultural Service – principally the various Asian communities, Afro-Caribbean groups, people with special needs, women and young people. The CDF report also contained an example of the work of a rural arts worker appointed by the North Kesteven District Council in Lincolnshire who became involved in organising exhibitions and workshops, and helping to commission new art and folk dance activities for children and adults. These activities helped revive community spirit through the bringing together of groups on projects of direct benefit and interest to local villages. A sense of pride developed in the creation of what was special about local culture and heritage from the past and the present (CDF, 1992b, p. 57).

Despite the statutory policy vacuum, some local authorities are active in encouraging a healthy and varied arts environment. In some areas local arts development officers have been appointed, some with previous experience as community artists and activists. The examples of practice illustrate an emphasis by local authorities on adopting a community development approach to the encouragement of community arts with a determination to develop the arts from within communities rather than parachute arts programmes in from the outside. Local authorities have also supported the development of representative and supportive bodies like arts forums with, in some cases, financial control of local arts budgets delegated to these bodies. This suggests the potential for local authorities in reorienting their services (a community services approach) so as to be responsive to community needs for active rather than passive involvement in the arts.

Community Arts, Diversity and Oppression

The desire to support diversity requires public bodies to adopt policies and practices that reflect a commitment to equal opportunities (ACGB, 1993). As Clinton (1993) has noted, artistic products are by their nature intended to be highly visible, and can in turn confer visibility on those who create them; community arts can help challenge inequalities and oppressions as experienced through ageism, ableism, sexism, homophobia and racism by explicit targeting and positive action through engaging with a variety of communities of interest and identity. Hutchison and Forrester's study of arts centres in the UK (1987) indicated that this is beginning to take place: over one-third of all arts centres in this survey organised arts activities specifically for the unemployed and for women; well over a quarter organised activities for the elderly; and about one-third organised activities for people with disabilities. The examples that follow indicate some of the ways in which arts-based work in communities can be inclusive, as opposed to exclusive, with new meanings and expressions for art and culture being generated.

Young People

When given the opportunity to be creative young people demonstrate talent, enthusiasm, new ideas and the ability to exploit mass and pop culture, fashion and style on their own terms. The rapid expansion of technology in the media is enabling young people to have immediate and direct access to the market-place of new sounds and images. All too often such developments are regarded negatively, as are the often self-organised large public gatherings of young people, such as raves. As Rubinstein (1993) notes, public authorities can play a role in creating spaces and sites that young people can control. Youth arts projects have helped young people to speak for themselves. For example, one of the Leicester-based Soft Touch Community Arts projects with young people led to the production of an audio play about 'joy riding'. In Leeds, Bannerworks' work with a girls' group as part of a cultural exchange project in Holland involved the production of a banner with images chosen by the girls and reflecting their perception of life in Leeds. The ten-year-old National Association of Youth Theatres continues to promote local theatre devised, rehearsed and presented by young people. More generally, and throughout the UK, Artswork, the youth arts development agency, has encouraged partnerships with other arts organisations and local authorities (including schools, youth and arts centres) on both projects and development work.

Older People

Theatrical and writing work with older people has had a bias towards reminiscence, social history and lessons from the political struggles of the past. Amateur arts in theatre and music has traditionally involved young and old alike. As a means of sustaining an active life in communities for older people, dances and arts activities provide an important form of social intercourse; the latter can also privide a forum for continuing education in craft and artistic skills. However, arts work with and by older people need not rely upon stereotyped perceptions of 'appropriate' art and cultural activities. In London the Laban Centre has explored with older people a range of arts activities that includes not only dance but also mime and movement.

People with Disabilities

The Scottish Convention of local authorities recently adopted a code of practice on arts and disability (Clinton, 1993). This recognised, for example, the need to include more people with disabilities in arts organisations and to ensure pricing structures that did not discriminate against attendance at events (e.g. the need to be near the front or adjacent to access and exit points). The Attenborough Report (1985) made positive recommendations relating to the access and information needs of people with disabilities concerning their use of concert halls, theatres and community arts centres. Some regional Arts Boards have initiated incentive fund schemes to help make arts venues more accessible, and local 'What's On' publicity has included information about the accessibility of events, venues and training programmes. In relation to active participation, SHAPE's network of independent organisations, theatre companies like Graeae and other initiatives like Hospital Arts enable and demonstrate the potential for people with disabilities to engage in creative arts production.

Women

Within the arts world women have been less well represented, first in comparison to male artists and second in relation to their position on management structures of Regional Arts Boards, local authorities and locally based arts organisations. Women's creativity traditionally has found expression through crafts and activities useful to everyday life. Given the relative 'invisibility' of women within other arts forms community-based arts has been a vehicle for providing opportunities for creative expression and active participation. Community arts projects and organisations have been established specifically by and for women, for example, Spare Tyre touring theatre company, Vera Productions (video work) and the Black Women's Radio Workshop. More often than not it is the smaller arts organisations that have attempted to schedule arts events to suit women, to include crèche and playgroup facilities in their planning, and, in recruiting women community artists, to take a positive attitude to career breaks and the need for flexible working arrangements.

Gays and Lesbians

Opportunities for artistic expression by gay and lesbian people are limited. Local authorities have been specifically restricted by Clause 28 of the Local Government Act 1988 from public expenditure on services and activities that promote homosexual ways of life. In interpreting the Act many potential funders have felt reluctant to support arts opportunities for lesbians and gay men.

Few funding bodies or locally based arts organisations have written policies that take gay and lesbian people into account. The reform of such restrictive legislation could contribute not only to promoting greater acceptance of the rights to sexual equality but also to reduce discrimination within the arts.

Ethnic Minorities

In relation to the arts and cultures of ethnic minorities progress has been erratic and confusing (Clinton, 1993). Commentators (CDF, 1992b; ACGB, 1993) have noted that while some Regional Arts Boards have increased their funding for minority arts and some councils (like the former GLC) have given a positive lead, pressures on local authorities' budgets have raised questions concerning the evenhandedness of funders. Consequently, among ethnic arts organisations there is a lack of confidence in the commitment of the funding system (ACGB, 1993, p. 75).

Various strategies have been suggested as a response to these concerns. On the one hand Owusu (1986) urges that black arts organisations should build up an 'independent organic cultural infrastructure that combines production and consumption' (p. 159). Demands for a fair share of arts resources from the state should go hand in hand with struggles to press for funding criteria that would guarantee black groups organisational and aesthetic autonomy. At another level, it is argued (ACGB, 1993) that the aims of funding bodies themselves should be to reflect, encourage and support cultural diversity in their composition and policies. Others (CDF, 1992b) argue for a national black arts organisation to help lay the foundations of black and cultural industries and promote a network of organisations for mutual support. All commentators support the movement towards securing ways for black and ethnic minorities to be more involved in policy making.

To summarise, then, as a strategy for promoting equal opportunities and social justice, community-based arts is committed to according people equal rights to attendance, participation and involvement in policy formulation. However, there remains much work to be done in terms of finding ways for such work, once produced, to be distributed and marketed (Kelly, 1984; Sones, 1993).

Towards Creative Futures

Community-based arts derives from commitment as well as authentic and participative artistic production; its future requires support that is neither benevolently paternalistic nor excluding because of rigid predefined notions of artistic excellence. The diverse range of community arts activities emerging and evolving demonstrates the need for people to engage directly in creative expression. However, financial support for community-based arts is regionally variable; local arts development has been disparate and certain groups of people have had restricted opportunities for their active enjoyment of arts and cultural activities. At the same time, providers have been subject to public spending cuts. The need to find creative ways of maintaining arts venues on a commercial basis and yet respond to community needs remains a major concern.

A way forward has been suggested in the Arts Council document 'Towards a National Arts and Media Strategy', which was produced in 1992 for consultation, comment and improvement and then submitted to the Secretary of State for the National Heritage in the form of the ACGB HMSO publication *A Creative Future* (ACGB, 1993). Its opening statements reaffirmed the centrality of the arts to the individual in society and to community and national life. The importance of recognising the diversity of cultural interests and traditions was stressed, as was the need to strengthen support for community-based arts activity. Local authorities were identified as having key roles in supporting arts and cultural activities and, in unison with the CDF report (1992b), it was recommended that:

> the Local Government Act 1988 should be amended to make arts spending by local authorities a statutory responsibility, and that the costs of such responsibilities should be designated as eligible for revenue support grant from government. (ACGB, 1993, p. 102)

Perhaps more so than in other 'official' reports, there was a commitment here to support participatory community-based art work as national policy. Drawing from this and previous reports, and the views of various practitioners (CDF, 1992b; Clinton, 1993; Kelly, 1984; Owusu, 1986), we conclude by suggesting five interrelated strategies for the implementation of a national strategy to support community arts.

First, a *flexible framework* for the development of cultural policies is required so as to involve wide-ranging consultation and decision making about priority targeting. Such policies need to reflect and respond to a diverse range of local amateur and cultural arts activities. In as much as the success of European arts and cultural policies rest on their ability to enhance and embrace regional identities, so too must a national cultural policy ensure inclusion through a widening of opportunities for the voices of local community and minority interests to be heard.

Secondly, the *development role* of providers and, in particular, local authorities needs to be strengthened. There is a need to develop local infrastructures of arts resources and facilities to respond to the diverse needs of communities and support community arts projects. Arts audits of the range and take-up of resources should be conducted. An assessment of their accessibility, both physical and perceptual, as well as their usage by different population groups will give an indication of the extent to which equity in access is being achieved. Furthermore, support and training for arts workers using a community practice approach to promote participative involvement in communities needs to be encouraged both to develop these skills and to enhance their status.

Thirdly, local funding strategies should *guarantee funding* for community-based arts. A simplification of grant-making and accounting procedures supported by clear written guidance with outreach officers helping groups to present their case can provide valuable encouragement. Those managing arts venues and resources can introduce sliding scale charges and incentive/matching schemes and can seek sponsorship for specific events to subsidise arts programmes. For community arts projects, local fundraising efforts and obtaining multiple funding sources are worth pursuing in spite of a difficult economic climate, the time and organisational expertise required. In themselves these activities promote wider community involvement. They also reduce a scheme's financial vulnerability to the overtures of any one funder, particularly when community arts is being employed in campaigns as a sociopolitical tool.

Fourthly, there needs to be a continuation of work to foster a range of *networks and alliances* in localities, and on the basis of distinctive art forms (e.g. Aditi: the South Asian Dance Education Forum, Community Radio Association, Community Dance and Mime Foundation). A national bid has been made to the Arts Council for funds to develop links between them. It should help to complement the existing Voluntary Arts Network and provide another national lobby for those groups with an explicit participatory arts and cultural focus.

Finally, given that community-based arts are often like carers in the community, hidden from all but the participants, it is important to continue to *document the range of activities* involved in community arts. This will help not only to enhance the status deserved by community arts but also to provide models of good practice for those directly concerned with its development, with performance indicators including processes related to 'excellence of participation and access'.

Potentially, the scene is now set for a radical change and positive response to diversity in the artistic and cultural quality of people's lives provided that national policy allows for a flexible framework able to respond to regional and local conditions and interests. The knowledge, enthusiasm and skills in communities needed to create a vigorous and diverse cultural life can be embraced so to enable the movement towards active creative futures.

7 Community Enterprise

Jenny Lynn

Introduction

Tackling issues of jobs, money and people's futures means touching some fundamental realities and, as the occasional spectacular collapses of giant conglomerate businesses testify, every enterprise involves risk. When those involved in the enterprise face additional problems, like lack of access to funds, transport, contacts and, most crucially for women, adequate free time to plan and develop projects, then the risks of failure are magnified.

Community enterprise involves people getting together to develop activities which will have a beneficial economic impact on the people involved and the community to which they belong. This community-based economic activity can take many forms: co-operatives, credit unions, community businesses, community development trusts, positive action training schemes, workspace for local small businesses and so on. Whatever the form, the common underlying theme is one of working together to tackle problems of poverty, unemployment and lack of resources that may be affecting the community concerned.

So how do we define in detail just what each of these various initiatives means?

Co-operatives

The co-operative movement in the UK began with the creation of consumer co-operatives, in which customers or consumers set up retail shops to sell good quality food at fair prices. These consumer co-ops were owned and controlled by their members, who elected committees to oversee their activities. People who joined the co-operative not only supported the spread of a new concept in retailing, but also received a dividend in proportion to the amount they purchased.

In the 150 years which have elapsed since the start of the first co-operative shop in Rochdale in 1844 the co-operative movement has developed a range of forms, all based on the concept of democratic control of trading activities by the members.

More recently intensified competition and changing retail patterns have forced many of the larger co-operatives to amalgamate, often rationalising the distribution of their shops by closing less viable outlets, abandoning dividend payments and so on.

Yet in some cases, this very contraction has breathed new life into the co-operative concept. Communities faced with the closure of their local co-operative shop have rallied round and created new community-controlled co-operatives, in which local people buy shares in the business and ensure that it continues to provide much needed services to the local community.

Thus when the people of the Upper Afan Valley in South Wales found that the co-operative store in the village of Blaengwynfi was scheduled for closure in 1983 they raised money through a share issue to the local community and a bank loan and succeeded in establishing a brand new community co-operative that is now a base for a thriving village store and home to several new small businesses (Land and Urban Analysis, 1990).

Worker co-operatives are businesses owned and controlled by the people who work in them. They offer a form of business structure in which everyone involved is entitled to a say in the running of the business, and to a share in the profits. Worker co-operatives are also expected to pursue social objectives, though the definition of just what these should be is left very much to the co-operative itself.

One further element of particular interest to community organisations considering support for worker co-ops is the concept of 'common ownership' which now underpins the vast majority of worker co-ops currently operating in the UK. Common ownership enterprises are collectively owned by the workers, who will benefit individually in terms of wages and profit distribution, but who cannot sell or pass on their membership of the co-op as they could if they held individual shareholdings (Industrial Common Ownership Movement (ICOM), 1992).

Worker co-ops vary in size from tiny two- and three-person businesses run on a collective basis to large commercial and industrial undertakings like Tayside Buses with some 960 employees, or the Scott Bader Commonwealth, a Northamptonbased chemical company employing nearly 700 people. In many cases these larger co-operative businesses have chosen legal structures based on the common ownership of part of the shares, with the remainder being held by one or more major investors in the enterprise.

The basic co-operative principle of working together for a common purpose can of course take many forms in addition to the consumer, community or worker co-op model.

Thus the last few years have seen a growth in what have been described as marketing, service or secondary co-operatives, in which a small group of individuals or small businesses join together for the provision of common services. Examples include Abbacabs in Swansea, where the city's 60 licensed hackney carriage taxi-owners pool resources to run a radio-operator service for themselves, or the Manchester Craft Centre, where local crafts-people jointly rent an unusual old building in the city centre in which they can retail their products, and benefit from joint marketing and promotion.

Again, these co-operatives are democratically controlled, with decisions about who can join, fee levels for services, capital investment and disposal of surplus being taken by the members themselves.

Community Business

Another type of economic initiative which has grown in popularity in the UK over the last 20 years is the community business. Pioneered particularly in Scotland, community businesses are described in a 1990 study for the Department of the Environment as 'trading organisations which work for community aims rather than distribute profits' (Land and Urban Analysis Ltd, 1990, p. 3).

Community Business Scotland defines a community business as 'a trading organisation which is set up, owned and controlled by the local community and which aims to create ultimately self-supporting jobs for local people and to be a focus for local development. Any profits made from its business activities go either to create more employment or to provide local services or to assist other schemes of community benefit' (Land and Urban Analysis, 1990, p. 7).

It is important to note that the wider definition of the concept of community (see Chapter 1) has been an important basis for the development of some businesses based on a 'community of interest'. Examples of community business based on community of interest include businesses serving the black or gay and lesbian communities, as well as disabled people's organisations.

Credit Unions

Credit unions are another form of community enterprise gaining rapidly in popularity, with more than 200 now operating in communities throughout the UK (Bayley etal, 1992). Like consumer co-operatives, they often have their roots in a self-help approach to problems of poverty and lack of service.

A credit union is a co-operatively owned financial institution which provides low-cost savings and loan services to its members and is administered normally by committees and officers who are democratically elected by, and accountable to, the membership of the credit union.

Credit unions thus enable people to start a regular pattern of saving, and then to have access to loans at reasonable rates of interest (Association of British Credit Unions, 1993).

In order to be legally registered by the Registrar of Friendly Societies each credit union group must prove that its membership will be held together by what is known as a 'common bond'. Thus there must be some sense of belonging to a community of interest, so that members of the credit union know and understand each other's needs, and the loans given to members are allocated and repaid on the basis of a strong bond of trust between people.

Local Employment and Trading Schemes

In many communities throughout the UK, people are beginning to experiment with a return to the age-old system of barter, through the mechanism of Local Employment and Trading Schemes (LETS), in which members of each scheme can regularly exchange goods and services in return for credits without money changing hands.

There are more than 30 such schemes at the time of writing, operating as far afield as Findhorn in the North of Scotland and Totnes in Devon, with a combined total of over 4,000 members. Each scheme decides on its own unit of credit (the Manchester LETS deals in 'bobbins' while members of the LETS in Rhayader, mid Wales, barter green pounds) and cheque books are used to record exchanges, debits and credits.

Typically members exchange domestic services such as babysitting, painting and decorating, gardening or hairdressing. Supporters of the schemes see them as an efficient way of enabling people to derive real benefit from their own skills, as well as a way in which people within a community can widen their circle of contacts (LETSLINK, 1992; Lee, 1993).

Community Development Trusts

A relatively recent addition to the spectrum of community economic initiatives has been the community development trust. Drawing to some extent on models of partnership between local communities and the private sector developed in the USA, community development trusts are organisations set up specifically to play a leading role in the economic and social regeneration of their communities.

The Department of the Environment's *Creating Development Trusts: Good Practice Guide* (HMSO, 1988) offers the following definition of development trusts:

> Development trusts are independent, not for profit organisations which take action to renew an area physically, socially, and in spirit. They bring together the public, private and voluntary sectors, and obtain financial and other resources from a wide range of organisations and individuals. They encourage substantial involvement by local people and aim to sustain their operations at least in part by generating revenue.

Thus they are essentially a partnership between representatives of the local community, interested and supportive representatives of private-sector companies, and local and central government.

They frequently attempt to draw substantial numbers of local people into membership, and often have ambitious goals of running large workspace projects, taking a lead on training and employment initiatives, or themselves becoming promoters of various forms of community business and enterprise support.

One of the longest established trusts of this kind is the North Kensington Amenity Trust, created in 1972 following protests at the building of an elevated motorway through north-west London. Starting with an endowment of 23 acres of land beneath the new motorway, the trust developed a whole range of workpiece and other projects, finally becoming commercially self-sufficient in 1987.

Thus community enterprise has taken a variety of forms, with each new venture trying to learn from the experience of others and yet striving to develop and sustain its own definition of what it wants to achieve and how it intends to do it.

The Starting Point

Many of the earliest examples of community enterprise occurred where there was a clearly identified need for a local service of some kind and yet neither private enterprise nor the public sector seemed able or willing to meet that need. Shopping, transport and banking facilities are examples of amenities taken for granted generally but often absent in remote and/or deprived communities. In many ways this approach can be characterised as 'community entrepreneurship', where an individual or group spots an opportunity or 'gap in the market' and begins to organise in response to it. Examples include the community transport undertaking developed on the peripheral estate of Hattersley near Manchester, and the provision of shopping, fish landing and other missing amenities through community effort in the Highlands and Islands (MacFarlane, 1988).

In some cases the initial stimulus was a negative one. People got together to respond to the threat of closure of a local shop or launderette, and then set about the task of investigating whether they could somehow or other run it for themselves, as we have seen with Blaengwynfi Community Co-operative.

Often a vacant or underused building may provide a focus for the new venture. Thus West Calder Workspace came into existence when a large co-operative bakery and warehouse complex closed down in West Lothian, while the former Stonebridge bus garage in north London was eventually converted into a workplace complex housing activities as diverse as recording studios and catering companies.

All of these initiatives began life in response to a clearly perceived need or opportunity. Often, in the process of development the original idea or concept may have been modified or even discarded in favour of better options which emerged later. But the initial impetus was focused upon a specific project area.

Yet an equally important source of community enterprise activity in the UK has been groups of people who have set out to regenerate their local community through some kind of economic project or activity and have faced the task of working out how to put their ideas into practice.

The mission statement of the Moss Side and Hulme Community Development Trust in Manchester describes it as 'an independent, not-for-profit partnership promoting action to renew the area economically, socially and in spirit, both directly and by enabling and supporting other organisations' (Moss Side and Hulme Community Development Trust, 1992). In pursuit of this aim, the Trust has converted a former church into small workplace units, set up a community recruitment and training organisation called Joblink and now manages a construction skills training centre, a database designed to facilitate the use of local businesses and a local labour scheme which channels local people into jobs created as a result of the City Challenge redevelopment programme in Hulme. There are similar examples of such umbrella bodies seeking to create and sustain a variety of community enterprises in Scotland especially.

Key Issues for Successful Community Enterprise Development

1. Promoting the Concept

Community enterprise development needs people, resources and markets. Increasingly, as more and more people come into contact with credit unions or community development trusts because they know someone who is involved in one, have read about them in the local paper, or work for a local authority which promotes worker co-ops, they will become an accepted part of the landscape.

With nearly two decades of community-based economic initiatives behind us the sheer existence of 'positive role models' should make the work of promoting this type of activity progressively easier. Yet there is also evidence, particularly within the inner cities, of growing scepticism about what are often perceived as alien regeneration initiatives offering little in the way of permanent solutions to poverty, unemployment or rising crime. In such circumstances, ensuring that community enterprise has the backing of key individuals within the community whose views command respect has frequently proved a crucial catalytic factor in transforming short-term external interventions into the kind of 'sustainable development' called for by Nigel Roome in his chapter in Part Three.

Matching the advocates to the target audience is an important technique. Thus when West Glamorgan Common Ownership Development Agency held a seminar for bank managers and accountants to overcome fears about worker co-operatives they used a local computer software co-operative to present the business benefit of the worker co-operative structure, while their Cooperative Youth Initiative regularly used teachers involved in co-operative educational activities to promote the benefits of this type of curriculum work to other teachers and educationalists.

A key issue at the initial promotional stage is how to ensure a balanced presentation which highlights the very real benefits of community enterprise to both individuals and community, but is also honest about the difficulties likely to be encountered by a new group, and the amount of hard work and sustained commitment that will be required to make the venture a success. Credit union development workers, for example, rightly promote the very real benefits of setting up a community-controlled financial institution in an area which may not even have a bank. Yet at the same time they have to stress that a year or more's intensive training will be required before any would-be credit union steering group is sufficiently skilled and experienced to launch what is in effect a small banking institution that will be subject to stringent financial regulation and control.

Given that people are the most crucial resource for any successful enterprise there is now a growing emphasis on promoting concepts of community enterprise and co-operatives to young people to ensure that the next generation of community leaders will be much more aware of the potential of community enterprise and the roles they could play in promoting it. One of the first in this field was the Cooperative Youth Initiative in Swansea which, along with colleagues at the Humberside Youth Initiative and the Schools Curriculum Industry Partnership, has developed a whole range of exciting co-operative activities for young people in schools and youth clubs.

2. Forming the Group

Many community enterprise initiatives are developed initially by a small group of people brought together either as a result of a common interest in tackling the economic and social problems of their community, or because they have a specific business idea which they want to develop along co-operative or community enterprise lines.

The first task for anyone involved in supporting the group is to help it to achieve a common vision of what it hopes to achieve. While this may seem like stating the obvious, it is all too easy for a group to be carried along on the enthusiasm of one or two individuals, and to discover only too late that not everyone shares the founder members' view of what the enterprise is really all about.

Community development skills can play a vital role at this point in helping the group to identify its goals, and to question whether a community enterprise really *is* what is needed to achieve the common objectives. It can be all too easy in an area of high unemployment and few local facilities to assume that setting up a new business will appeal to everyone. It won't, and indeed for some people who may be fully stretched already in another form of community activity such as a tenants' association or women's group, community enterprise development may actually distract the group from its primary focus.

On the other hand, many successful community enterprises have been developed by groups concerned about apparently social issues who found that a community enterprise could help them achieve social as well as economic objectives. A number of community security businesses have been developed, in places such as Allender, Middlesbrough and Manchester, where concerns about crime, vandalism and the need for good community safety have meshed with a desire to create an employment alternative to the insecure, badly paid jobs as security guards that were often virtually the only work available in the area.

Pre-school childcare ventures are now an established part of the community enterprise scene in many parts of the country, and they are being joined by a growing number of parent-managed after-school initiatives like the Brookburn Out Of School Hours venture in Manchester or the Radnor and Treganna After School Club in Cardiff. The core aim of such groups is normally to provide affordable and enjoyable after-school activities for children whose parents work full time, but may also include other objectives such as a commitment to provide part-time work opportunities, or training placements for young people.

While the majority of organisations involved in community enterprise or co-operative development have adopted the 'community development' approach which takes the group itself as the starting point there are a number of examples of a more interventionist method.

Bootstrap Enterprises in Hackney and Blackburn consciously set out to create employment in co-operatives using a structured approach to training and development which involves the organisation in a great deal of 'hands on' business development activity, including where necessary recruiting a new set of co-operators if the first group are unable to make a success of the venture (McEnery, 1989).

3. Supporting the Development Process

Over the past 15 years support for community-based economic initiatives has becoming increasingly sophisticated, as local co-operative development agencies, community development trusts and local authority economic development units have sought to ensure that the groups they support have access to good quality business training and advice which is tailored to the specific needs of the business sector in which the group plans to operate.

Some local authorities used the Government Urban Programme to offer grants towards the cost of feasibility studies for new co-operative or community enterprise initiatives, and these were especially valuable where the group needed access to specialist skills, such as an architect or surveyor to draw up plans for a building conversion, or marketing advice relating to a specific business sector.

However, as the Department of Environment's own guide to Community Business acknowledges, 'Many agencies involved in cooperative development and small enterprise support work feel that a feasibility study should not be done entirely by an outside consultant' (Land and Urban Analysis, 1990, p. 33). As the guide goes on to stress, the development of a feasibility study and business plan is essentially a learning process, which will be omitted if the group is simply handed a glossy business plan produced by a consultant with no input from themselves.

The Community Security group in Manchester began their research with a visit to a similar venture in Middlesbrough. With support from the local authority's development officer they prepared a questionnaire in advance of their visit, then wrote up their findings as an initial report which was to guide their subsequent investigations.

Over a series of meetings with the development officer the group then wrote a research brief covering all the main aspects they would need to investigate in order to produce a sound business plan, including the security industry environment, market size, key players, cost structure of contracts, legal constraints, training needed, start-up finance required, and so on. Then the group divided the research work between them and agreed a timetable with the development officer for the completion of their research.

This whole process helped to build the cohesiveness of the group, identify different strengths and weaknesses within it and, most crucial of all, develop a sound understanding of the key forces affecting the industry in which they intended to operate.

Analysing the skills that will be needed to run the enterprise will often reveal gaps that can be filled either by consciously setting out to recruit someone who already has the required skills, or alternatively by ensuring that members of the group acquire the necessary training. Often development agencies will run courses in basic bookkeeping and financial control, sales techniques and so on, which in some cases are tailored specifically to meet the needs of people with little or no previous experience in these fields.

Coventry Cooperative Development Agency pioneered a ten-week training course in 1984 designed as an action learning programme to introduce participants to all the key elements involved in researching a business plan; and Strathclyde Community Business runs a vocational training programme for community enterprise members funded through the European Social Fund.

Likewise a comprehensive series of training materials is available for use with groups setting up credit unions. The series covers all the essential elements of setting up and running a credit union in line with the regulations laid down by the Registrar of Friendly Societies (Association of British Credit Unions).

Manchester City Council's Local Action Team used a small Urban Programme budget earmarked specifically for what they termed 'skills development'. This was used to help facilitate the decision-making process for community enterprise management groups as they chose their legal structure or learnt about their forthcoming responsibilities as employers.

Bootstrap Enterprises in Blackburn employ a mixture of 'bottom-up' development work with individuals and groups, and 'top-down' techniques in which they research and develop the business idea, and then recruit and support a group of people to put it into practice. One of the more successful examples of this approach is Dovetail Furniture in Blackburn, which provides employment and training in furniture restoration to some 14 people, including ten with special needs. This business was entirely researched by Bootstrap Enterprises who not only produced the business plan but also secured over £54,000 of private-sector finance then went on to recruit the management committee and staff for the new venture.

With funding for specialist co-operative and community enterprise development increasingly threatened by local authority spending cuts, there is growing pressure on the mainstream business development sector to adapt and tailor programmes to meet the needs of community enterprise. Thus the Welsh Development Agency has had a specialist community business unit since 1988, while more and more training and enterprise councils are developing specialist business programmes targeted at inner-city residents, young entrepreneurs and so on.

4. Securing Resources

Community economic initiatives have tended to develop precisely in those areas where the conventional financial infrastructure may be weak, and where the local community may already be experiencing severe poverty and a range of other difficulties which make resourcing a new project unaided virtually impossible.

To offset these disadvantages it is vital that the group develops a sound business plan, with well-researched financial projections which they understand thoroughly and can justify to potential funders. This means that there is a continuing need for business training which builds the confidence of the group based on a recognition of both its specific needs and the business sector in which it intends to operate.

Finance may well not be the only resource in short supply for the project. Often there may be a lack of suitable premises, and many would-be enterprises have disintegrated as members have become downhearted after hunting for months for premises and drawing a blank. The provision of managed workplaces was a key element in the successful growth of community business in Scotland, and it lies at the heart of the business strategy of many community development trusts. Investment of public-sector finance in this way ensures that the workplace is owned by the community, thereby adding social value to the economic benefits of supporting small business development.

Once the business plan has been completed and the group embarks on the quest to secure the resources they need to launch the venture, they are likely to need all the stamina and commitment they can muster. There is a real need for development workers to ensure that the group does not lose momentum, and that the programme of preparation and training continues so that the project remains a 'live issue' for everyone involved.

What Future for Community Enterprise?

As Part One of the book has argued, the depth of the social and economic crisis affecting many communities in the UK is bringing about a re-evaluation of public policy in favour of new forms of economic partnership with local communities.

Community enterprise in its many forms is beginning to be incorporated into mainstream economic regeneration programmes, after 15 to 20 years' moving in from the margins.

This results in part from the increasing credibility of the range of community enterprise initiatives attempted over the last few years coupled with the growing influence of the organisations they have created to network and lobby on their behalf (the Industrial Common Ownership Movement, Community Business Scotland, the Scottish Co-operative Development Company, Community Business UK, the Association of British Credit Unions and the UK Co-operative Council).

It may also be said to derive from the growing interest throughout Europe in what has became known as the 'third sector' of the economy, that part of economic activity which is neither public- nor private-sector controlled. Sometimes referred to as the social economy, the concept includes both community-based economic initiatives, large-scale worker-owned enterprises such as building co-operatives in Italy or privatised bus companies in the UK, and a whole range of employment and training initiatives which operate as much for social as for economic reasons.

Organisations involved in supporting these types of initiative have made considerable headway in recent years in lobbying EC institutions to secure inclusion in a wide range of economic and social programmes, as well as seeking to harmonise legal frameworks for co-operative and community enterprise across Europe.

Indeed as the resources for community enterprise from local and central government within the UK have diminished through budget cuts, UK organisations have turned increasingly to European programmes to fund their training and enterprise development activities. Often this has been achieved as part of a transnational project designed to facilitate the exchange of experience between projects across Europe, such as the 'Quartiers en Crise' network which has provided an opportunity to compare comprehensive urban regeneration programmes in Paisley, Belfast and Manchester with similar initiatives in cities and towns across Europe. In addition, the changes which have occurred in eastern Europe have given added impetus to the development of third-sector initiatives which offer an acceptable alternative to wholesale privatisation of the economy.

There is every reason to assume that these European inspired trends are likely to continue and intensify throughout the 1990s, giving added weight to the arguments for more active involvement of local communities in their own economic regeneration.

The incorporation of community-based economic regeneration models also owes a great deal to the growing interest in the USA in concepts of corporate responsibility within the private sector. Indeed, over the last ten to 15 years there has been something of a paradigmatic shift in conventional management education wisdom about the role of major companies. Where once the role of business management concentrated almost exclusively on maximising shareholder wealth, management education programmes focus increasingly on the need to consider the company or corporation as an organisation which is answerable to a variety of 'stakeholders', with the local community included among their number (Oster, 1990).

These concepts of wider corporate responsibility have been characterised in the UK by the increasing influence of organisations such as Action Resource Centre and Business in the Community, who see their primary role as facilitating effective links between the business sector and local community organisations committed to tackling poverty and unemployment.

In the USA corporate involvement in community regeneration has been greatly assisted by changes in the legislative and taxation framework, such as the Community Investment Act, which has provided substantial financial incentives to companies willing to commit resources to projects of direct benefit to the community.

The strength of transatlantic influence on UK policy development has been well documented by Professor Robin Hambleton and others. There is every reason to suppose that corporate support for the community role in economic regeneration is likely to grow in importance throughout the 1990s, particularly as organisations like Business in the Community and others continue to facilitate opportunities to exchange experience with communities in the USA, along similar lines to the European networks that have been established.

Finally, there is likely to be a continuation of the trend towards greater direct community involvement in urban regeneration activity of all kinds. Programmes such as Estate Action and City Challenge have laid the foundations by beginning to insist on both community involvement and the importance of ensuring that major physical redevelopment fully incorporates the economic dimensions necessary to tackle issues of high unemployment and poverty.

Building on the work of local authority planning departments and others, who pioneered concepts of 'local benefit' and 'planning gain' in the 1980s, more and more communities affected by major redevelopment are demanding the creation of structures which will ensure that a significant proportion of jobs created will be actively targeted at local people.

Indeed, many leading construction companies are coming to accept the obligation to recruit and train local people as a normal part of the trading environment of urban regeneration (MacFarlane, 1991; Manchester City Council, 1991, p. 75).

In some cases, such as the City Challenge programme, this concept that major redevelopment should bring tangible *benefits* to the local community has been surpassed by a stated commitment to ensure that the local community becomes an equal and active *partner* with government and the private sector in the very process and outcomes of regeneration itself.

Such concepts of ownership and empowerment have been taken up with particular vigour by the black community, for whom the rhetoric of the benefits of 'trickle-down' economic policy has traditionally held little attraction.

Yet there are those who would argue that much of the talk of partnership and consultation has been hollow, that communities can easily find themselves on the sidelines when the big projects are being discussed, that community enterprise may be simply the latest in a long line of utopian solutions to macro economic and social problems.

Indeed, a survey of the decision-making structures of the new partnership organisations set up to run City Challenge initiatives found wide variations in the extent to which community representatives were able to exercise any real power within the process (MacFarlane and Mabbott, 1993).

For a century and a half both local and central government have developed a corporate culture which assumes the right to determine programmes and allocate resources, justified by only an occasional appeal to the ballot box. Gradually the concept that communities have a right to be consulted about what affects them has gained ground, to the point where it is an accepted feature of planning and other similar legislation. The challenge facing community enterprise in the 1990s is to make the major transition from margin to centre, from consultation to genuine partnership, from involvement to ownership. It will not be easy, but many of the pieces are in place, and a key one is community practice.

8 Community Policing

Mollie Weatheritt

Introduction

During the 1980s something called community policing came to be widely accepted as the answer to problems of acceptability and effectiveness, problems which, since the 1960s, have come increasingly to dog the British police service. These problems were not new – indeed how to secure public consent to policing was a major preoccupation of the first Metropolitan Police Commissioners in the nineteenth century – but in the decade and a half before the urban riots erupted in the early 1980s concern about the state of police public relations, about allegedly remote and abrasive policing styles, and about the apparent inability of the police to cope effectively with rising crime had already become established on policing and political agendas. Since that time a powerful, if unlikely, combination of pressures from those on the streets who are prepared forcibly to protest against the imposition of unwelcome policing activity and those in the corridors of power who are concerned to ensure that the police give value for money have ensured that these issues have retained a prominent place on those agendas. In this context, community policing, with its emphasis on the preventive and non-conflictual aspects of policing, on local service delivery, on public participation and public responsiveness, and on voluntarism and self-help, appeals to a broad spectrum of interests. Community policing is, therefore, a potent combination of ideology and practical politics. It promises much in terms of what it symbolises about what the police stand for and how we would like them to behave.

The term 'community policing' is often associated with the work and ideas of John Alderson (from 1973 to 1983 the chief constable of Devon and Cornwall). His diagnosis, which has become part of received wisdom, is that as police forces have increased in size and complexity they have become more remote from the people they serve; and that as police have taken to patrolling in cars rather than on foot, so their work has become more reactive and, hence, conflict-ridden. As a result, the police themselves have come to believe that their capacity to react and, where necessary, to exert their legal powers, provide the essence of policing (Alderson, 1979).

That policing has indeed become more conflict-ridden is undeniable, although whether the police themselves can be held solely, or even primarily, responsible for this is more debatable. Broader social forces – a decline in notions of deference, a burgeoning in the 1960s and 1970s of political protest and industrial strife, and the growth in crime – have acted to bring more people into actual or potentially adversarial relationships with the police. Relations with young people, with black people and with the economically marginal groups on whom policing activity tends disproportionately to bear, are, as they have always tended to be, marked by tension and conflict. And while, overall, the police rate relatively highly in general public esteem, there is recent evidence that dissatisfaction with police services extends beyond those groups with whom the police generate adversarial contacts to include those people, for example victims of crimes, who turn to the police for help (Skogan, 1990).

Community policing is widely seen as a way of addressing the problems of excessive conflict and poor service delivery that lie at the heart of this diagnosis. Alderson's prescriptions, which have been widely supported, are that first, the police need to invest heavily in activities which provide a non-conflict meeting ground with the public. To this end he advocates increased police work in schools and greater use of 'community constables' – officers attached to particular neighbourhoods whose job it is to get to know and understand the people who live and work there. Secondly, he advocates that the police work co-operatively with other agencies 'to remove or foil criminogenic conditions', in other words, to prevent crime. And thirdly, he recommends the police consult more with local communities over both the substance and style of police work (Alderson, 1979).

Alderson has used the term community policing to imply a total – and fundamentally altered – approach to policing but the term is probably more often used to imply something both more modest and more disparate. Community policing has come to be used as a catch-all phrase, covering a variety of policing activities and initiatives of which its advocates approve. Thus, in one of a series of papers published by the Policy Studies Institute looking at the role of community in social policy, Paul Ekblom (1986) lists as features of community policing: community constables, specialist community liaison offers, crimes analysis, police discos and clubs for young people, schools liaison, police shops, community surveys, inter-agency approaches such as victim support, juvenile bureaux and local consultative committees. Behind this varied set of activities lies values stressing partnership, consultation, negotiation, service and prevention. Whatever advocates of community policing want in practical terms, they would no doubt agree that these values should be given more prominence within police forces and made more concrete in police activity.

For the purposes of this chapter I shall concentrate on what can be regarded as three main defining characteristics of community policing practice. They are:

- the greater use of foot patrol and the posting of officers to specific geographical areas for which they have continuing responsibility
- the development of partnerships in crime prevention through multi-agency problem solving and informal social control measures
- the development of methods and structures for consulting local communities about their policing priorities and for involving them in the design and delivery of solutions to policing problems.

Community Policing and Patrol

Patrol has always formed the backbone of police work so it would be surprising if it were not also to feature prominently in community policing tactics. For most people the visibility and behaviour of police officers provide the most concrete evidence available to them that policing is being done and the behaviour of patrol officers is quite rightly seen as being crucial to the state of police public relations. It is taken for granted by advocates of community policing that these dual aims of ensuring police visibility and of encouraging appropriate behaviour are best served by having police officers out and about on foot getting to know the people in a locality.

Surveys of the public have repeatedly shown that this is indeed what most people want (see, for example, Weatheritt, 1987).

Chief constables are well aware of these popular preferences and by the late 1970s many of them had begun to broadcast the virtues of returning more police officers to the beat. This policy was not just good for public relations, it also made economic sense. Many forces had introduced vehicle mileage restrictions as a response to the large petrol price increases of the 1970s thus forcing patrol officers out of their cars. And the police service as a whole was going through a period of relatively rapid growth in staffing which, since all police officers begin their careers on the beat, would have been translated directly and disproportionately, in the short term at least, into an increase in patrol strength.

At the same time, research findings were emerging which showed that the police role was a much more all-purpose one than the traditional emphasis on crime fighting and law enforcement had implied (see Reiner, 1985, pp. 111–12 for a summary of this work). And once it had been documented that the police were called upon to deal with a wide range of interpersonal and other problems for which recourse to the criminal law was unnecessary or inappropriate, it was but a short step to conceiving of the police as 'social workers in uniforms', providing a '24-hour social service'. Most senior police officers would agree that this broader aspect of the police role ought to be recognised and made explicit and are well aware of its importance in securing police legitimacy (see Reiner, 1991, Chapter 6 for the views of chief constables).

Just as studies of what police officers actually do have been influential, so, equally, have studies of policing effectiveness. Of particular relevance has been a series of studies of the effectiveness of patrol and of detective work, summarised in what were later to become two influential Home Office Research Studies published respectively in 1981 and 1984 (Morris and Heal, 1981; Clarke and Hough, 1984). These showed first, that the capacity of police patrols to prevent crime was strictly limited; and, secondly, that most crime was detected not through the unaided efforts of the police but because members of the public volunteered relevant information. Here was more rigorous evidence of what advocates of community policing were beginning to argue: that the key to effective policing lay in public co-operation and that traditional patrol strategies were failing to deliver the preventive goods.

The political acceptability of these messages and the will to act upon them have undoubtedly been increased by the interest shown by successive Conservative governments in promoting economy, efficiency and effectiveness in the public sector. While the value for money spotlight has been turned on an increasing number of aspects of police organisation, patrol was an obvious early candidate (see Burrows, 1989, pp. 26–9), not least because of the amount of police personnel that it absorbs (probably about 40 per cent – there are no national figures) and the fact that a large proportion of patrol time is spent in effect passively, waiting for something to happen. There have been repeated attempts, some of them promoted by central government, to encourage officers to use this 'uncommitted' time to better effect by, for example, engaging in community problem solving. Thus in 1983 the government issued a circular to police forces asking chief officers to set clear objectives and priorities for their force, to give a high priority to crime prevention in doing so, and to define and explain their objectives in such a way as to engage the experience and affect the behaviour of junior operational officers (Home Office, 1983).

No explanation of the value and attractiveness of community policing approaches to patrol could be complete without reference to the urban disturbances of the first half of the 1980s and, in particular, Lord Scarman's recommendations about what was needed to repair the fractured police public relationships of which those disturbances were both symbolic and symptomatic (Scarman, 1981). Scarman's discussion of the importance for the police of balancing the need to enforce the law against the need to ensure public tranquillity has, in many areas of policing, been instrumental in promoting a more sophisticated and self-conscious weighing of sometimes conflicting imperatives. However, in other important respects, for example in recommending that 'community' and other operational officers co-ordinate their efforts more effectively, Lord Scarman did little more than to reinforce an approach to policing which had long been officially recognised as desirable and which, for the reasons I have described above, was also proving attractive on very different grounds.

Patrol in Practice

It is a reflection of the difficulties involved in separating the reality of community policing from its rhetorical underpinnings that no statistics are available which could throw light on senior officers' claims to have returned more officers to traditional beat work. The best (and most up-to-date) information on the deployment of patrol officers shows that at the end of 1988, 18 per cent of them were assigned to community constable duties

(Bennett and Lupton, 1992a). While this figure (which tends to be higher in rural forces) is not insignificant, it tells us nothing about *patterns* of policing – whether freeing officers from the demands of shift-based general duties work significantly changes the nature and purpose of their contacts with the community.

The available evidence suggests that this has not happened to any great extent. About one-fifth of community constables' time is spent away from their beats doing other types of police work. Even when assigned to their beats, community constables spend a significant proportion of time (over one-third) inside the police station and only a small amount of time (8 per cent) on community contact and on preventive work (Bennett and Lupton, 1992a and b; all figures relate to 1989–90). Given the number and weight of official endorsements of the importance of focused, community-related and preventive approaches to patrol over the last decade, it is perhaps surprising that community constables' work patterns have not greatly changed over this period (for a comparison see Brown and Iles, 1985, who surveyed community constables' activities in 1981); that their work remains substantially similar to that of general patrol officers (Bennett and Lupton, 1992b); and that their apparent lack of involvement in community activity should have persisted.

What are the reasons for this? If officers are to plan their work so as to maximise their contacts with the community in the interests of joint problem solving, they need to know that this is expected of them, be provided with appropriate organisational back-up and access to resources in both defining and helping to solve problems, be supported by their supervisors and be judged in terms of whether they do this work well. There is scant evidence that this approach to policing has begun to take root in police forces. Yet without it, community policing (at least in terms of patrol activity) runs the risk of being little more than a public relations exercise, a convenient, and in some respects persuasive, way of implying that something different is being done while obscuring the fact the core activities of policing remain unchanged. This is not to say that there are not individual officers who are able to rise above these difficulties and whose work is highly valued by the police force and by the public. But an approach to policing which is dependent for its success on the exceptional qualities of individual officers is unlikely to become pervasive or routine.

It is equally difficult to judge whether the assignment of officers to relatively small geographic areas with a brief to get to know the people who live and work there significantly affects the *style* of policing. *Prima facie* arguments are strong. Officers who have a continuing rather than a one-off investment in the relationships with those whom they police are unlikely to jeopardise the basis of that investment by ill-considered action. Officers who deal with those they police on the basis of personal knowledge rather than anonymity are more likely to use their power covertly and in acceptable ways than overtly, coercively and unacceptably.

There is some evidence that community officers *are* more able to tune their responses more finely to particular situations than are their colleagues (Fielding et al, 1989). The moves in some police forces to assign *all* patrolling officers to small area teams will provide a more exacting test of this possibility. Those moves may also provide a more propitious environment than has existed hitherto for problem-based policing to flourish.

Partnerships in Crime Prevention

Multi-agency Partnerships

It is a commonplace of policing that it is the primary duty of every police officer to prevent crime. Yet it also becomes increasingly clear that preventing crime is precisely what the police are least good at. Attempts to resolve this paradox have invariably involved recourse to the work of other social agencies and to ideas about community.

It has long been recognised that the causes of crime lie outside the control of the police. During the 1960s this formed the pretext for two developments in the way in which the police thought about their preventive remit and organised their preventive activity. The first of these involved the police in taking on a much more proactive social role, aimed primarily at preventing crime committed by young people. Schools liaison schemes were set up by many forces, and the police provided leisure facilities and activities for young people. By the end of the 1970s these developments were being explicitly encouraged by central government (Home Office, 1978), not so much in the name of community policing (although to many people activities such as I have described form an important part of what they understand community policing to be) but, rather, in the name of better crime prevention.

Parallel to but organisationally separate from much of this, crime prevention in police forces was becoming a specialism in its own right. Police crime prevention officers have tended to work to a fairly narrow brief, being concerned primarily with disseminating crime prevention advice and advising on physical security. As with patrol, assumptions about the effectiveness of this specialist activity came under increasing official scrutiny during the 1970s. (The most important of the relevant research projects are reported in Clarke and Mayhew, 1980.) Specialist police crime prevention, it was concluded, was too diffuse and insufficiently problem oriented; too reactive and too individualistic; and too preoccupied with physical measures without taking adequate account of people's motivation to use them.

In 1984, partly as a reaction to this critique, the various strands of crime prevention policy were brought together in a circular issued jointly by five government departments and aimed not only at the police but also at education, health and social services (Home Office, 1984). The circular urged that preventing crime was 'a task for the whole community'; that 'police effectiveness cannot be greatly increased unless the community can be persuaded to do more for itself'; that the police should work in partnership with other agencies in order to tackle specific crime problems; and that those problems should be identified following consultation with local communities to assess their fears and concerns.

This promising approach to the development of crime prevention policy and practice seems, however, to have been more successfully promoted than implemented. Nine years have now passed since the circular was issued, during which time the police have repeatedly stated their commitment to pursuing the partnership approach, and the government has publicised many apparently successful examples of multi-agency crime prevention (Home Office, 1990). It is therefore unfortunate that a recent review of progress concluded that the partnership approach 'has hardly been tested', with crime prevention remaining 'a peripheral concern for all agencies and a core activity for none' (Home Office, 1991). The main reason for this is that multi-agency crime prevention has developed ad hoc and in response to the enthusiasm and initiative of committed individuals rather than within the framework of an overall strategy and structure designed to secure effective co-operation. Whether it is a police responsibility to provide such a framework is debatable; yet with some notable exceptions local authorities themselves have been slow to take the lead, being handicapped by lack of resources and with priorities lying elsewhere.

The development of more effective partnership approaches to crime prevention has also been hampered by lack of information. In the face of political and practical pressures to get on with the job, monitoring and evaluation are widely considered to be the weakest features of many, and probably most, crime prevention initiatives (Home Office, 1991; Bottoms, 1989). Moreover, where rigorous research has been undertaken it has suggested that tackling crime can provide a fragile basis for creating and sustaining a community of interest among different agencies (see, for example, Sampson and Farrell, 1990; Saulsbury and Bowling, 1991). Many of the problems are organisational: agencies can fail adequately to think through their intentions in coming together and the precise commitments required of them in terms of changed spending and policy priorities and changed organisational procedures. Other problems are more fundamental. It needs to be explicitly recognised that different agencies (for example, the police and social work departments) have different functions and that these functions will necessarily limit the extent to which co-operation between them may properly and ethically extend (Bottoms, 1989). These points echo some of the discussion in Chapter 2 concerning inter-agency work as part of community services approaches.

Community Partnerships and Informal Social Control

The exhortations of the Home Office circular have been aimed primarily at official institutions. But the circular also identifies the importance of collective grassroots action in generating effective crime prevention. Here the reasoning has been that involvement in local action against crime will create increased social interaction and stronger community feeling and, hence, more effective informal social control. The most widespread policing response to this has been the encouragement and support of neighbourhood watch schemes.

Neighbourhood watch has on the face of it been a runaway success. According to official figures, by 1990 there were over 100,000 schemes. In 1988, the British Crime Survey found that around one in six households in England and Wales was a member of a scheme (Mayhew, Elliott and Dowds, 1989, Chapter 6).

Judged on this basis, neighbourhood watch has quickly attained the status of a major movement in community-based crime prevention.

Neighbourhood watch has sought to generate community-based activity in two main ways. First, it has been used as a means of encouraging people to become more security conscious: to deploy more physical protection against crime and to engage in increased neighbourhood surveillance. Secondly, by building on and promoting shared concerns about crime, neighbourhood watch has been expected to create new patterns of interaction between neighbours and thereby promote informal social control.

Neighbourhood watch seems to have done some of these things but not all of them. Neighbourhood watch members tend to be more security conscious than non-members, they are more likely to report suspicious incidents to the police, and they report a greater sense of security from having their home watched. But they are unlikely to derive a greater sense of neighbourliness from membership (Mayhew et al, 1989, Chapter 6). Neighbourhood watch, moreover, tends to have taken root among better-off owner-occupiers in affluent suburban areas with a low risk of burglary rather than on crime-prone estates and in inner-city areas (Mayhew et al, 1989). This raises questions about the need for an existing consensual basis for order if grassroots, community-based crime prevention is to take off; where the basis for order is fractured and contentious, harnessing the activities of the police to the concerns of a particular group or groups runs the risk of exacerbating neighbourhood tensions.

Finally, it seems appropriate to ask what precisely is meant by those advocates of community policing who want the police to promote and mesh with systems of informal social control. To begin with, where informal social controls are working well, people tend to have less need of police. It is where they are lacking that the police will be called upon to intervene. And while it may be possible for caring and welfare agencies to forge constructive relationships in order that informal community resources might be identified and harnessed, for the police to try to do so is a far more perilous enterprise.

Police Community Consultation

Perhaps the main legacy of Lord Scarman's report on the Brixton disorders has been his recommendation designed to ensure a greater community involvement in policing policy and operations. Lord Scarman was persuaded that at least part of the responsibility for the riots lay in the failures of both the police and community leaders to use existing liaison machinery, with the police taking a more parsimonious approach than was desirable to the sharing of information with community leaders and failing to heed what Lord Scarman considered to be legitimate criticisms of local policing methods and styles. He recommended that a statutory duty be placed on police authorities and chief officers of police to establish consultative arrangements. This recommendation was given legislative effect by section 106 of the Police and Criminal Evidence Act 1984. The Home Office has subsequently advised in a series of circulars that among the issues that consultative committees may legitimately discuss are: community attitudes to local policing, police procedures, the causes and pattern of crime, crime prevention, and the needs of victims of crime (Home Office, 1982 and 1985). The more recent circular adds that 'the police should be as open as possible in their dealings with consultative groups and should be ready to discuss all aspects of police aims and policy' (Home Office, 1985, para 4). By the end of 1991 well over 500 groups had been established throughout the country.

Like multi-agency crime prevention, police community consultation has had mixed success. There is good geographical coverage, with formal schemes existing in all police areas, but doubts persist about the motivation and ability of consultative groups to promote open and informed discussion of policing policy at local level.

In a highly critical review of the then existing state of play, Morgan (1990) has argued that, with some conspicuous exceptions, consultative groups have been excessively dependent on the police for information and support. Police knowledge and expertise, their access to resources and their ability to maintain a consensual line in public, coupled with consultative group members' relative ignorance of policing, have meant that the police have been able to maintain control of discussions and promote their own agenda (see also Stratta, 1990 and Home Office, 1989). Consultative groups are, moreover, generally composed of people who are well disposed towards the police and who fail adequately to represent local organisations and interests. Groups and individuals who are the most likely to have adversarial relations with the police tend not to participate, with the result that groups fail to provide an adequate forum for the resolution of conflict. The level of public attendance at group meetings tends to be low. Few groups have sought to identify and try to solve specific local problems.

Conclusion

I began this chapter by describing community policing as a potent combination of ideology and practical politics. The intervening review has sought to explain why the policing ends and policing values that community policing seeks to promote have proved attractive to policy makers. From a police point of view, the renewed emphasis on prevention and partnership that community policing requires, with its corollaries of shared values and joint action, has considerable legitimating potential at a time when the police service has come under the critical spotlight. And for a government concerned to reduce public expenditure and to get a better return from an expensive resource, an approach which emphasises joint problem solving and harnessing the voluntary efforts of others is potentially cost effective.

Community policing has not, however, emerged as part of a grand design but rather as a response to a number of disparate developments which, for varying reasons, place an emphasis on localism, partnership and prevention. Community policing ideas, particularly in relation to patrol, have tended to build upon and develop prior orthodoxies rather than introduce new ones. While some community policing developments, particularly in relation to crime prevention, have, through the device of advisory circulars, been given strategic direction by central government, none – with the exception of police community consultation committees – has had legislative backing. And while much has been done to put in place new structures to promote police/community dialogue and action, in important respects community policing practice has been left to develop somewhat piecemeal.

It is probably fair to say, too, that community policing has achieved more in presentational than in practical terms. At a working level community policing ideas have proved difficult to operationalise other than superficially and in an ad hoc way. I have identified a number of reasons for this. In relation to patrol, it is that 'community' is too vague and all-inclusive a term to guide action and that, as a result, community officers have not had a distinctive job to do. In the case of partnership approaches to crime prevention, it is that crime prevention ends cannot be promoted in the absence of better local structures and a better understanding of organisational priorities and a greater willingness by participants to tackle them. In the case of local consultation it is that consultative groups have, on the whole, failed to generate any useful role for themselves other than as recipients of police education and are unrepresentative of whole communities.

None of the above is meant to imply that the police should abandon the values of service, responsiveness, consultation, localism and partnership to which appeals to community commit them. One of the more encouraging developments in policing over the past decade has been the greater preparedness of the police to submit themselves to scrutiny by outsiders and to engage, less defensively and more constructively than in the past, with their critics. The proliferation of community forums in which these debates can carry on has to be a welcome development. And it is also clear that appeals to something called 'community policing' have served as an important legitimating device, as a handy shorthand for all that is presumed to be best in British policing, at a time when such legitimation was urgently required. Thus, at a political level it can be argued that community policing has served its purpose well.

If, however, as I have argued, community policing intellectually and practically leaves much to be desired, it is incumbent upon those charged with making it work to take seriously the evidence which is now available about its deficiencies. It is, therefore, encouraging that some reassessment has been and is being provoked by other developments which, although not parading themselves under the community policing banner, may, nonetheless, turn out to have important consequences for the delivery of police services.

The most important of these is the way in which appeals to the 'customer' rather than to the 'community' have begun to inform progressive police thinking. In 1990 the police service published an extensive research review which pointed up, amongst other things, the gap between the views of the public and those of police officers about what should count as effective policing (Joint Consultative Committee, 1990). Hard on the heels of this came evidence from the 1988 British Crime Survey which showed a decline in public support for the police over the previous four years, much of which was attributable to mounting dissatisfaction among people who had contacted the police: support for police diminished with the need for their services (Skogan, 1990). The police service responded immediately with a collective public statement committing itself to improving service delivery within an equal opportunities framework. As a result, a number of police forces have set out to implement 'total quality management' approaches to service delivery; many are committed to carrying out regular surveys of those who come into contact with them; and all are moving towards setting explicit standards of service (for example, response times) for which, under the provisions of the Local Government Act 1992, they are to be held accountable locally. Forces are also committed to programmes of decentralisation. As already indicated, in several forces this has meant reorganising police officers into teams with responsibility for smaller geographical areas.

It is too early to say what the impact of this changed emphasis will be on the future and effectiveness of community policing. The emphasis on user surveys will provide the police with a much clearer picture than they have had hitherto of how people react to their encounters with them and will enable them to monitor changes over time. The move towards standard setting will generate information not previously within the public domain. For example, local police commanders might agree to keep local officers on their beats for a specified number of hours per day and days per month. The onus would then be on them to demonstrate whether these standards had been met, and to present it in an accessible way, neither of which is done at present. The availability of such information, collected specifically to promote public discussion, might help promote more informed and focused debate within consultation forums. It would undoubtedly increase local pressure for the police to make available more resources, but it would also force the police to be more explicit about the uses to which they currently put those resources. None of this would guarantee more community policing, but it would enable people to make better judgements than they are currently able to make about whether community policing is being done.

It is important to remember too that, crucial though it is that individual officers are discouraged from acting in ways that exacerbate conflict, it is the social and economic context in which they operate, not police action *per se*, that generates the amount and type of conflict with which the police are called upon to deal. Where the consensual basis for order has itself broken down, or where the police have to operate with conflicting and irreconcilable definitions of order generated by different sections of a heterogeneous community, their task becomes both more difficult and more contentious. Just as appeals to the wishes of customers will fail to provide a basis for police action when those 'customers' are in an adversarial relationship to the police, so will appeals to 'community' fail to provide an unequivocal basis for action where that community is itself divided. Increasing social and economic divisions not only create the problems with which the police have to deal, they also erode further the consensual basis for police action on which advocates of community policing would wish the police to act. Policing can never be a harmonious activity; nor can the *police* make it so. The challenge for community policing is to seek out and apply the bases for consensual action where these exist; to create, sustain and use a network of relationships which support that endeavour; and for officers to approach the job they are required to do in that spirit.

9 Community Government

M. Habeebullah and David Slater

The Concept of 'Community' in Local Government

Community government stands somewhat apart from the themes dealt with in other chapters in Part Two. It represents more than a slogan, but it cannot yet be said to be an area of established community practice or policy development. It can perhaps be most usefully and accurately summarised as an aspiration, consistently present in British politics, which materialises in various forms, and as partial developments of practice from time to time. Our interest in this chapter is to examine these various manifestations in local government, and to consider to what extent they represent a movement towards, or a potential for, a form of government in which there is a genuine scope for communities to assert themselves in political/decision-making processes in their broadest sense.

We have seen in earlier chapters (Chapters 1 and 4) of this book the way in which the term 'community' has been deployed by the state in relation to an increasingly wide spectrum of its activities and policies. The use of the term may be varied but, as has been said, it is far from aimless. The point of earlier analysis was to identify the motivation, intentions and underlying needs within the state for vesting its activities in the clothes of 'community'. Of particular relevance to this chapter is the theme of a state responding to and struggling with an increasingly diverse, fractured and yet assertive society (Chapter 3).

Here we are dealing with the application of the term 'community' to the process of government itself. While government in Britain has in many decisive respects become increasingly centralised since 1945 and especially since 1979, the language of government and of political ideology is ever more prominently spattered with 'involvement', 'participation', 'citizenship'. Our purpose is to examine the spectrum of ideas and policies which have some reference to what might be called 'community government', or 'community in government'; and to consider to what extent they represent a significant countertrend to this process of centralisation.

We will begin by looking at traditions and trends of thought or philosophy within the main political parties which refer to community. Butcher et al (1990) identified the way in which the established post-war model of local government had been increasingly subject to questioning, from the centre and left, as well as from the Thatcherite right in the 1980s:

> From all sections of the political landscape . . . there is a question of the relations between the principles of local democracy and the function – regulatory, promotional, direct provision – of local and central government. This questioning addresses fundamental issues concerned with the overall remit of local government: the proper relations between local government and central government and between local government and the public; questions about the nature of effective organisation and sensitive administration; and contested ideas about the proper role of the public service professional. (Butcher et al, 1990, p. 139)

Conservative responses, promoted from the libertarian right, have focused on substituting market mechanisms and elements of 'consumer choice' in favour of standardised service provision by local authorities. The effort to hive off services to the private and voluntary sectors extends now into housing, education and social services. Community preferences are viewed as synonymous with consumer or market choices, and are therefore seen to be given greater weight via decentralisation through the market.

The Liberal Party approach to 'community politics' developed in the 1970s and represented a form of activist electoral politics aimed at enabling and empowering people in their own communities; it did not identify any concrete goals in terms of the focus of power in local authorities. By the early 1980s community politics had been extended to 'community government' (Liberal Party policy document, 1982). Here the Liberals stressed their belief in political as well as administrative decentralisation within local authorities, to ensure that local priorities held sway over centralised and departmental policy making.

The Labour Party's growing interest during the 1980s in local government reform and localised modes of service provision also stemmed to a large degree from concern for its electoral base. The broadest point of consensus within the party was that Labour local authorities needed to respond to the ideological and political onslaught from the right. But crucial differences centred on whether this response should amount to no more than reforming the existing mode of service provision or should extend to fundamental changes in the relationship between local state and community.

Local Government: Trends towards Reform

Within these strands of political thought are contained the roots of a number of key concepts and modes of implementation which refer to or have a bearing on the relationship between government and community. Those with which we are mainly concerned are the following:

- enabling
- political devolution
- support for the voluntary sector
- consumerism.

Enabling

A theme which spans the political spectrum from right to left is that of moving local government into an 'enabling' relationship with other social actors, rather than operating primarily as a provider of services. Needless to say, the way in which the concept of enabling is interpreted differs widely.

The right, *pace* Nicholas Ridley, would wish to push forward an agenda of reducing direct provision by local authorities across many major service areas, substituting for this provision a role of enabling other agencies and specifically the private sector to become the providers.

This view of a circumscribed role for local government is countered on the left by the idea of local authorities taking a proactive role in providing the necessary support and framework for an active and participative democracy. Gyford describes this as an 'infrastructure for citizenship' (Gyford, 1991, p. 186), which can focus on either 'enabling people to achieve things for themselves' or facilitating the individual's 'full and active role in the political community'. The Association of Metropolitan Authorities (AMA) echoed this in its publication *Community Development – the Local Authority Role* which took the view that 'such an enabling orientation should become part of the culture of local government as a whole' (AMA, 1989, pp. 15 and 20). Gyford himself proposes a third possible approach, in which local authorities resource 'active citizens' collectively in their roles as support service, training agency and resource centre; this approach addresses itself to grassroots politics and sustaining an active civic culture rather than to alternative forms of service provision.

This wider conception of the enabling role opens up the question of whether local authorities should be seen as the sole or even the primary movers in this respect. In British political culture there is a big question mark over the role of the political parties in relation to civic society. In their concentration on electoral politics and the achievement of power they barely address the wider functions of political parties as social organisers. This is a theme to which we will return later.

Political Devolution

Most prominent among the recent political projects to give communities a decisive or central role in local government has been that of political devolution. The term 'community government' is, for example, currently being used by Bradford City Council to summarise and project such policies since the Labour Party resumed control. It has been used by the Liberal Party (as referred to above) with the same intent, something reflected in the policies of Liberal Democrat local authorities, notably Tower Hamlets. The Conservative Party and Conservative authorities have shown some interest in themes of local government decentralisation; for example Hertfordshire County Council was considering forms of devolution before the Conservatives lost control there in the 1993 county council elections.

The trend towards devolution of power has characterised the genuine but problematic efforts being made by many local authorities to move away from the management/client relationship that local government has had with the public. The underlying problem is that those whom local government serves have indeed been consumers, and have experienced themselves almost exclusively as consumers of the services concerned, with little say in policy formulation or implementation.

The growing themes of citizenship and involvement in local government have been an expression of the difficult position which politically hard-pressed local authorities find themselves in: of having to seek to engender an active local democracy, from the top down, in very unpromising circumstances. It is a call to communities to play a part in government which has not historically been available to them.

The attempt to alchemise a client relationship into a political one is beset with problems. Local government's historical role since 1945, as part of the conveyor belt of service delivery, brought with it a distinctive political and bureaucratic culture. The terrain on which more democratic or community government might develop has been affected by the controlling influence of Whitehall, but also by the managerial outlook of local authority politicians and officers and by the reduction of the role of political parties to adjuncts of town hall politics.

The difficulties of recovering or recreating this terrain has been reflected in the history of the 'new left' during the 1980s, and by the way in which decentralisation emerged as a political phenomenon. The 'soft left' activists who drew their experience of political organisation from outside the Labour movement (through the women's movements, community politics, the student movement) brought with them a different set of political values from those of the machine politician of the old school. They also brought a strong awareness of the political vulnerability of local government, brought about by years of bureaucratic politics and the alienation which it had created. The realisation of the need for fundamental change in the relationship between local authorities and the communities they serve was the starting gun for much of the political development of the decade in local government. Combined with the need to secure a political powerbase against Thatcherite incursions, this was the basis for the advent of decentralisation.

Throughout the 1980s Labour and to a lesser extent Liberal Democrat authorities have struggled with schemes which have attempted to get varying combinations of both neighbourhood-based services and direct participation elements into place at the same time. Many of these schemes have been reduced in scale and ambition during implementation, with participation often being the first element to be sacrificed. In some cases, such as Manchester, they have imploded for financial and/or electoral reasons. A major cause of this failure, in our view, has been the inability to distinguish between service decentralisation and political decentralisation. A more recent trend emerging in the last few years has been that of less ambitious projects, dispensing with capital intensive decentralisation to neighbourhood centres, but seeking to inject greater community involvement into the delivery of services through existing structures. Nevertheless, the gap between designing a structure (something which comes naturally to local government) and developing a culture of active involvement (something which doesn't) remains.

In the mid 1980s, as decentralisation was adopted by different authorities, there was considerable discussion of the underlying reasons for its uncertain progress after the first flush of enthusiasm. The debate focused on factors constraining change within local government (declining resources, resistance from unions) and factors relating to the spectrum of political opinion within the party itself (Hambleton and Hoggett, 1990). The detailed discussion of various decentralisation programmes, their strengths and weaknesses, and different ideological perspectives did not deal with the wider political context. Concentration on programmes of change coming from within local authorities leaves more or less untouched the question of the enormous amount of work to be done on the relationship *between* local state and community. Again, this is a theme we want to take up later.

Support for the Voluntary Sector

The relationship between the local state and the voluntary sector is another area in which the strategies of left and right contend. The Thatcherite perspective has been one of promoting the voluntary sector along with the private sector as an ideologically acceptable alternative setting for service provision, and one which should expand as 'social' provision by local authorities is broken up.

The vision has been one of community-based organisations expanding their role and scope of operation (e.g. in housing special needs, in the care field), to take up the spaces in provision vacated as local authorities' roles are reduced. To date this approach has shown little sign of producing concrete results – voluntary organisations remain sceptical, not only about the scale and contract-based nature of the funding on offer but also about having their self-determination, values and models of provision distorted by the need to operate at levels they had not previously envisaged.

The impetus from the left has been to expand and transform the relationship between the local state and voluntary sector. Butcher et al (1990, p. 148) refer to this approach as 'cultural pluralism':

> This strand of local pluralism involves use of non-state agencies as part of a strategy to both recognise and respond to diversity in local culture, lifestyle and needs. In this model increased 'sensitivity' and 'responsiveness' is seen to come less as a consequence of market competition and more as an outcome of the promotion of indigenous community control over local services.

The example held out as the most advanced and developed move in this direction by a local authority has been that by the Greater London Council (GLC) during the Livingstone regime of the early 1980s. Significantly the GLC had considerable resources and none of the more politically draining responsibilities such as housing. It chose to throw this weight behind a strategy of 'giving power away'. In 1983–4 the authority handed over a total of £40 million in grants to voluntary organisations in a programme of active and coherent support with a clearly identified set of overall objectives.

This strategy of the GLC's took the authority into territory which extended beyond the 'purse-holding' role which characterises the traditional relationship of local government to the voluntary sector. Reflecting on the GLC experience in 1986 after its dissolution, Campbell and Jacques commented on the dynamism the GLC introduced to its relationship with communities and with the voluntary sector. The unique quality of the GLC in the Livingstone era was that:

> [it] allowed for the factor of self-determination, a quality of the voluntary sector which the left has never really understood. What the GLC did was to develop a new concept of the relationship between the state and the voluntary sector . . . [it] was pro-state *and* [our emphasis] pro-voluntary sector, for a new symbiotic partnership . . . the GLC responded to the [Thatcherite] challenge in a way which the left has generally failed to do, to create a positive pro-state, pro-public solution . . . Instead of seeing the state – in this case the local state – as the fount of all things good and positive, the GLC saw the state in part as enabling the voluntary sector, resourcing people in their own things, in being creative, in having an

identity. Put more theoretically the GLC was pro-civil society, not just pro-state. (Campbell and Jacques, 1986, p. 8)

While this approach to reforming the role of local government remains a consistent theme at a theoretical or intellectual level, it has been little replicated among Labour local authorities at large. And certainly funding patterns have not extended to enabling voluntary sector organisations to meet local authorities on a more equal footing over policy issues in the locality. The voluntary sector is seen all too often as a second string to the local authority bow, and a troublesome one at that.

Consumerism

The drive by the right to break up the statist model of service provision has led to the introduction of the concept of 'consumer choice' in the public service sector.

The Conservative government has sought, accordingly, to legislate for and promote alternative systems of provision for housing, education and community care, for example, through the private sector, voluntary sector or quangos. The extent to which these measures will give rise to a coherent and equitable alternative to state provision remain very much in contention. But the degree to which it has changed the face of local government is incontestable. Local authorities are moving further and further down the road towards becoming supervisory and monitoring bodies, rather primary service providers. Local authority professionals have to engage in new roles, negotiating access to and between services.

In this vision of the future the guarantor of standards is the market, influenced by consumer choice. So, for example, parents now choose between schools for their children according to the school's 'performance'; provision for those in need of care is being privatised or relocated towards the voluntary sector, so that choice is exercised by consumers within a local market.

The degree to which this has removed important areas of provision from any kind of democratic or community control, and the extent to which consumer sovereignty is an adequate alternative safeguard, will be touched on later.

Models for Community Government

Having discussed the various concepts through which the relationship between state and community is mediated, we will now look at the way in which these concepts, and the political traditions they reflect, emerge in the form of different models for community government. We will confine ourselves to four basic models, although there are many variants of each. These are:

- community government as 'hole in the road' politics
- community government as devolution
- community government as decentralisation
- community government as empowering consumers.

Community Government as 'Hole in the Road' Politics

Here an authority is responding to the most basic demands on its services at a local level. In essence the model offers to residents additional opportunities to communicate individual demands or complaints regarding services, to local ward members, or to relevant officers. An authority may, therefore, introduce local 'committee' meetings at ward or area level, which members of the public are invited to attend on a regular basis. The system works as a form of listening and responsive local government. There is also the scope to develop a corporate approach at local levels, involving other public bodies and agencies. However, there is little or no opportunity for residents of an area to develop a wider or more informed perspective on services to, or needs in, their area. The system does not aim to develop skills, knowledge, organisation or strength in communities.

The model therefore has the overall result of providing feedback on existing services but does not provide a real basis for a fundamental reshaping of the scope and delivery of those services.

An example is Middlesbrough Borough Council which has one of the longest established systems of neighbourhood consultative committees in the country. Its community councils take the form of open meetings, chaired by a ward councillor and with officers of departments in attendance. The principal innovation is the nomination of a senior 'lead officer' for each community council, whose responsibility it is to activate responses within the borough to issues raised at meetings.

Its main limitations are dependence on the quality of chairing, on the level of commitment and powers of persuasion of the 'lead officer', and on the commitment of different departments and agencies in turning up to meetings. The community councils are public forums to which individuals (or sometimes community groups) bring problems, complaints and local issues on which they require action from the local authorities. They do not actively engage in community development.

Community Government as Devolution

In a devolutionary model the power of decision making over policies and priorities for a locality is to one degree or another lodged with a committee or forum of representatives from the area. In principle devolution of power is closely associated with decentralisation of service delivery; ideally the two would parallel each other. Moves of any significance towards devolved power, though widely canvassed and discussed, have been rare in practice. Islington, one of the earliest and most comprehensive decentralisers, also set up neighbourhood forums in a model which went as far down the road to devolution of power from the centre as that promoted by any local authority. The forums had control of local budgets, and an advisory role in the working of neighbourhood offices. Even so, the authority retained the core of its central committee system, and some central departments. In an analysis of the experience of this system in 1989, Khan identified several areas of difficulty:

1. In the early phase local budgets were underspent due to lack of initiative from forums and lack of understanding of the budget process. With time the budgetary problems were overcome, but largely as a result of the Neighbourhood Officer taking a leading or predominant role.
2. The relationship between officers and forums had been co-operative, but based on the primacy of officers and a secondary role in decision making on the part of forums.
3. Decentralisation had not significantly lessened the problems of departmentalism; and forums had been given little guidance on the matter or how to challenge it.
4. Officers tended to see forums in a supportive role, with their involvement being principally around officer initiatives. Officers related most readily to the forums in the role of funnel for information, and sounding board for new ideas and policies.
5. Most importantly, no detailed guidelines were developed by Islington to govern the relationship between forums and central departments. The lack of a formal structure through which forums and central committees could work proved to be an inherent weakness, leaving the relationship highly

ambiguous. Forums tended to be successful in getting their views accepted by central committees if they coincided with the established direction of policy; but found it very difficult to get appropriate responses where their views were opposed to existing Council policy. (Khan, 1989)

These tensions within the Islington system are symptomatic of problems for voluntary-led bodies in asserting themselves within the local authority system, of the unwillingness of politicians to devolve power in any clearly delineated way, of the limitations to influence over broader policy issues which can be achieved even within a devolved system.

Community Government as Decentralisation

The intentions guiding decentralisation strategies vary widely between authorities, and are often uncertain or contested within individual authorities. They range from the pragmatic – that service delivery will be improved by the physical nearness of frontline staff to the communities or neighbourhoods to be served – to the politically more far-reaching – that decentralisation is a part of the effort by local authorities to move away from the traditional, standardised management/client relationship between local government and the public.

Common themes running through the various approaches to decentralisation have included the following: location in particular neighbourhoods enables service managers to be much more closely attuned to the particular needs of the area, and to focus priorities and service delivery accordingly; and the bringing together of previously departmentally based services into multi-service teams creates scope for addressing need in a much more coherent and fluent way at a local level.

Rochdale Metropolitan Borough Council, Labour controlled until 1992, introduced a model of decentralisation which was described as 'community driven'. The authority went a long way toward breaking up traditional departments and bringing together the different professional disciplines in neighbourhood teams. However, it eventually backed away from linking decentralisation with the devolution of decision making in the overt way seen in Islington. While there were to have been neighbourhood forums, the direct linkage between them and the working of neighbourhood teams was eventually substituted with 'working parties' on specific policy areas. Nevertheless this did open up the possibility of worthwhile, if uneven, intervention at policy level by residents' representatives, community organisations and the voluntary sector.

Community Government as Empowering Consumers

Another strand of the movement away from the 'town hall knows best' approach of old is one in which the consumer-responsive models of the commercial world have been adapted to varying degrees by local government. Hambleton and Hoggett (1990) refer to this approach as a 'new managerialism' since, despite its emphasis on the shake-up of bureaucratic culture, 'it leaves managers, professionals and administrators firmly in control of their hierarchies'.

The effort to redefine clients as consumers, and to refocus management style and priorities accordingly, has revolved around themes of greater choice, flexibility and customer care. Its rhetoric is one of listening to the customer, 'service sampling', mission statements and market research.

York City Council, for example, has been a leader in the field of customer orientation. It pioneered the concept of the 'citizen's charter' in the late 1980s, with its associated commitments to service standards. It has made a substantial commitment to communicating what it is doing as an authority, and to consulting widely over specific projects. It has pursued a policy of examining its individual services 'from a customer viewpoint' and implementing management changes through departmental management teams.

While it would be generally accepted that it is an advance if authorities become more responsive and the quality of service improves, Hambleton and Hoggett point out what they regard as six serious limitations to the consumerist ethos:

- It fails to shift the power relationship in favour of the consumer, let alone the disadvantaged consumer.
- The movement has been dominated by the 'charm school' approach, which offers largely cosmetic change.
- It has difficulty in coping with the needs of *groups* of consumers, though many public services are consumed collectively.
- Consumerism concentrates on individual and material issues rather than social or community needs.
- The use of the word 'customer' is inappropriate for the framework within which local authority services are provided.

- The focus on consumerism encourages the view that local government is simply an instrument for delivering public services, whereas accountability to the citizen is as important as responsiveness to the consumer. (Hambleton and Hoggett, 1990)

Conclusion

We have surveyed some of the ideological grounds for the introduction of the concept of community into the process of government. We have also examined some of the main modes of implementation emerging from these political foundations, and specific examples of models of reform introduction by particular local authorities. We now want to examine, in general terms, what these developments have meant for the relationship between community and government, communities and local state.

The new right, as we have seen, wishes as far as possible to substitute the state and political mechanism for making choices with the market as the mechanism of individual choices. The new left proposes, rather, to expand the political processes by which social choices are made such that there is a fundamental shift in the nature of the relationship between community and state; this would mean a dispersal of power, and a desirable diversity and autonomy of communities and neighbourhoods. Between these polar opposites lies a spectrum along which individual authorities have located their reform programmes.

For the sake of simplification we will examine the outcomes of the past ten years in terms of the left and right extremes. Within the terms of the debate set by this chapter the right almost excludes itself in the sense that it wishes to dispense with the local authority role as far as possible rather than reshape its relationship with the community. To the extent that we confine ourselves to the question of how 'choice' is made, however, we can examine the results of market-led thinking. The most penetrating criticism of the principle of choice exercised in the 'market-place' of services is that it depends entirely on the ability of the individual to exert choice in practice. In the political universe of the libertarian right every individual is able to exert influence over the ultimate choices made in the market-place, whereas, in the words of Malcolm X: 'I am not a diner until I may dine.' The purity of the theory excludes from consideration the fact that many 'individuals', and many social groups are, for a variety of reasons, not able to exert choice in the same way as others. The market is in fact a highly exclusive form of social decision making excluding, for example, those with insufficient spending power and those from minority groups who cannot secure provision to meet their specific needs. In this conception, the 'community' is reduced to more affluent, more vocal and more powerful interest groups.

The intellectual framework of the right also has the effect of narrowing the legitimate considerations of government, and specifically local government, down to questions of efficient management and contracting out of basic services. It is not concerned with wider questions of government as the means by which we all decide how to live together; rather, it wishes actively to exclude government/the state from as many areas as possible. The left on the other hand proposes to enlarge and simultaneously transform the government/community interface. The question mark here concerns seriousness of intent as well as realisability.

There is no established tradition in Britain of communities and community politics having an assertive role *within* the boundaries of the state. Even in those local authorities where a relatively radical approach to devolution of decision making has been adopted there have been clear signs of hesitancy on the part of the left, over the direction in which a dispersed form of power would carry policy and policy making. Taking Labour authorities as a whole, their approach to community politics and to the relationship with communities is hedged around in a number of important ways which suggest that significant change is a long way off. These fall under the headings, broadly, of *structure, funding* and *process*.

We referred earlier to the way in which the neighbourhood forums in Islington continued to have an ill-defined relationship with the central decision-making *structure* of the local authority, and how this reflects unresolved doubts about the political benefits of the politics of empowerment. In other authorities, where the weight of political conviction behind devolution has been considerably less than in Islington, the structural limitations on devolution have been more emphatic.

One feature that we have observed, in Rochdale for example, has been the way in which the more determined decentralisers have had to carry those in other camps with them, by selling decentralisation in politically pragmatic terms, in order to carry programmes through ruling Labour groups. The result has, ironically, been that the shift to neighbourhood government has been endorsed by councillors who have been persuaded to see it in the light of reinstating themselves in their rightful kingdoms of old, lost with reorganisation in the 1970s. Where community involvement has been structurally disengaged from service provision as part of political brokering, then neighbourhood offices have a tendency to become part of the local politician's fiefdom.

The issue of *funding* mirrors these structural restrictions on the genuine dispersal of power. The nature of funding to the local voluntary sector is such that it can respond at a primary level to the weaknesses and omissions of local authority provision but cannot effectively challenge them at a policy level. It is ironic that those most aware of need at a primary level are least able to press the issue at a policy level in a sufficiently developed way to engender a response.

The point about *process* refers back to our earlier comments about political parties. There is a vacuum in the political process in Britain which ensures that policy cannot be developed in any adequate sense, from the political grassroots upwards. Party politics at the local level is conducted largely at the level of 'mud slinging', rather than as a process of concrete policy debate, and popular involvement in substantive issues. Policy formation at the national level is arrived at either as a result of the competitive lobbying of fringe 'think tanks' and pressure groups, or, increasingly, through market research. Political parties, including the Labour Party, have historically failed to provide the organic link between grassroots activity and policy formation, seen for example in the parties of the left in European countries. This is a fundamental weakness in the political fabric, and a serious disablement of any movement towards anything which could be called community government.

In concluding this chapter we have, then, to strike a pessimistic note about the prospects of progress towards models of government in which communities can assert more than an intermittent influence. Both right and left have promoted reforms which purport to bring government closer to community. Those of the right revolve around a restricted interpretation of 'community', while the stated objectives of the left face fundamental obstacles that have not yet been approached with anything like sufficient conviction. Community government will continue to emerge as a strand in British politics in various guises and in limited forms.

It will not, however, develop beyond the germination stage without significant changes in the political culture. In an ideal world this would mean:

- political parties developing a much more bottom-up approach to policy formation
- support from central government to the voluntary sector for a much more proactive role in policy making
- local authorities providing resources to local community groups and organisations to develop policy on issues of concern to them.

In the meantime a welcome beginning, even in the context of limited resources, would be for local authorities to think in terms of community government in a limited form, to take a more active approach to promoting an infrastructure capable of supporting community involvement at a policy level.

10 Community Care

Liz McShane

Introduction

The concern with 'community care' in current social policies for health and social services is not new. The policy was first officially proposed over 30 years ago to enable people to receive treatment while living in the community rather than being admitted to hospital. It was not, however, translated into action. Alan Walker (1982) describes the lack of political will, planning strategy and resources from the early 1960s onwards that has characterised community care policies and led to a cynical view that in many areas community care is a myth.

From a policy that was honoured more in the breach than in the observance through the 1960s and 70s (in spite of mounting evidence of the failures of large total institutions) community care has nevertheless emerged as a cornerstone of major changes in health and social services policy (Griffiths Report, 1988; White Papers *Caring for People*, HMSO, 1989, and *People First*, Department of Health and Social Security NI, 1990). The policy identifies the need for a 'mixed economy of care' in which community care services are purchased by the statutory bodies and provided by a mix of statutory, voluntary and private agencies. Partnerships between the state and the private and voluntary sectors to provide contracts for care within the community are to be set up and implemented by managers in social services.

Wide-ranging administrative and managerial restructuring has taken place in local social and health services in preparation for the changes in policy, but it remains doubtful whether the resources needed to implement the changes fully will be allocated. Lack of resources led to the original date for implementation being put back from April 1991 to April 1993. Public spending plans for 1993–4 show that community care funding for local authorities will fall well short of requirements, by approximately £250 million a year (Ivory, 1992). Taking into account the budget capping of some local authorities and a skewing of spending towards authorities with the most independent-sector residential care, the bleak picture is of cuts in jobs and care services at a time of rising poverty and unemployment.

Care objectives such as enabling vulnerable people to live in the community rather than in institutions, responding flexibly to people's needs, and encouraging the choice and independence of vulnerable client groups require a massive shift in existing resources. Without adequate resources the complex task of co-ordinating different contracts into a package of community care could mean 'no care' for those who slip through the net of family carers and hard-pressed professional staff.

The debate on community care must also confront the different interpretations that exist of the concept of 'community'. The policy objectives conjure up a picture of the community as a place where people will receive support, understanding and acceptance from others (the 'rosy view' of community, sceptically identified by Titmuss, 1968). It is also assumed that dependent service users within those communities will make their needs and choices known, liaise with helping agencies, accept the help offered and move on to become more independent and less in need of help.

All these assumptions overlook the negative attitudes towards traditional 'client' and 'patient' groups demonstrated, for example, by those who mobilise activity to prevent aftercare facilities being located in particular areas. They also ignore conflict within communities, notably racial conflict which targets vulnerable families in the inner-city, or sectarian conflict in Northern Ireland. Finally, they assume the continuing existence of local kinship networks, but social change in Britain (as described in Chapter 3) seems to make this less likely. The image of service users participating in provision alongside professionals belies the stereotyped roles that are often the reality in this situation.

Given these dilemmas, current community care policy presents a considerable challenge to planners and professionals in health and social services. Much has been written about such challenges (e.g. Bulmer, 1987; Bornat et al, 1993) and it would seem pointless to rehearse them further here. More useful, and more consistent with the focus of this book, would be to explore what a 'community practice' approach to community care planning would look like, and to assess how far such an approach would offer solutions to the professionals, users and policy makers searching for ways of making community care a reality.

An innovative pilot programme in community care in Northern Ireland, one which embraces considerable user involvement and active community participation in the support of vulnerable people, provides insights into what such a community approach can offer.

The Community Support Programme

The Community Support Programme is a pilot programme funded by the Department of Health and Social Services Northern Ireland and Urban Aid programmes in Belfast and Derry and administered by the Northern Ireland Voluntary Trust in Belfast (an independent trust supporting the efforts of community groups tackling social and economic problems in Northern Ireland). The programme was set up in 1989, when policies on community care were about to change, to demonstrate a community development and mutual aid approach to community care, with user involvement as central to the process. Ten pilot projects in different parts of Northern Ireland were each funded £20,000 a year for three years from 1989 to 1992. They cover a wide range of social policy, including mental health, learning difficulties, physical disability, alcohol and drug dependency, carers of dependent relatives, parent support, childcare and residents' participation in housing and inner-city development. Users of the project and local people define their own needs and then participate in planning and running activities to meet them. The work is not intended to duplicate that of the statutory services but to complement it and to try out innovatory responses to needs. A full-time co-ordinator is employed (McShane, 1991 and 1993).

In Northern Ireland the mainstream agencies providing health and social services and implementing the community care policies are four area boards appointed by the DHSS, with board units of management providing services at local level.

The ten pilot projects are all small-scale community or user groups which have set up and run their own services. An analysis of the projects suggests that they demonstrate three different categories or models of community support, as detailed below (although there are overlaps, and some show more than one model in their work).

Model 1

This relates to three neighbourhood projects involving local people in meeting locally defined needs, two in inner-city areas of Belfast and one on a peripheral estate in Derry. All three areas have been profoundly affected by the troubles. Two projects are concerned with the needs of families and children and one with a range of housing, health and social needs within a depressed estate. These projects correspond to the community development approach defined in Chapter 2.

An example of a Model 1 project which provides support to parents and children is the Corner House in the inner-city New Lodge area of Belfast. It provides a daily drop-in with a crèche, and runs a range of groups and activities. There are mother and toddler groups, education classes, a young single parents' group, an adolescent group, a parents' support group, an alcohol education group and an after-school club. All of these groups began as a result of locally expressed needs, either by users of the drop-in or from a survey carried out by members of the management committee. The committee is made up of local users of the house, Corner House staff and a health visitor and social worker. The house is seen as part of the local community and as an accessible place in which users have a say.

The young single parents' group grew from just two young women calling in for support and for 'something to do', to about 18 members, of which a core of nine to ten meet regularly. Some came along through neighbourhood contacts, others through a referral system set up with social work staff in the local maternity unit. The group is helped by staff to plan its own programme of activities in the house. There are discussion groups and information on health, child care, budgeting and careers advice. There is also space to meet and chat, and there are social outings and shopping trips. A drama group also developed which played a role in building up members' self-esteem and confidence. Local social workers who have referred people to the group stress its preventive role, and feel that for some babies and young children it has made a significant difference, enabling them to remain in the community with their families rather than being taken into care. The acceptance and self-help ethos within the Corner House group means that it has an image which is less stigmatising than a nearby social services facility for families 'at risk'.

The committee employs a project manager (funded by social services) whose remit is to encourage users to express their needs and to take part where possible in the various programmes. Feedback from users themselves and from relevant professionals shows that this community/user-owned project succeeds in meeting needs in a way that encourages users to help each other.

Model 2

These projects each reflect a community of interest rather than a small geographical neighbourhood. They represent a self-help and advocacy approach, with groups tackling their own problems and providing support to their members. They are: a carers' association providing information, advice and support to six carers' mutual support groups; a group of young deaf people providing youth services, advice and liaison for the isolated 'deaf community' in a number of areas; and a group of people recovering from alcohol and drug dependency who run their own alcohol-free social centre. These projects could be seen as falling within both the community action and community services approaches.

An example of Model 2 projects with a particular relevance to current community care policies is the Newry and Mourne Carers' Association. It is now recognised that the considerable number of dependent elderly people and people with disabilities who remain in their own homes in the community manage to do so because of the efforts of informal carers. Carers are usually (but not always) women in the family who, having taken on the main caring role, are often left to shoulder it unaided. It is not so much the community that is personally supporting its vulnerable members, but hard-pressed women carers. The resulting stress and isolation can become an intolerable burden on the carer whose own health may suffer and who ultimately may be unable to continue.

The Newry Carers' Association aims to meet carers' needs for mutual support and relief from isolation, to provide them with information on the services available (often sadly lacking), and education on the skills needed for caring. Its six carers' support groups are spread over a wide rural area. With assistance from the three part-time staff each group organises its own programme of speakers, information and social activities.

The aim of the project is to bring isolated carers together so that they may gain support, information, confidence, friendships, and a recognition of their own role as carers and their right to support in that role. Feedback from carers in the local groups endorses this:

> 'What I get out of it is talking to people who have the same problems, just basically sharing, as they understand what you're talking about.'

> 'Knowing there are other people in the same boat as you, that's relief in itself.'

> 'Some of the speakers are excellent, and the courses are really great . . .'

> 'They (the staff) listen to everything you have to say.'

The association organises functions, such as seminars or Christmas parties, which bring together all six support groups, and a quarterly newsletter goes to all members. An important source of support has developed via the association's office telephone, with carers seeking help on a range of problems or just finding a listening ear when stress becomes too much.

There is a question as to whether a project supporting carers is in fact trying to help people to tolerate the intolerable. While the carers in the local groups often vent stress and anger at their situation, most do not see an alternative, though they feel that they deserve better financial and social recognition. The assumption, in these traditional, largely rural communities, that women will act as carers, remains relatively unchallenged. The association sees as part of its role the promotion of greater awareness of carers' work and needs. It acts as an advocate and pressure group on the carers' behalf.

The six carers' groups have members from all sections of the community in terms of the religious/political divisions in Northern Ireland. In the groups' experience, religious differences in the wider society, while being something of which all members are aware, do not permeate into the work of the carers' groups in any disruptive way; the common bond between carers is more important.

While the carers themselves do become involved in running the local groups or become members of the association management committee, their acute needs often make it difficult for them to participate actively. The community support grant, which enabled staff to be employed, was crucial therefore to the success of the association. It has been found, on the other hand, that ex-carers, although still needing the understanding and support of their local group, often have more time available and are able to provide a carer's voice and an important source of help on the management committee.

In terms of co-ordination with local health and social services, the carers' project has a social worker and district nurse on the management committee and has had close links with local social services from the beginning. When the pilot programme ended, the association entered into a partnership arrangement with the Southern Health and Social Services board to continue its work, with joint funding from the Board and the Princess Royal Trust for Carers.

The local residents on the Corner House management committee and the user members of the carers' association have a sense of ownership of their respective projects, an awareness of their autonomy and of responsibility to try and ensure that the projects continue. However, some projects falling within the third model of community support, below, are aimed at people whose situations make it unlikely that they will be able, or that they will wish, to be closely involved in running their own self-help project, at least initially.

Model 3

These projects have a participatory 'rights' way of working with vulnerable groups, most of whom are in contact with statutory services. The level of need is high and includes help with resettlement and integration into the community after institutional living. These projects comprise: a drop-in centre and outreach programme for people who have moved out of psychiatric hospital; a resettlement service for people moving out of a hostel for the homeless; a scheme for people with learning difficulties moving from hospital or the family home into supported accommodation and more independent living; and a community-based project providing counselling and group support for people suffering from mental health and stress problems. The first three projects are located in small towns but also serve the surrounding area, and the fourth is on a new town estate. These projects can be seen to involve a community services approach but with the important difference that they originated within the local communities rather than from statutory services, and that they consciously seek to implement participatory values and methods (see Chapter 1).

It might be thought that these projects would be outside the limits of community-based support or user groups, and that they lie within the realm of professional statutory services. It is true that the initial level of user involvement, either on the committee or in the work of the projects, was quite low, but all of them now have committees made up of people from the area. The programme shows that, by starting with small steps, working on people's own terms, and especially respecting people's rights and views, project users can and do contribute in a number of ways.

The Omagh Beacon Centre drop-in and lunch club for people with mental distress has an active members' committee which meets regularly, organises its own activities and sends two members to the project management committee. The Larne Simon resettlement service includes users on its local committee but also enables people who have been through the resettlement experience to advise and lend a hand to others moving out from the hostel. The CHARM trust project run by a committee of parents and friends of those with learning difficulties, providing supported accommodation for them, has residents taking part in interviews for staff in the houses. There is an ongoing planned programme of supporting residents to achieve more independent living for themselves based on the principles of normalisation.

Working in Communities

Having drawn together the experiences of ten varied projects into three models (summarised in Table 10.1) it is possible to offer a number of generalisations about the role of a community practice approach to community care.

The process of people stating their own needs and working with other users and relevant professionals to try to meet them is at the core of the *participatory approach*. This is especially true of those community action projects that were clearly user led from the beginning, perhaps in the face of an initial lack of recognition of their needs by statutory bodies. The Deaf Youth Association run by and staffed by young deaf people (a first for Northern Ireland) was formed to combat the isolation and neglect of young deaf people and to improve their quality of life, as well as to promote deaf awareness among the statutory agencies.

The Roden Street Action Team in Belfast used a community support grant to embark on a broad-based action plan to improve

Table 10.1: Models of Community Support Projects

	Name	Area of support
Model 1 Neighbourhood	Creggan Parent and Toddlers' Association, Derry	Children and parents
	New Lodge Corner House, Belfast	Parents, children and adolescents
	Roden Street Action Team, Belfast	Residents in a community under stress
Model 2 Community of interest	NI Deaf Youth Association	Young deaf people 12–35 years
	PANDA, Belfast	Those recovering from alcohol and drug dependency
	Newry and Mourne Carers' Association	Carers and their dependants
Model 3 Rights	Beacon Centre, Omagh	People discharged from psychiatric care
	Larne Simon Resettlement Project	Homeless people resettling in the community
	CHARM Trust Coleraine, Ballymena Ballymoney, Ballycastle	People with learning difficulties moving into independent living
	Stepping Stone, Craigavon	People with mental health and stress problems

and 'turn around' their own small estate of 300 houses. They employed their own community development worker to help them identify and tackle issues such as housing improvement, security and safety of residents, health and childcare on the estate. Over the three years they developed working relationships with statutory agencies, secured a major housing and environmental improvement scheme for the area, provided security grilles for houses that had suffered sectarian attack, and played a key role in bringing together a number of community groups to run a local family centre. All of these concrete achievements not only brought resources into the area but also gave local people a sense of having a voice. This is in an area where the troubles and urban redevelopment have produced widespread apathy, cynicism and a feeling of helplessness.

The community support pilot programme I have described suggests that a project which provides effective, ongoing support on a face-to-face basis is at any one time probably reaching between 40 to 180 people, depending on the nature of the work and the level of need. Over the space of a year the number of people benefiting from the project is considerably more. This support work would be run by a local committee of between ten and 15 people (with an active core of four to five) and from one to three full-time permanent staff, backed up by a variable number of part-time workers or volunteers. However, crude quantitative measures alone are inadequate as a measure of assessing the role and impact of community-based projects. While the active members involved in an organisation may be relatively small in number, their range of work and their ability to reach the most vulnerable is clear.

The information from the pilot programme also shows that *personal support* can be a reality for people belonging to communities of interest, and not just territorial communities. Six of the projects succeeded in bringing together people who share common problems and in a way that encouraged mutual aid and a wider view of the issues involved. These projects included the centre for people recovering from alcohol and drug dependency, families of people with learning difficulties, ex-patients from a psychiatric hospital, as well as the carers' groups and young deaf already described.

Informal networks of kin and neighbours are known to be of central importance in communities. It is clear from the descriptions of their activities that networks of relatives, friends and neighbours are often the means by which people make contact with projects. The exceptions are three projects whose users were referred only by statutory agencies. But these projects, like the others, have their base within the life of local communities where they are seen as being informal, accessible, flexible and different from a more formal and controlling statutory level of provision. All included informal and social activities and outings and recognised the value of these in enabling users to have a sense of belonging. The Christmas party and seasonal celebrations are not extras but very much part of what these projects are about.

If these are small-scale projects attracting a certain number of users, how do they relate to *other groups and agencies* either within their own communities or further afield? In all cases there were boundaries to be drawn, and sometimes tensions between the projects and other community and voluntary groups in the field. In this situation there is value in the adoption of a community practice approach which recognises the problems and works to overcome or prevent them, so that people can come together to work for change and specific goals, instead of dissipating energies in rivalry and duplication.

The projects which supported people with a high level of dependency, such as those dealing with mental illness and stress, learning difficulties and homelessness, demonstrate that it *is* possible to work towards the involvement and participation of service users. This has important lessons for statutory agencies working in the same area, who must examine their own culture, values, practice and organisation. Given a supportive environment there is considerable untapped potential for 'clients' and 'patients' to move towards choice, independence and mutual aid.

Policy Implications of the Community Practice Approach

The community support pilot programme demonstrates that it is possible for dependent groups to be supported by local community or user groups, working within the values of self-help and mutual aid. But this does not mean that the same people do not need statutory services and support. It must be stressed that the community care evident in the pilot programme requires real resources of money and staff support from social and health services if it is to work successfully. Thus the programme shows the capacity of community and user groups to give support, but it also shows the resources that would be necessary if this were to become part of a community care policy.

The ten pilot projects operated within an infrastructure of continuous support provided by the programme co-ordinator. This spanned the initial stages of setting up and employing staff, to running the project and finally the development of long-term strategies and fundraising. All the projects were visited by the co-ordinator at least once a month for the first year, and were in regular contact with the worker by phone and through visits for the remaining two years. Feedback from project staff and management committees at the end of the programme showed that they saw this support as vital to the development of the work.

The issues and needs that arose in the support of the projects over the three years included the need for training and support for management committees, which are made up largely of project users and people from the local community. While some projects made use of short courses on management within the field of community practice others worked with the programme co-ordinator in sessions on: working towards the project's objectives; the respective roles of committee and staff; communication within the project; preparing reports on progress and evaluation of work. In most projects it was found that at some point user members of the management committee had to reduce their high level of commitment for a period due to ill-health or family commitments. Sometimes project workers needed to perform the difficult dual role of working for and giving support to a local committee. Where this was done successfully it enabled projects to move ahead and make remarkable gains, both in the work carried out and in the confidence, insights and skills of local committee members.

Conclusions

The findings provided here have major implications for community care policy as a partnership between statutory and community organisations, as well as for the concept of community as a social system that is able to provide support for its more vulnerable members. Further, it underlines that community-based care projects require a range of support from statutory agencies if a partnership with them is to become a viable reality.

A reorientation to community-based community care implies that statutory agencies need first of all to validate and embrace this approach to working with local or user groups. This will mean a reassessment of the values by which people work and the role of the 'professional' in relation to service users. Training in community practice will be needed for staff at all levels, as well as training and support for staff and committee members of the local groups to enable them to participate as equal partners in planning and delivering services. Statutory staff will need to be delegated responsibility to work with local groups, and in turn these staff should be backed up with support within their own agencies. Crucially, adequate resources must be allocated for this purpose. The evidence demonstrates that the community can care, but the process needs recognition and adequate financial support.

There is much to commend this sort of approach to community care. While the rationale for it is written into the policy white papers, other developments are not encouraging. Local authorities are setting in train a managerial and often highly technical structure of planning and implementing care. So far this seems to lean heavily on the ethos and ideas of the private or commercial sector, and user involvement and clients' rights do not figure strongly in it. As already discussed, the wider political and economic context is one of insufficient money and resources for the broad sweep of the community care plans. Failure fully to implement these will mean that the needs of people discharged from institutions will not be met. Indeed, current shortages of resources in social services departments mean that this is already happening.

In view of this situation the lessons from the community support programme are doubly important. They demonstrate that local community and user groups have the capacity to provide services and support for a range of vulnerable groups in a way that enables service users to be involved in the process. They show that the objectives of providing flexible care in the community and giving choice to users are possible. But this must not be interpreted as care 'on the cheap'. The projects were funded to cover their core costs and were given a comprehensive support system, and both of these factors were crucial to the groups' success in meeting their users' needs. Adequate resources are just as necessary for this user-based model of care as for a more traditional one devised entirely by professionals. While the securing of adequate resources may be doubtful in the present climate, the programme gives planners an opportunity to move community care policy in the direction of a responsive and preventive support for service users, and one in which users can play a part.

Part 3 Critical Perspectives

In this part of the book the contributions move to an exploration of the ideas and ideologies which underlie the development of community policy and practice. The authors reflect upon the preceding analyses and descriptions from a critical perspective and from key value positions. The three themes or values selected – equality, environmentalism and democratic citizenship – are shown to be central to public policy.

Helen Meekosha begins her chapter by identifying the 'politics of identity': the interconnections of race, class, sexuality and gender. She places this within a theoretical context and discusses the dimensions of public policy which relate to identity groups: managing diversity, social justice, the establishment of specific units and national agendas, equal opportunities and the use of community strategies. She argues that community policies have been deployed at the same time as there have been reductions in resources, and she links this to a discussion of the emergence of differences within feminism. The dilemmas posed by the equality/difference debate constitute the kernel of the chapter, which concludes with a perspective on how the development of identity politics has impacted on community practice. She suggests that solidarity which recognises differences could be a key concept in future, reviving possibilities of coalitions, alliances and networks between groups.

The need for policy makers to engage with the implications of environmentalism is the basis of Nigel Roome's chapter. He outlines different theoretical green perspectives and identifies core principles. He then discusses the role of community and public policy from a green perspective, and suggests how different forms of green ideology connect with social movements and political structures as well as with community practice. The chapter contains a historical overview of the ways in which policy in relation to community practice and environmental action has developed, and the author gives reasons for optimism that environmental agencies will adopt a more community-focused approach. However, he advises caution on how to encourage local action and argues that new tools to help discussion and choice about futures are essential.

In their chapter Hugh Butcher and Maurice Mullard set out to clarify the concepts of citizenship and democracy in the context of community policies, and suggest that these are 'contestable' concepts. They identify four dimensions of citizenship and argue that competing models of democracy are also located in different philosophical assumptions. They bring together the strands of citizenship with the different assumptions about democracy and point to the connections between the two. In the final section of the chapter they make community policy itself the focus of attention and discuss the extent to which community policies have informed different versions of democratic citizenship. Community policy, they argue, is central to democratic citizenship and its practical realisation in contemporary society.

11 The Bodies Politic – Equality, Difference and Community Practice

Helen Meekosha

Prelude

A middle-aged white professor is taking his evening run, following his regular route past a park in a city in the north-east of the USA. In the darkness he passes two male black adolescents who turn on him, tripping him and beating him, tearing at his clothes. He manages to escape, runs through the park and flags down a passing police car. The police chase and arrest the youths. At the police station the youths claim that the man had made homosexual advances to them, and they had fought him off.

In the movie *City of Hope*, directed by John Sayles, the leaders of the black community centre defend the young brothers. Meanwhile the professor is approached by the gay members of his faculty who offer their support in his case against the black youths, claiming this is an issue of homophobia/'fagbashing', even though the professor is known to them to be straight. In a further twist to the tale, the only black city councillor in a city of police corruption and harassment of young blacks, formerly a colleague of the professor's, has been challenged by the community centre leaders to defend the youths publicly. He is challenged as a middle-class former academic who is now 'inside the state' – a traitor in the eyes of the black Muslim community leaders – to stand by 'his people' and assert his belief in the truthfulness of the youths, despite his knowledge of their guilt. The event is being presented by the community centre as a black versus white issue, with racism as the overarching if not exclusive issue.

All this is set within the context of the proposed redevelopment of condemned housing which nevertheless is some of the only accommodation available for low-income Hispanics and blacks. The mayor, the district attorney, council employees, the police, and the developers are intertwined in graft and corruption associated with the building of a 'City of Hope' and 'Renaissance Centre'.

The interconnection of race, sexuality and gender provokes a politics of identity often resulting in opposition between and inside different minorities and within feminist politics. These dimensions of 'difference' have generated overwhelming issues for practitioners in the 1990s: community workers, social workers and policy makers. For community workers complexities such as these have replaced or extended or modified the 'working class versus the state as agent of capital' agendas of the 1970s. Current social problems resist such skeletal reduction – as Sayles's film shows, individuals caught within these community politics have multiple identities and competing loyalties. The surfacing of essentialist politics – claiming that solidarity with the identity group transcends all other competing claims to loyalty – simplifies complex layers of interacting oppressions into crude dichotomies or polarities: black/white, gay/straight, male/female, disability/ablebodiedness. The politics of difference, diversity and identity have given a new edge to demands for equality and social justice.

Practitioners and activists are increasingly finding themselves concerned with the implementation of policies of equality of opportunity, anti-discrimination, and access and equity. Respect for difference and acknowledgement of identity are also part and parcel of contemporary strategies. As a woman who has been an immigrant, who has experienced disability, who has worked both as a community worker and a teacher of community work, I have felt a growing frustration in recent years as I have moved between different spheres of my life and politics. I have become increasingly aware of the impact of what is known as post-structuralist thinking on the way in which people perceive and project their own and others' identities (Nicholson, 1990). In these apparently diverse situations the same tensions reappear, tensions which have as their resolution the erections of boundaries and barriers. This chapter is written in the belief that these boundaries can be crossed and the barriers dismantled.

The chapter begins by outlining some of the structural and policy questions raised by the involvement of the state in equity issues and in 'managing diversity'. Some of the complexities of political, administrative and professional issues are canvassed, and some implications for effective practice are outlined. The chapter then examines the way in which the state increasingly uses community strategies to deliver services to disadvantaged and minority groups. The concepts of equality and difference are considered in the light of theoretical developments emanating from post-structuralist critiques of structural and feminist analyses. The implications for practice of the new theorising is detailed and some of the current dilemmas for community practitioners noted. Finally some considerations are presented for breaking out of the impasse that I have identified.

Introduction: the Big Picture

During the 1980s theoretical developments, particularly post-structuralism with its rejection of materialist and structuralist accounts of social inequality, claimed to question the grand theories which had explained social problems in terms of one 'big picture' – usually Marxist or socialist feminist. Hugh Butcher, in Chapter 4, argues that such trends have had an impact on those who make policy even though 'they may operate at a level once removed from the concrete day-to-day agenda'. The impact of post-structuralism means that for many practitioners and community activists there is no longer one story to guide them. There is no agreement on the ends or the processes, or indeed who constitutes 'the enemy'. The enemy may be the state, big business or even other stigmatised groups in society as exemplified in John Sayles's film. Poor whites rage against immigrants and refugees, unemployed youths attack gay men, and so on. The community practice espoused by the grand (usually male and white) theorists of yesteryear is today under question, and seen as failing to come to terms with contemporary realities.

Concepts such as 'gender' and 'community' have been criticised as too totalising to be useful, subsuming as they do a range of diversity and shifting definitions of identity (Spelman, 1988; Cain and Yuval Davis, 1990). These concerns debated in theory have been paralleled for policy makers, community practitioners and activists in practice. For example, black women in the USA and Britain, and Aboriginal and immigrant women in Australia, have questioned a feminism which has claimed to encompass women's issues while it fails to acknowledge their experiences or to recognise their agenda (Meekosha and Pettman, 1991). They see this feminism as speaking *for* them rather than *with* them, while recognition of this diversity has at times overwhelmed those attempting to pursue collective and communal approaches to discrimination and social justice. At the same time, Conservative governments, with fiscal crises and economic priorities ranked above social agendas, have been at pains to stress individual and family concerns over collective solutions, even though ideas of community are promoted as a means of delivering social programmes.

Demands by groups for sensitivity to difference and for the recognition of the specific experiences of marginalised minorities arise on the one hand, while on the other 'managing diversity' has become a catchcry in government bureaucracies and in capitalist enterprises. Are demands for sensitive and appropriate community and state services claims made in the context of 'equality', an icon of liberal democracy? Or are they claims which dispute the usefulness of the idea of 'equality' in societies where the most powerful strata are perceived as atypical and unattractive as role models for wider emulation – for instance, older, white, Anglo bourgeois men? This debate will be pursued in more detail later in this chapter. It is important to note that the concern with equality emerges in a period when government action on discrimination against minorities has been institutionalised, yet overall, economic inequality has been steadily worsening in the USA, Britain and Australia (Williams, 1989; Raskall, 1992; Smith, 1981).

The State and Public Policy – Difference and Equality

Public policy, given an apparent failure to advance on equality goals, suggests major structural problems in state perceptions of issues. In Britain, Beveridge's proposals of the 1940s and T. H. Marshall's ideas about the development of citizenship rights have carried great weight. However in recent years such values have suffered major ideological attacks under the impact of neo-conservatism, the new right and governments which seek to minimise the role of the state in individual welfare. Such broad arguments about the role of the state in welfare have continued, while 'equality' and 'access and equity' programmes have been developed by governments. These programmes, which are aimed in part at making 'mainstream' services more relevant to those who were structurally excluded, have had to respond to critics who demand specific programmes and entitlements based on identity (race, culture, disability, sexuality, gender).

As a result of state policies recognising issues of inequality as they affect social groups, the 1980s have seen some members of hitherto excluded groups making gains through appointments to government bureaucracies, academia and large corporations. For example a number of white middle-class women have permeated the higher echelons of power in the Australian public service. In the USA and the UK they have been joined by some black men in the public and civil service (Eisenstein, 1991; Yeatman, 1990; Cockburn, 1991). This mobility has occurred during a period of increasing poverty for the rural and urban populations in the USA and Australia, particularly among some racial and ethnic groups, and among women in these groups. In Britain gains for minorities have been made in a climate of increasing racism and feminisation of poverty.

The policies relevant here are those which carry labels associated with:

- managing diversity
- social justice
- establishment of specific units and national agendas
- equal employment opportunity (EEO)/equal opportunity (EO) and affirmative action (AA)/anti-discrimination
- community.

Managing diversity signals that the state is both the recipient of demands for action by identity groups and a constructor of categories in the interests of maintaining harmonious social relations (Meekosha and Pettman, 1991). Various agencies of the state may seek to absorb the appropriate minority cultures where these are making demands and claims against them. 'Managing diversity' within the state also means the provision of social welfare by 'drip-feeding' marginalised groups, such as Aboriginal communities in Australia. One effect is the emergence of a second-class welfare state within the voluntary sector (Marcia Langton, quoted in Pettman, 1992, p. 90). A clear strategy emerging from both government and the market-place constructs 'managing diversity' as a profitable exercise for both the public and private sectors. Thus 'diversity' can become a code word for the less powerful and more marginalised sectors of society, while the management of diversity in an unequal society requires each category to be presented as homogeneous and harmonious.

Social justice has been the concept used by the Australian government moved to reconceptualise its activities, defined by four elements of 'equity, equality, access and participation' (Australia, Department of Finance and Department of Prime Minister and Cabinet, 1989), managed through a social justice secretariat. The government requires all departments and agencies to take these elements into account, whether or not they were specifically focused on social goals, in all their programme development, implementation and evaluation. Social justice programmes are given concrete expression through national agendas. These agendas have been produced by the government-appointed advisory councils to the offices with support from the bureaucracy, following wide public consultation and active lobbying by organised interest groups. In the decade since 1983 there have been the launches of national agendas on women and for a multicultural Australia. These agendas find one expression in budget statements released annually, which demonstrate in which ways government expenditure in all departments of state support the agenda goals.

The establishment of specific units was introduced by the Whitlam Labor Party government in 1972 in Australia with the creation of the office of women's adviser to the prime minister. Since then, there have been a plethora of specific units and advisory bodies covering race and ethnicity, gender, disability, sexuality and age. In Britain this was mirrored by units established by the Greater London Council (GLC) (abolished under Thatcher), various London boroughs, and local authorities which pursued the municipal socialist road.

The limitations of *equal employment opportunity (EEO/equal opportunity (EO), affirmative action (AA) and anti-discrimination* legislation are widely recognised. The promotion of privileged members of each category as a result of equal employment opportunity regulations can often result in tokenism (Hutchison-Reis, 1989; Zavella, 1991), with the recruitment of small numbers into the dominant elites. This recruitment can integrate 'minority' elites into the dominant systems of surveillance, so that they in turn may become managers of the system of control against which they may have previously struggled. Their movement into the elite can also lead to isolation from their 'community', while their minority status can keep them ghettoised within the state.

Governments are increasingly using *community strategies and the language of community practice* as part of a reformulation of the welfare state. One of the main avenues for the implementation of this community perspective remains the family, as the concept of the 'community caring' becomes translated into caring by families (principally women), without support, outside institutions, in the 'community'. Why, then, have central, regional (state) and local governments funded the development of programmes delivered through community groups? The reply seems to lie in the fact that governments have been seeking to withdraw from centralised provision of services, for example moving people out of costly institutional care into 'community care' which in fact is only cheaper if it is provided by voluntary effort. Interest and lobby groups demanding that governments support the community definitions and delivery of services 'targeted' on 'special needs' categories has also put pressure on governments. In Australia this latter perspective explains the development of ethnic childcare programmes, while in Britain it serves as a rationale for the development of Muslim girls' schools. The demands by groups should be seen in conjunction with a deterioration (either numerically and/or qualitatively) in many state provided and supported services.

In Australia feminists who were concerned at the lack of appropriate and adequate services organised from the early 1970s for women's services, particularly women's health centres, and these have proliferated as a consequence of successful action over the last 20 years (Broom, 1991). Yet the support for such services is still constrained by the priorities of the state as governments look for 'substitute' rather than 'oppositional' ideologies in the community sector. Thus one finds that in Britain, in the area of ethnic and race issues, community projects with an emphasis on political rights fare less well than those campaigning for better services in receiving government funds (Cain and Yuval Davis 1990, p. 15). Those organisations seeking specific group service delivery have the greatest chance of success, those seeking broad political change the least.

The use of community care by the state can lead to a number of directions for minorities. Given the emphasis on flexibility, and the long history of institutional insensitivity to their needs, it may well be that the 'community road', that is the provision of programmes in the community through non-institutional means, actively improves opportunities for minorities through opening up the possibility of participation and local control. Alternatively, there may be little change to the structural position of minorities, who experience in the restructured welfare state the same system of structural discrimination that existed previously in the large bureaucracies and institutions. Finally, the changes may actively disadvantage minorities – people of ethnic background without strong familial or community networks, who find as they age that they are isolated linguistically and culturally in the community, may prefer some type of institutional/collective care where their own language is spoken and their behaviour is sympathetically received, to isolation in the 'community'.

Such a polarisation of opportunities between those who are advantaged by public policies and those who remain the most oppressed and subordinated demonstrates that the process tends to benefit a minority of the 'minorities', while many actually experience a decline in life chances.

Equality and Difference – What's in a Concept?

Introduction to the Debate

Over the last two decades two distinct trends have emerged within feminism. First we have seen the growing recognition of differences between women: black women, immigrant women, lesbians, women with disabilities, Aboriginal women, third world women, older women . . . at times the list seems endless. Some groups of women have reacted harshly to what they have perceived to be a privileged group of white middle-class women who have seemed to say they speak on behalf of *all* women. The theory and practice of feminism may not yet have come to terms with one of its unintended consequences – the power to exclude some women and include others.

Secondly some women have moved to a position of celebrating their difference from men and have sought to re-establish a community of women where values of nurturing and caring are given prominence as women-only values. Yet such a position often denies or downplays differences between women on the basis of race, class and so on, with problematic consequences for women whose differences are not recognised. Furthermore the position says little about those sociopolitical and economic power relationships which sustain the unequal distribution of goods, services and wealth between men and women, and between women and women.

Along with the emergence of differences within feminism other social movements around identity have developed. From the early 1970s Afro-Caribbean groups and Asian groups became significant political actors on the British scene and in Australia the ethnic rights and Aboriginal land rights movements gained momentum. The International Year of the Disabled Person (IYDP) (1981) marked the turning point for people with disabilities. Their struggle to organise around their shared sense of oppression took on a more structured and extensive framework, drawing on the campaign for civil rights articulated by other social movements. Similarly the mid to late 1980s witnessed the rising political profile of older people, as well as a resurgence of the gay and lesbian movement around the politics of HIV and AIDS.

While the impact of post-structuralism may have decomposed the political thrust of a 'women's movement', it provided a crucial range of insights for theoretical understanding. Central issues of concern included the use of language, the rediscovery of 'the body' as a social construct – black, white, able or disabled – and the deconstruction of the universalising and homogenising consequence of the concepts of gender and race. This perspective raised a further question for community practitioners who are committed to 'responding to the needs of women' – which women in which context?

So public policy and community practice, traditionally based on a notion of equality and social justice, have had to be rethought in the light of these debates. While these ideas may be held at one step removed from community practice, they intrude through their influence on broader strategies of social change.

Conceptual and Theoretical Issues

There is a fundamental paradox to be addressed: any attempt to discuss commonalities undermines attempts to discuss difference and vice versa (Spelman, 1988, p. 3). Minority groups have experienced and attempted to work through these contradictions, often with considerable trauma, during the last two decades.

Demands for equality with current power holders can often seem neither feasible nor desirable, indeed they seem a fantasy in a highly stratified society for those whose perspectives are strongly influenced by their differences from this hierarchy. Equal opportunity in its most liberal form has clearly not been about equality of outcome. The language of identity and discrimination avoids focusing attention on structural considerations, couched as it is in terms of individual and group rights.

The valuing of and respect for difference has been developing as the humanitarian and political goal of the 1990s. Yet an emphasis on difference, in terms of developing theoretical analyses of the nature of social systems, could lead to the impossibility of making any generalised statements. One could ask whether this is a movement towards endless ethnographic reporting of difference, which is no replacement for the theory it seems to want to supersede (Di Stefano, 1991).

The concept of difference has become a substitute for more critical concepts such as privilege, conflict of interest, oppression and subordination. Difference can avoid discussions of power. For example, the experiences of Aboriginal women, immigrant women, black women, women with disabilities, are not simply different; they are part of overall power relations and at the same time intersect with and influence each other (Gordon, 1991, p. 106). In some situations the same individuals or groups of women may have power and in some they may be powerless. Respect for difference also throws into relief issues of class, political and religious values and beliefs. Does respect for difference mean that we value all others' positions equally and uncritically – religious fundamentalism, nazism? Should we 'respect' differences that seek to become dominant and oppressive forces in themselves (Connolly, 1990a; Phelan, 1991, p. 136)? The equality/difference debate is widespread; in community practice, public policy formulation and implementation, gender studies, sexuality studies, black studies and in the emerging area of disability studies. A variety of other conceptual tools has been brought into the arena, notably 'specificity', with its translation in public policy as 'special needs'. Yet in many ways the setting of equality as an alternative goal to difference and vice versa offers a false dichotomy, and advances neither theory nor practice.

The idea of specificity offers the potential to bring back together the currently diverse threads of feminism. Both equality and difference privilege the white male as generic and thus 'An emphasis on specificity . . . aims at disrupting hegemonies, calling out differences for question and rendering everyone accountable for her positions and actions' (Phelan, 1991, p. 133). Yet such a view, while bringing forth ideas of the 'special group or individual', leaves dominant forces untouched, and can at the same time create for those who have been identified as 'special', a soothing and soporific sense of self (Minh-Ha 1989, p. 87). In the context of policy making, 'difference', 'specificity' or 'special needs programmes' can either legitimate inequality or hide inequality from view, as can be demonstrated in housing, health, education and welfare services that become even more selective and 'targeted' as time goes by.

The 'big picture' concepts – race, gender, class, community – become problematic under the influence of post-structuralist theory. If we cannot generalise about women in practice, can we theorise about 'women' at all? Theoretical debates focus on the shifting nature of socially constructed concepts. What constitutes the notion of 'Aboriginality' in Australia or 'black' in Britain or the USA, depends on the context in which the category is mobilised, either by the state or by claimants (Pettman, 1992; Lilley, 1989). 'Gender' is often considered a central, fixed concept. Yet current campaigns in Australia to have the government recognise transexuality as a ground for complaints of gender discrimination demonstrate the malleability of the idea of gender and its highly contingent qualities. The possibility of a feminist practice as such can be destroyed if activists and practitioners avoid the use of the concept of gender.

'Community' has always been considered a problematic concept (see Chapter 1 by Butcher; Bryson and Mowbray, 1981; Anthias and Yuval-Davis, 1992). It is a concept used by minorities to mobilise resistance, and for groups and community workers to claim legitimacy in the political processes. In the last decade more than ever before it has become integrated into policies of social intervention by governments at local and central levels. Yet that integration has had the curious effect of revealing a plurality of communities which share only their marginalisation from the assumed 'mainstream'. As the welfare state contracts under the influence of neo-Conservative ideologies of public policy, only those groups exposed as critically or multiply disadvantaged are sanctioned to seek specific community resources from the state. The 'community' can be said to be reduced to categories of equal opportunities, defined ultimately through their previous exclusion from the mainstream (Cain and Yuval Davis, 1990). 'Community' is now far more prevalent in discussion of public policy and practice than reference to class or poverty, or income and wealth differentials.

Current conceptual and theoretical frameworks are inadequate to deal with the context of contemporary politics and policy making. For example, we have few ways of speaking about intra-group violence and conflict, such as in Aboriginal male violence against Aboriginal women in Australia, or black on black violence in South Africa (Meekosha, forthcoming). We need to refocus on theoretical developments which *can* contribute to a more aware practice (Parmar, 1990; Segal, 1987). At the same time, we *do* need to substitute a feminist for a 'malestream' story, or an account of a colonised people for an imperialist world view; we should expect these accounts to be more valid. If we fail at this task, then we are set adrift in a sea of relativity (Cockburn, 1991, p. 212).

New Theorising – Implications for Practice

Collective and organising implications loom large for practitioners and political activists concerned with social justice goals. Are individual experiences all that matter, and are inequalities and degrees of oppression simply questions of relativity?

> Everyone seems to be clamouring for 'difference', only too few seem to want any difference that is about changing policy or that supports active engagement and struggle (another no-no word; . . .) . . . (Hooks, 1991, p. 54)

The language we are allowed to use, who is allowed to speak, organise, who is employed, all reflect these current dilemmas being debated within the walls of the academy. What is perceived as endless theorising by feminists at the level of the political correctness of concepts has contributed to political practice and policy making, at times inhibiting action.

Criticisms of 'essentialism' in feminism and in particular feminist social policy, arise from a reaction to the assumption that all women have the same experience and needs, and that there is something innate and/or essential about the category 'woman' or 'black' or disabled (Morris, 1991, 1992; Williams, 1989; Meekosha and Pettman, 1991). Other critiques reflect the perception that some women are not so much subsumed as excluded or shut out of the account. Essentialism serves to mask the privileging of women who were white and middle class in feminism, and the privileging of men in race and ethnic politics. (Hence the title of the path-breaking book by Hull, Scott and Smith in 1982 *All the Women are White, All the Blacks Are Men, But Some Of Us Are Brave*.) Meanwhile disability remains largely ungendered and lacking a race dimension. Might specific/category claims in social policy simply reinforce the essentialist nature of the category? Is childcare for women reinforcing a stereotyped role? Why is childcare not as important for men?

Demands for equality, and recognition of difference and specificity have together resulted in the emergence of 'additive strategy' (Meekosha and Pettman, 1991), whereby different minority groups are added on to the 'mainstream'. Nowhere is this clearer than in some equal opportunities programmes, in particular where the category 'women' is privileged as in 'women and other minorities'. Such strategies leave the structures of inequality untouched; moreover it is not possible simply to add the experience of disability or Aboriginality to the experience of being a white or able-bodied woman.

Feminist theory has repercussions for practice, while practice continues to inform theory. Arguments for single-sex schools and arguments against women working in the dangerous workplace (such as the lead industry) are put forward by some feminists on the basis of 'difference'. Such arguments have also been put forward by conservative, anti-feminist forces. Feminist strategies in the workforce, such as the fight for 'comparable worth' (with men) in female dominated industries as the basis for determining wage rates, and the entry of women into non-traditional jobs, reflect political choices along a 'difference–equality' continuum, with the emphasis shifting in accordance with the ideological positions of the women concerned.

The pursuit of 'difference' carries in its train the potential for separate women's development, in environments from which men are excluded. For some women, who have been forcibly segregated from both men and the outside world (as institutionalised women with disabilities) such a strategy is problematic. Current feminist discourses of difference rarely mention disability, as if celebration of difference was not able to encompass an experience perceived as only negative. The politics of race, class, gender and sexuality are often imbued with pride and self-affirmation. Disability politics are still seen by many activists and policy makers to lie solely within the province of welfare. The political debates about identity and difference have often led to a one-dimensional symbolisation of the complex needs of people – the multiplicity of categories brings in turn a reduction to crude equivalence between 'groups' and 'needs': women need childcare, disabled people need access, and so on.

The important contributions of the new theorising lies in the acceptability of analyses which illuminate the contradictions and conflicts within oppressed groups. Asian women who supported Salman Rushdie's position on *The Satanic Verses* in Britain (Connolly, 1990a) demonstrate the existence of power struggles within oppressed groups, and the importance of their appearance in public debate. Issues of representation and accountability have materialised in the wake of feminist questioning of totalising concepts, raising again an exploration of the meaning of power on the margins and the implications when the powerless move into positions of power – as when Australian women bureaucrats ('femocrats') move into positions of control or influence in the institutions of the state. Is the empowerment of marginalised groups sometimes only a way of changing the dominant 'bodies' at the top of the power hierarchy?

We have to reconceptualise ideas of power and authority, and move beyond the important arguments about whose voice is controlling and whose voice must be heard to political community and solidarity in difference (Jones, 1991). Two current under-standings of authority – that it must be accessible to all women and men currently excluded so that we can each control our own lives, or that we should resist authority as a tainted practice anti-thetical to feminist principles – may contribute little to struggles for equality or recognition of difference. A redefinition of authority would move from a concept of 'border-patrolling and border-engen-dering [to] meaning-giving' (Jones, 1991, p. 123). Re-examining the concept of authority would open up a debate in community practice that is in danger of being closed – that of leadership and expertise. In this sense we can look at authority as having its basis in the possession of skills and knowledge which need to be passed on, rather than as an excluding power-ridden concept.

Community Practice – Difference and Equality

A number of elements of analysis come together at this point. First, the emergence of arguments for equality in the earlier phase, and for recognition of difference later on, have been interpreted by the state and incorporated into public policies and programmes. Secondly, the influence of post-structuralist theory and developments in feminist thinking have interacted to produce layers of interpretation and interrogation of experience, with outcomes that are far from clear in their implications for practice. In parallel to these discursive intersections, debates and struggles have been occurring within social movements, while for community practitioners the environment in which they operate has become highly coloured by the reflections of these debates.

There are wider issues raised by the diversity of women's voices, by anti-racist and multicultural analyses emerging from the black, Aboriginal and ethnic rights movements, and by explorations of the meanings and needs of people with disabilities and gay men and lesbians. While these may well be fairly widely discussed in the general literature in social and public policy, they have not been addressed in any sustained manner in relation to community work practice. Much professional practice material on community work tends to tell of how to undertake specific tasks. They are for the most part general skills guides rather than intellectually rigorous and theoretically informed approaches to professional practice in a complex, multidimensional and culturally diverse social environment. Indeed the poverty of articulation of identity issues with community work theory has obvious repercussions for practice, even though 'training' in community work often includes the compulsory sections on race, class, gender, and sometimes disability.

The 'community of bodies' is in many ways the new heartland of struggle and gives rise both to the intellectual ferment and to the increasingly complex responses within public policy. Declining and broken class-based movements have been overtaken by movements which are by and large concerned with identities – sexual, racial, ethnic, lifestyle, age, disability. Even within these movements there have been calls to difference, with even smaller and more fragmented identity groups emerging (Meekosha and Pettman, 1991). These differences have challenged the calls for equality, by eroding the clarity of goals espoused in earlier demands and supplanting them by modes of self-affirmation in separate identities: at times the desire to become 'equal' dissolved in the statements of individual uniqueness.

The very language and intent of community practice has changed considerably as a result of these developments. The language of difference has been embraced, although often in an 'add-on' way. Some definitions of community work call on workers to 'acknowledge the specific contribution of black people and women' (Federation of Community Work Training Groups, 1990). Others argue that they should confront 'practices or institutions which discriminate against black people, women, people with disabilities, religious groups, elderly people, lesbians and gay men and other groups who are disadvantaged by society' (Standing Conference on Community Development, 1991). Community workers have quite rightly addressed criticisms of the predominance of white, Anglo male biases inherent in practice. They are working with a range of identity groups composed of women, blacks, immigrants and so on, in the community and inside local authorities and local councils in Britain and Australia, as well as continuing to argue for the legitimacy of these activities.

Within the arena of race and ethnic politics, a number of distinct trends have emerged in what has been termed the 'ethnic revival' (Smith, 1981) and the rise of nationalism. The weakening of class-based political action in the face of the strengthening of post-war capitalism in western democracies has highlighted the social awareness of inequalities which take 'ethnic' as the line of social cleavage and oppression. One consequence has been for ethnic groups to form and mobilise around the push for the maintenance (in some cases re-creation) of ethnic heritage, and the search for an 'essential ethnicity' to which they can lay claim. Here we see the intertwining of the demands for equality and 'freedom', with ideas of ethnic separation, resulting in quite novel constellations of actions and ideologies – in some cases with horrendous consequences, as in the former Yugoslavia. The privileging of essentialist claims – as for instance in the acceptance of fundamentalist and ethnicity-linked religious groups – has brought with it very real dangers as these ideologies and beliefs are allowed to flourish unchallenged in a climate apparently more tolerant of difference.

The primary objective of attacking essentialist notions of community (which assume white privilege) by highlighting race issues has often resulted in treating race as a homogenous category, thereby creating a new essentialist category with its own problems. In Australia community workers with ethnic groups have for the most part focused on the ideology of multiculturalism, raising awareness of cultural values, norms and heritage. They have often failed to examine internal power within ethnic communities on the one hand, and racism within the wider community on the other. In this context a simplistic, superficial and ahis-torical practice based on respect for difference can *reinforce* inequalities.

If a woman is 'different' her feminist loyalty can be called into question by the most powerful segment – usually white middle-class women imposing their own definitions of legitimate feminist practice. One example can be found in those anti-rape organisa-tions in Los Angeles established in the early 1970s which included very few black women; the situation led black women to establish rape crisis programmes specifically for the black community. These organisations became primarily community service oriented, leading to accusations by white women in the anti-rape movement of black women's conservatism and having too close an associa-tion with the bureaucrats responsible for funding (Matthews, 1988). On the other hand, the assumption of the need to be different can elicit the opposite response. In Britain, an attempt to set up separate girls' nights in a youth project for black women was unsuccessful. Young Asian women did not go to separate groups as they believed it would reinforce an identity harmonious with their families' wishes and they wished to rebel against such ideas (Connolly, 1990b).

White, Anglo able-bodied community workers and community groups ask why 'they' (the 'others') do not join, come to meetings, organise? These workers and groups often assume apathy as the reason, without addressing issues of who is setting the agenda, does the group dispense power equitably and what is the relevance of the existing group to the 'others' being requested to join? For instance, few voluntary and community organisations have made much headway towards equal employment opportunity (Cockburn, 1991, p. 230; Meekosha et al, 1987). So while the paid workers may be either drawn from the dominant groups in society or 'community leaders', those who are clients or make up the con-stituency of the organisation may remain marginalised.

An awareness of these tensions has played a part in the devel-opment of a politics of identity. Identity politics has provided a decisive response to the assumptions and ethnocentricity of much mainstream theory and community practice. First, it has provided a critique of notions of community and shown that community is indeed permeable with ever-changing boundaries. Secondly, identity groups have become actors in community politics, rather than disadvantaged objects of community work intervention. Thirdly, non-directive community work, with the role of the worker as facilitator rather than leader or spokesperson, has been shown to be an idealised and unhelpful notion in understanding the role of, for example, gay workers organising around AIDS or disabled workers around public transport (see also Chapter 3 for a discussion of the roles of workers and their agendas).

We do not expect these workers to come value free to their positions, carrying a bundle of neutral skills with which to aid the community. Workers who share the characteristics of their 'patch' or constituency group are usually more able to understand the issues and relate to the individuals affected than benevolent outsiders who have often put themselves in the position of mediating between the authorities and the oppressed group.

While acknowledging these advantages, it is important to note that identity carries three possible dangers. First, it has at times become *the* qualification for the position. Bitter and conflicting scenarios have developed regarding the role of those not part of the identity group. Employing a member of the category at all costs has led to workers being set up to fail as a result of inappropriate appointments coupled with lack of support and training.

Secondly, there is a danger that this interpretation of the 'respect' for difference will allow no role for those outside the category. It can become an excuse for white workers not dealing with racism, men not dealing with sexism, and so on. If the only legitimate speaking position on such issues is accorded to those individuals/agents directly experiencing the situation/problems, then 'experts' are demobilised. As a consequence, the constitution of the criteria for legitimate speaking and/or acting positions has become a central tension both in community organising and action, and in social planning.

Thirdly, the recent shift towards the funding of community groups around identity has resulted in pressure exerted by the state for the groups to respond to bureaucratic demands, with clear outcomes which may erode the original political goals of the constituency. Groups become trapped by the need to continue to demonstrate oppression or disadvantage or victim status for funding purposes, rather than continue the project of social change. At the same time given the fiscal and legitimation crisis of the state (see Butcher, Chapter 4), some types of community practice with discrete groups has met with little resistance. It is cheaper to develop services for specific groups than provide good, accessible universal services.

Crossing Boundaries

Community development in Britain, the USA and Australia tended in the 1970s to concentrate on working-class neighbourhoods and the development of networks and the organisation of local action to achieve locally articulated goals. As we have seen, this pattern of intervention has become transformed in recent years under the impact of social movements which, transcending locality, have now focused on a politics of difference and the specificity of smaller group experiences of discrimination and disadvantage.

As community work becomes increasingly moulded by the pressures of market models of welfare, the historic focus of community work as a profession of activism and commitment to the achievement of social justice becomes translated. It has now become a mode of work in which ever more tightly delineated minorities and sectors of society experiencing discrimination are channelled into organising the provision of specific, usually volunteer-operated, services. Despite these pressures, innovative practice is occurring, with community workers and activists taking risks, crossing boundaries and re-examining practice in the light of both theoretical influences and direct experience.

Major questions confront community practitioners as we move through the 1990s. How do we transcend the political moralism of separatist tendencies of identity politics in community practice on the one hand and the 'additive approach' on the other? How can we prevent the relentless task of maintaining good relations with government and external funding bodies on whose funding we rely, eroding the energy needed to develop and maintain the community empowerment process at the local and national levels? How do we establish priorities for community practice in the face of 'market-driven' community work and ever increasing demands on what the 'community' can achieve? How do we move beyond the doubt, uncertainty and sense of defeat characterising much of community work in the 1980s? The important task may not be constructing *unity*, but achieving *solidarity* from the vantage point of our differences.

Dominant groups have a great deal invested in people staying in the correct categories for the purposes of policing, immigration, social security administration and justification of state surveillance/violence, to name but a few examples. It is therefore important that fixed and repressive aspects of categories are challenged as part of strategies of resistance.

This flexibility should not cause a lack of commitment or direction vis-a-vis a transformed set of social relations. It should not be reactive for its own sake, but should be part of an alternative vision. New categories can be forged in the process of resistance as in the case of the Australian Aboriginal Gungarakyn people who re-evaluated power relations between men and women, allowing women 'to assert their importance as reproducers of people-land-society' for the purpose of land claims (Lilley, 1989, p. 90). Thus challenging and crossing boundaries allows us to move beyond the paralysing effects of identity politics without moving back to a mainstream practice largely undifferentiated by race, gender, disability and so on.

Moving beyond 'additive' strategies requires reassessment of concepts of universalism, collective provision, multiculturalism and responsible citizenship. Demands on governments to respond to the specific needs of identity groups in terms of the provision of housing, social security, education, health and so on have been a double-edged sword. On the one hand, notable victories by groups making claims on the state have improved services. In some cases they have allowed segments of distinct communities such as Aboriginal people and immigrant groups in Australia and Asian and Afro-Caribbean groups in Britain to follow desires for self-determination and collective provision. On the other hand ghettoised provision has protected the mainstream services, and in some areas new services are moving in the direction of specific provision only. Universal entitlement to quality, cheap, accessible housing, education and health is only debated in what remains of progressive left circles in industrialised countries.

The practice of the 'politics of location' (Mani, 1990; Zavella, 1991) has emerged as a strategy for working around simple categories which have become rigidly interpreted and imbued with political and community moralism. There are many sites of power, many sites of resistance, and struggles are temporary and changing. This has implications for community practice. It means that the social location of each group, project or activity is as important as the substantive issue. Following this argument, community practitioners need to articulate their location vis-a-vis the 'community' with whom they work. For example, where do workers themselves stand in terms of race, gender, class and education? Similarly gaps and commonalities between individuals within the group need to be articulated. The social locations of members of the group are taken as points for departure, for it is increasingly the case that the social response to an individual's identity leads to his or her involvement in community politics. Thus identity is an important but not the sole factor in community practice. While identity may be the point of departure – single mothers getting involved in a campaign for childcare – identity demands need reformulating in a way that does not reinforce their essentialist nature, in this case that childcare is an issue only for women.

Is there a danger that the emphasis on the politics of location is simply a return in disguise to the politics of localism, a method of working much criticised in earlier literature (Mowbray, 1984; Dyen, 1989) for failing to come to terms with systemic problems that go beyond the immediate situation? The politics of location and position also need long-term liberating goals and alternative visions of a more just society. There is a continuing problem that the emphasis on the politics of location could further highlight the current preoccupation with the individual at the expense of collective, national and international solutions, so that one is left with fragmented activity, typified by 'Generalization is out; particularity is in' (Di Stefano, 1991, p. 91).

Many community workers and feminist activists increasingly believe in the need to revive the idea of coalitions, alliances and networks between marginalised identity groups. In some ways the philosophy and practice of coalition work runs counter to the intent of identity politics, in so far as the interests of the minority may be sacrificed in the interests of the majority; so new forms of networking, alliances and coalition structures need to be discussed. Some argue this is a crucial way to fight back following the demoralisation of feminist and popular community movements suffering the unprecedented effects of 'uncaring' governments.

Coalition building has been compared to leaving home; leaving the safety of your own barred room. 'You don't go into coalition because you *like* it. The only reason you consider trying to team up with somebody who could possibly kill you, is because that's the only way you can figure you can stay alive' (Reagon, 1983, p. 357). As we have seen, diversity has been used in recent years by governments to divide and rule, so there is clearly value in taking the alliance route. Alternatively some argue that their distinct needs are best met by organising autonomously (Radford-Hill, 1986, p. 165); they fear the loss or marginalisation of their 'claims' by premature entering of coalitions and alliances. Universal 'sisterhood' as an unwelcome spectre can easily re-emerge when some groups are less powerful than others.

The effort, time and energy required for coalition work may also threaten the survival of your own group and compromise your goals. This is particularly true for some people with disabilities whose capacities are limited by shorter days and reduced physical endurance. It is notable that disability is the last 'cab off the rank' in identity politics. Sadly, too often the simple requirements for the involvement of people with disabilities, such as access, are still avoided when organising coalition work. Within the more institutionalised practices of feminism there is still much fear of women with disabilities. Some feminists, in the rush to move gender issues away from welfare, can refuse to be in alliances with women with disabilities. Alliances between identity groups are still the exception. Not all the new social alliances are progressive in nature; they can easily be co-opted by conservative and business groups on the new right. There is similarly nothing inherently caring or progressive about being a woman, a disabled person, an immigrant and so on. For instance, a campaign in Haringey, London, occurred where the Black Pressure Group on Education and the Parents' Rights Group took a homophobic stance against policies directed towards educational equality (Mercer, 1990, pp. 48–9):

> Was it a paradox of the postmodern condition or just everyday life in post colonial Britain that what resulted was an 'unthinkable' alliance between Black People and the National Front? Welcome to the jungle, welcome to the politics of indeterminacy in the twilight of modernity. (Mercer, 1990, p. 49)

Conclusion

In the final analysis post-structuralism has drawn us into many deep divides and has not indicated new forms of practice capable of dealing with the complexities of the post-modern world. It has, however, led to the experiences and knowledge of many of the marginalised, hitherto overlooked, being recognised for the first time. It has ensured that community practitioners have begun to challenge the old ways and old texts. What remains is to devise new structures to bridge the divides and new forms of collective action to transform the many destructive sources of power in society.

Community practitioners should be able to move beyond the simple respect for difference on the one hand or the uncritical acceptance of the push for equality on the other. The invocation of the equality litany – race, class (though not perhaps in Australia where rumour alone suggests class does not exist), gender, disability, age, sexuality – carries a great danger, that all these differences are understood to incur the same quality of disadvantage. The majority of the population encompassed by these categories in their totality suggests a very real potential power, even though in practice there may be hostility and tension between and within them. While the issues formulated by these groups have been very important in reframing the practices of the welfare state and the provision of communal services, it is important to be aware of what has been let slip and the effects of this dissolution of earlier views of social needs including universal provision. We have seen the individualisation of social relations, the competitiveness between categories introduced in order to reduce overall state expenditures in the name of respect for difference, and in particular in regards to community work practice, the loss of the capacity to mobilise communities for action through struggles for power rather than the cheaper management of targeted state services.

12 Green Perspectives on Community and Public Policy

Nigel Roome

During the past 20 years increasing attention has been focused on the problem of the world's environment and the importance of balancing environmental needs with the pressures for development and economic growth. There are no simple answers here; however, the quest for balance implies that there is potential for harmony between development and environmental protection. Yet the challenge to humanity, society and the individual in the search for that harmony should not be underestimated. The reason that the world confronts environmental problems is due to the aggregate effect of our decisions and actions. These decisions are informed and guided by the theories and models we construct about our economic, social and environmental worlds. And our actions are conditioned by the organisational and power structures within which we operate. Shaping a changed approach to our environment which aligns our actions with the achievement of environmentally sustainable forms of development will oblige us to accept new ways of thinking and new forms of practice.

The environment/development (green) debate is therefore essentially a debate about the capacity for progress through modified behaviour, reformed social thinking and organisation. That debate manifests itself in many forms. For some, it is captured by physical issues such as global warming, the depletion of the ozone layer and the loss of important global habitats (for example rain forests) and their associated genetic material. For others it centres on the north/south paradox with its attendant issues of equity and the politics of third world debt, where a wealthy north is seen to have achieved relative material prosperity at the expense of environmental degradation and where a poor, indebted south, rich in natural resources, sees the development of its forests and mineral resources as an inevitable way to service debt burdens or to secure improvements in economic well-being. Yet others are aware of the importance of ecological, economic and cultural diversity and seek to retain the richness of environmental resources and human traditions.

At times these concerns are a focus for debate in our neighbourhoods, as when we address plans to site a motorway or airport in a greenfield location running across an area of wildlife interest and adjacent to our homes. At the same time these proposals create opportunities for employment and provide the speed and ease of transport expected within developed economies. At other times we address more distant concerns: to save species from extinction, such as whales, which most of us would not ordinarily see in our lifetime, but about which we have strong ethical, moral and emotional convictions.

Whatever way these concerns are constructed, they are invariably deep-felt, multifaceted and complex. They embrace economic, political and cultural perspectives as well as involving scientific and social scientific explanations. They are embedded with moral, philosophical and meta-physical meaning. Often they are rooted in human responses of alarm, anger, frustration and passion – responses which often find expression through individual and shared action. Shaping solutions to environmental problems of a global or local kind therefore requires the agreement to a coherent set of goals and a solidarity of purpose which can only be generated successfully through decisions and actions based on participation.

The purpose of this chapter in the context of this background is to address the connections between community policy and practice and the green debate, with its emphasis on social reform and revised frames of thinking and action. The essential need is to explore the extent to which the resolution of environmental concerns is mutually compatible with community policy and practice. To this end the chapter is divided into three main parts.

The first part provides a theoretical background to discussion about community policy and practice and green perspectives. It explores the nature of the green debate and examines a number of the issues which underpin green perspectives. Particular attention is placed on the ideological foundations of green thinking and the extent to which community policy and practice is consistent with these alternative ideologies. The second part focuses, more specifically, on the development of policy which builds on community and environmental perspectives. It draws on both the literature and the practical experience of local environmental action in Britain to explore the rationale for policy, to chart the emerging shape of policy, and to illustrate the issues that arise in seeking to achieve environmental change through the processes of community policy and practice. The third part considers the future prospects for developing the links between community policy and practice together with environmental action.

Green Perspectives

In order to appreciate the principles of a green perspective it is important to explore some of the characteristics of environmental problems, and through that the nature of the interaction between social systems and environmental resources. Environmental problems have been defined as meta-problems: that is, they are problems, or sets of related problems, which are not easily resolved within the boundaries of conventional analysis and specialised social organisation (O'Riordan, 1971). In this sense, environmental concern should be seen as a human construct through which individuals place value on the quality or quantity of their environment. This value is dependent on our experience, culture and socialisation. Invariably it shifts over time with changing expectations and experiences. It finds expression and is mediated through political, economic, scientific and social institutions.

Contradiction is inherent in environmental concern. At the individual level we confront ambiguities in our lifestyles which must be resolved. For example, in the choice about the type of transport we use, there is a need to reconcile factors such as convenience and need, cost and environmental consequences. These are complex choices, often made on the basis of imperfect information and under the influence of broader social pressures stemming from mores, customs and values. It is quite common for apparently dual standards to arise; for example, as commuters we expect new and improved roads, and as residents we object to road-building programmes. In order to make sense of these ambiguities there is a need to consider the complex connections between the options available to us as individuals, as members of communities and as part of wider societies; to anticipate the implications that follow from pursuing these options; and to balance our different perspectives and interests when making choices.

At a collective level there is a wide set of environmental concerns expressed within society. These range from wildlife protection, the quality of air and water, soil conservation, the risks to health or damage to historic buildings, to name but a few. Synthesising these concerns into a coherent set of social objectives at different levels of organisation – neighbourhood, national and global – is fraught with difficulty. Part of that difficulty is bound up with the adequacy of social knowledge and part with the mediating power of social structures. In terms of social knowledge, single disciplinary interpretations of environmental problems provide only partial explanations of environmental realities. There are a number of dimensions to this problem.

First, science is able to offer only limited explanations of environmental processes and it has even greater difficulties predicting future environmental states. This is evidenced by the continuing discussion about the extent and effect of global warming. Because science is uncertain and ambiguous it is difficult for individuals and policy makers to make clear choices about ways in which to benefit the environment. It is therefore difficult for individuals to assess the real trade-off made in choosing, say, between products on the basis of convenience, cost and environmental performance.

Secondly, the choices people make could be simplified if the true cost of environmental damage were to be incorporated in the cost and price structures of goods and services. However, conventional economic systems do not easily take account of environmental concerns. The economic explanation of environmental problems is that many environmental features have characteristics which place their value beyond the operation of normal markets. The so-called 'free good' and 'common property resource' characteristics cause normal markets to fail in accounting for the value people place on the environment. The exclusion of environmental values from conventional economic structures means that the measures we use of economic progress also fail to take account of changes in environmental values (Pearce, 1989).

The response to this failure of market systems has not been resolved. Some authors argue for the use of 'environmental economics' to capture and incorporate environmental values into extended accounting systems (Pearce, 1989). In this way the cost of pollution damage would be built into the cost structure of the industry which produced the damage. This approach embodies the 'polluter pays principle' which is advocated by many environmentalists. Others argue that problems of measuring and valuing (environmental) damage are so imprecise that the resolution of what is socially acceptable must rightly lie in the domain of political choice (Self, 1975).

At present both the political system and the economic system are being used to resolve disputes about desired environmental futures. This happens through the activities of national pressure groups and local activists creating a climate for legislative action, such as the Environmental Protection Act 1990. It happens through international agreements on the European Community or world stages (as is the case with the Montreal Protocol on CFCs emissions or the work of the 'Earth Summit' in Rio de Janeiro in 1992). This raises important questions about the adequacy of social structures and institutions to mediate and resolve the environment as a meta-problem. The experience of the Earth Summit indicates that global environmental imperatives, which by nature transcend the boundaries of nation states, are singularly difficult to resolve because of the need to reconcile local, national and global interests. But the difficulties of resolving environmental problems do not arise simply on the international stage: there are equivalent difficulties at the local level. These small-scale problems arise because local development is often an expression of global and national trends – say towards greater energy consumption or the use of natural resources. As a result the loss of rain forests can be viewed as both a global and a local phenomenon which requires resolution at both global and local levels. Consequently, local level environmental disputes are just as difficult to resolve as their global counterparts.

The boundaries of the environmental debate are extremely elastic and are constantly being extended. Moreover, environmental concerns are often bound up with other meta-problems such as poverty and wealth, population and human rights. However, there are core principles to environmental perspectives. These argue that humanity is only part of the life sustained by the planet. But, because we have the capacity to alter and change the planet and the life it supports, our potential power must be matched with the responsibility to consider and act in the interests of present and future generations as well as other living matter. In this way we are obligated to maintain the options available in the future by seeking to protect the diversity of life and environmental conditions.

This value system considerably extends current notions of social justice and the rights and responsibilities of individuals as citizens. It implies a commitment to respect individuals irrespective of their gender, ethnicity and cultural identity. It suggests that maintaining cultural and environmental distinctiveness is an important goal, and that individuals or groups should seek neither to dominate nor subjugate the identity of other peoples or species, their neighbourhoods or habitats.

Concepts and Dimensions

In response to these issues and principles, green perspectives reject reductionist views of the world and argue for a move towards *holistic* approaches, in which there is an emphasis on synthesising the contribution of individual disciplines, cultures and perspectives within social and political structures, at all levels, into a more integrated whole. This implies the adoption of a *systemic* view of the world (Vickers, 1971) to provide the framework within which the contribution of different views can be set. It places value on the improvement of dialogue within and between groups in society. These groups include territorial communities as well as disciplines, cultures, citizens and policy makers. It emphasises the *ways and means by which individuals participate* in decisions which affect their lives and the lives of others, including future generations. It is therefore about *fostering the active community*, which is able to take control and responsibility for shaping a *sustainable way of life*.

It implies improvements at the boundaries of organisations and institutions, so that *shared responsibilities* become more clearly defined and so that organisations do not blindly pursue narrowly conceived purposes without regard for common interests. Developing this approach demands a critical questioning of conventional wisdom and follows in the tradition of writers such as Galbraith (1958), Schumacher (1976), Commoner (1971) and Carson (1962). In this sense the environmental meta-problem demands the adoption of meta-solutions which challenge conventions across the board of social, institutional and individual practice.

Underpinning these ideas is an environmental ethic based on *respect* for people and their different perspectives, *respect* for other living matter and *respect* for the planet. Equally important is the acceptance of *interconnectedness* – the realisation that humanity and nature are part of an intricately linked physical, ecological and human system. Much of the social reform demanded by green perspectives, therefore, is concerned with building this environmental ethic into individual and social action and in developing and applying more holistic forms of thinking.

Suggestions for reforms of this kind are to be found in the work of international conferences and publications, beginning with the 1972 Stockholm Conference on the Environment and leading to the recent United Nations' Conference on Environment and Development, held at Rio de Janeiro. Many authors have offered responses to the challenges we face. These have ranged from the neo-Malthusian critique of the Club of Rome (Meadows et al, 1974) to individual countries' responses to the call for a world conservation strategy (see, for example, WWFUK et al, 1984). More recently, there have been stark commentaries on the perils of past notions of economic theory and practice and the need for new visions based on *sustainable development*. This is evident in the work of the UN's World Commission on Environment and Development (Brundtland, 1987).

However, this emphasis on sustainable development has raised issues about the difficulty of defining with precision what this term means, in an operational sense, and how we will know when we have achieved a sustainable society (IUCN, 1991). Nevertheless the clear message from these collected ideas is that society has been dominated by thinking which has taken insufficient account of the importance of the earth's environmental features and characteristics. Consequently, reconstructing the relationship between human society and the environment is critical as a means to limit the potential for future harm to earth and human society.

The Role of Community Policy and Practice in Green Perspectives

What, then, is the place of community policy and practice within the green debate, and the reconstructed relationships which many agree are required but which most of us glimpse only vaguely? O'Riordan (1991) has provided a useful framework for analysing this question through his work on the relationship between environmentalism, social change and environmental management. Many of the relationships he speaks about are captured in Figure 12.1, which is adapted from his work. The figure illustrates how different forms of green ideology connect with broad

Green labels	Deep green	Medium green	Light green
Environmental philosophies	Earth-centred nurturing mode	Human-centred or manipulative mode	Science first: reliance on scientific modelling and technology
Environmental management strategies	Gaian management strategies geared to retaining global stability	Designing with nature: eco-auditing for comprehensive accounting	Self-regulation through voluntaristic and enlightened use of a corrected market economy
Green movement characteristics	Green rights; earth survival first; global co-existence New age economics Self-reliant communities Devolved power	Accommodation adjustments to management and business via ethically acceptable production, marketing and consumption	
Community practice	Active communities		
	Self-reliant communities connected to global environment-sustaining programmes	Community participation	Community involvement
Political structures		Devolved power in international federated structure	Centralised national power with new international structures
Social movements	Animal rights	Pacifism Respect across genders Anti-oppressive	Right to know Right to health Consumerism

Figure 12.1: Environmentalism, Social Change and Community Practice
Adapted from O'Riordan, 1991

social movements and political structures. It also relates these to generic forms of community practice. More than this, it implies there is a range of green perspectives driven by two main philosophies; 'human centred' (manipulative mode) and 'earth centred' (nurturing mode). These philosophies in turn are linked with different forms of environmental management strategy.

The most formal of these management strategies (light green strategies) seek solutions to environmental problems through a reliance on scientific analysis and technological advance. In this way the identification of environmental problems associated with past technological advances will be resolved by new technological innovation. In the case of society's demand for energy, it can be argued that we placed faith in our ability to harness nuclear power as a safe and efficient means to generate electricity. This was seen as a way to retain our high energy use lifestyles in the face of the threat of diminishing fossil fuels. The problems of nuclear waste and the technical difficulties of decommissioning nuclear power stations were not anticipated at the time of the nuclear programme. We have been encouraged to believe in our ability to resolve these problems through further technological advance.

This characterises how human beings use the dominating power of technology to remedy environmental problems of their making, which are the product of their lifestyles. In its turn this belief in the capacity of human ingenuity means that there is no need radically to assess lifestyles because of the capacity of science to detect, and technology to correct, these problems. Implementing these technological responses causes the market economy to adjust in a way which accommodates aspects of the new environmental economy, such as nuclear waste reprocessing.

In the centre ground, medium green management strategies follow a deeper social transformation based on the acceptance of an environmental ethic which supports the idea of working with the environment. Clearly, an ethic based on respect for the earth is supportive of a respect for humankind and a capacity to share power through devolution, federation and greater participation. Within this framework there is space in society for traditional knowledge, as well as emotional and spiritual experiences of the environment, to complement the contributions of science and technology. Debate is therefore opened to a wider constituency of interests. With that move towards participation and active

involvement comes the responsibility and challenge of demysti-
fying science and technology.

To the right of Figure 12.1 is a managerial strategy grounded
in Gaian principles: a deep green strategy within which earth is
regarded as a system state in dynamic equilibrium which has the
self-regulating capacity to maintain life but not necessarily to
perpetuate human life (Lovelock, 1987). In this order of
management, humans seek to work with the earth to ensure that
they do not jeopardise the opportunities for this and future generations to remain as one of the earth's species. The implication
of this strategy is a substantive reorientation of beliefs and
behaviour grouped around a shared acceptance that the goal of
humanity is co-existence and the survival of life. It implies an
acceptance of humility: acknowledging that it would be arrogant
of human beings to adopt the view that they are stewards of the
earth.

One critical observation is that the boundaries between strategies
are not tightly observed in our individual or social lives. In other
words individuals and societies do not readily correspond to
strategy types, rather we have a capacity to adopt different
strategies under the influence of place and circumstance. In
English cultural traditions there is acceptance of the experience
of emotional or spiritual uplift in the face of dramatic natural
scenery, such as the Lake District, or the sight of our native flora
and fauna. In traditional Aboriginal and Inuit societies there are
even more profound forms of reverence for the spirituality and
nurturing qualities of the earth and nature.

In developed economies people devote considerable time and
resources to gaining the spiritual and emotional uplift provided
by the environment. But those same people may take responsibility for activities which degrade natural resources, for instance
through the careless disposal of household products, like paint
thinners, or through involvement in the management of polluting
industrial processes, where the capacity of technology to protect
the environment is balanced against the cost to the company and
the benefit to society. These shifts in the world view we hold as
individuals help to explain the apparent contradictions in our
behaviour and choices we make

As a process of empowerment and support for greater participation in decisions, community policy and practice is most closely
aligned with deep green and medium green thinking. Even so
community policy and practice does have a role in social organ-

isation under dominantly light green ideologies. The distinction here is that the purpose of community policy and practice differs depending on the type of green ideology prevailing in society. In deep and medium green perspectives, community policy and practice are an essential component of social organisation to maintain a social order which places value on the active community and participative styles of decision making and action. It perpetuates a sense of individual humility by recognising that power is vested in individuals by communities, not by individuals expropriating that power from communities. Community practice therefore offers the means to reinforce values in society which emphasise respect, participation through empowerment, and shared problem solving.

The purpose of community practice, in light green societies, depends on the underlying trends in social values. In societies that are moving from light green to deeper green perspectives, community practice represents part of the broader pressure to establish reformed social organisation and reinforce the communitarian values set out in Chapter 1. In societies where a light green stance is only a chimera, then community policy may be little more than a means to legitimate limited participation at the margins of decisions. Community practice under this scenario takes the form of limited community involvement. Interpreting the purpose of community policy and practice is therefore critically dependent on social context, especially the ability of social structures to cope with reform and the capacity for individual agents of change to progress ideas which influence social thinking as well as local practice.

The above discussion helps identify the ingredients of community policy and practice that are important to green perspectives. First, community policy and practice has an educative or re-educative function. It is part of a process through which people are empowered to consider, in a more complete or holistic way, the implications of their decisions, or the decisions made by others, as they affect society and the environment. This type of open debate and systemic thinking is a necessary part of effective participation in environmental decisions, yet it runs counter to notions of professional elites, with sole access to specialised bodies of knowledge and opinion. However, it is totally consistent with approaches to problem solving based on dialogue and sharing of experiences. It seeks to build broader ways of thinking into social systems, as a way to help people understand the real choices they face and the real outcome of any decisions they agree to make. Rather than rejecting the contribution of science, this approach advocates the encouragement of 'skeptical scientific knowledge', through which individuals and communities are able to appreciate the limitations of technical and scientific explanations. This demands the development of critical reasoning as well as systemic thinking.

Secondly, community practice contributes to personal reform in drawing out the consequences of individual decisions and actions in a way which encourages reflection on our choices and behaviours. It acts as a lever for personal and collective awareness and then transformation of behaviour. Finally, it supports organisational reform, where conventional practice, conventional wisdom and the power structures they perpetuate are regarded as potential candidates for change. This requires considerable vision, to think beyond the immediacy of the present day, to look for creative and innovative alternatives.

Policy and Practice

The first part of this chapter has discussed the mutually supportive elements of community policies and practice and green perspectives. It has explored the green debate and considered the ideological foundations of green thinking, especially the extent to which community practice is consistent with green alternatives. This second part focuses on the way policy, which builds on community practice and environmental action, has developed in Britain. The context to this analysis is provided by the observation that a range of institutions in Britain have a light green perspective and there is a growing body of opinion driving the move to deeper green ideologies.

Examples of this transformation are provided by reforms occurring in the environmental movement. Some of these institutional changes as they affect rural policy have been described elsewhere (Roome, 1986 and 1989). What we are experiencing here is a move away from elitist bureaucracies, agreeing policy objectives and approving management regimes which they, or their agents, deliver. There is an increasing recognition that environmental management and improvement is a participative exercise which involves discussion and transaction with local people. Environmental action is therefore increasingly bound up with community practice. While the process of institutional change which supports these developments is by no means complete, it cannot be denied that it will have increasing significance for communities and public agencies. Moreover, the environmental movement has also been successful in challenging the conventions of other sectors of British society, such as business (Roome, 1992).

The recent history of environmental policy and community policy in Britain shows evidence of a steady drawing together of these two separate strands. This process has not always been easy and is far from complete. Although it can be argued that the synergy between community practice and environmental policy and action is now established, it is not yet universally accepted or practised. In order to understand the nature of the current relationship it is appropriate briefly to chart the main events in the development of community environmental policy and practice.

From the viewpoint of environmental policy there have been longstanding commitments by environmental groups to engage in the process of policy formation (Lowe and Goyder, 1983) across a broad range of environmental concerns. Arguments for increased local participation in the planning process developed in the 1960s. Skeffington (1969) took the view that planners needed to understand more adequately the needs of local people and that local people needed encouragement and support to enable them to make meaningful contributions to the future destiny of their local areas.

However, the changing context of local government planning, at the time of the Skeffington Report, undermined the notion of community participation. Local participation has not been an easy issue for professional planners, who are separated from their communities by barriers of profession and divided responsibility (to the profession, to their political leaders on the council as well as to the community). These tensions were more acute at a time when local government reform was making it more remote from community, while the language and procedures of planning were adding to its obscurity. However, there was pressure for greater community involvement in planning as a result of disquiet about the environmental changes occurring in both town and country. On occasions these changes were sanctioned by local authorities and other public agencies, and sometimes they were inspired by public policies.

In the 1970s the membership of interest groups increased and this reinforced the opportunities for groups such as the voluntary amenity societies to argue their role and involvement in local decisions (Larkham, 1985). Planners, keen to observe the legal obligation for participation in structure and local plans, engaged with the comparatively well-organised and informed interest groups. There was an administrative tidiness in working with groups which understood the system and which had specialised and focused concerns. Similarly the environmental volunteer movement offered local authorities an opportunity to achieve their objectives using people beyond their own direct labour organisations (Simpson, 1981).

These comments do not detract from the contribution of volunteers or consultees in planning procedures. However, these activities are different in nature from the local participation in the policies and practice of local authorities and other resource agencies which develop out of community practice. At this stage the contribution of community development to environmental change was seen as radical and exciting, but not in the mainstream of policy and practice (Stevenson, 1972). Fashioning a relationship between environmental action and community policy was not really part of the consciousness of environmental thinking in Britain.

Community practice, as community development, was emerging at this time with a strong focus on urban areas. For example, the Community Development Project was formed in 1969 to develop action teams in twelve localities. In rural areas there was a track record of support for communities through the Rural Community Council network. However, this was mainly concerned with the strengthening of local groups and village infrastructure. It was not until the late 1970s that serious attempts were made at community development practice in rural communities.

The 1970s, then, were a period of developing experimentation with community development practice. At the same time there was a growing concern about the environment within particular social groups, especially the young, the educated and the middle class. The environmental movement could therefore reasonably be branded as the province of the elite classes (Eversley, 1974). The two strands – community policy and practice on the one hand and environmental action on the other – touched but took essentially separate courses and had separate constituencies.

Agencies and voluntary organisations advocating environmental improvement and protection did not devise their policy solutions around locally determined environmental agendas and actions. Neither did they place much emphasis on the role of participation and empowerment in environmental action. Community practice workers, for their part, reflected either the concerns of the agencies which funded their work or the needs expressed by the communities with whom they were working. Neither agencies nor community groups placed high priority on environmental issues compared with more immediate concerns about employment, health or the needs of minority and disadvantaged groups.

There was a further important distinction. Environmental initiatives tended to focus on resources and areas. In this sense, projects within the local community looked to draw on environmentally concerned groups and individuals for their support. Community practice, in contrast, was concerned about working with communities of interest, who shared problems, as much as with communities defined by locality. Community practice was much more directly involved with issues of cultural identity, and ethnic and gender concerns than with environmental projects and action. Moreover, environmental elites were often separated, in a spatial sense, from the areas where most community practice was developing.

The pressures which brought these two strands more firmly together arose on a number of fronts in the 1980s. The popularisation of environmental conservation was significant. The stolid ecological tradition of nature conservation, which emphasised protection of the spectacular and where people were perceived as threats to species and habitats (Warren and Goldsmith, 1983), was under attack from more radical perspectives. Mabey (1973) had long argued the merit of the enjoyment of the commonplace but it was not until the 1980s that these ideas were built on by the urban wildlife movement and the work of the early Groundwork Trusts in the north-west. By bringing nature conservation into the cities these pioneers confronted the need to manage wildlife with the consent and commitment of community interests. The need was to identify the synergy which came from the idea that wildlife was a resource for people and that people were a resource for wildlife (Bradley, 1986; Davidson, 1988).

A number of guides were produced at this time to help build the capacity of local people to tackle environmental problems in towns (Gibson, 1986) and country (King and Clifford, 1987). Some (Pinder, 1985) were more concerned with guiding communities in how to organise themselves. King and Clifford's contribution is particularly interesting because it offers insights into a range of environmental issues as well as the organisational problems of mobilising local opinion. It takes the view that small contributions to the environment are as important as large projects and that the environment is as much about emotional responses as scientific analysis.

In urban areas the trend in the 1980s was to move away from urban redevelopment, with its preoccupation with the reconstruction of the built environment, to notions of urban regeneration, where community issues were of significance in promoting community confidence together with the physical and economic rehabilitation of an area (Civic Trust, 1989). Equally, the 'Healthy Cities' initiative and city farms offered community project workers a broader set of environmental initiatives to develop as part of the agenda for local urban action.

Urban areas saw a strong ethnic dimension to community environmental action. Projects based on the use of vacant land to grow traditional foodstuffs important to non-white communities were established from the early 1980s. The pioneering Ashram Community Service project in Birmingham, Sparkbrook, the Bowes Street Allotments in Manchester, Moss Side, and the Walnut Tree Walk School Garden in Kennington, London, all demonstrate the growing importance attached to multicultural traditions in the use of the environment. Other urban community concerns about the environment include opposition to road improvement and development schemes on wild areas, community gardens, local energy-saving initiatives and community recycling schemes.

Many of these community projects had strong commitments from local authorities but there was also an increasing range of other bodies committed to supporting community environmental action. These include the Association of Community Technical Aid Centres, Royal Institute of British Architects' Community Architecture Department, Architecture Workshops, the Urban and Economic Development Group, the Civic Trust's Regeneration Unit, NCVO's Inner Cities Unit, the Black Environmental Network and many other local and national groups. The plurality of groups centred around a core belief in environmental improvement through local action. This represents a measure of the developing breadth of consciousness about community practice and environmental action in urban areas. In this way environmental agendas have been readily accepted in towns and cities to take root alongside the developing experience of community practice.

In the countryside the progress of community practice and environmental action has been more bound up with the capacity of state resource planning agencies to accept the need for greater community participation in policy formulation and implementation at a local level. It is therefore worth exploring these changes in rather more detail. A concept unifying community practice and environmental action in rural areas was provided by the notion of integrated rural development (IRD). The criticism of past rural policy was that rural resource planning had become the province of specialist bureaucracies operating within limited and inflexible remits, with little sensitivity to local environmental or community needs. IRD offered a means to bring together the strands of economic development, environmental management and community practice. Pioneering initiatives such as the Two Villages project in the Peak District National Park (Parker, 1984) acknowledged the importance of bringing the set of agencies, with an interest in rural areas, together with local groups and interests. This consultation would then shape more locally sensitive policies.

This work did not stand in isolation. It took place at the same time as the Community Projects Foundation was developing its experience of rural community practice through the Leominster Marshes project (Community Projects Foundation, 1986) and as the track record of Rural Community Council patchworking was expanding (Scott, 1985; Moseley, 1985). However there is little doubt that the Peak Park project was more concerned with the practice of institutional reform, in bringing together public policies and agencies, than with building local participation as the core to that process. However, the Rural Community Council projects with their greater commitment to community practice acknowledged environment as one of many local concerns.

A fresh impetus to the development of bridges between community practice and environmental action was provided by initiatives from the environmental agencies in the early 1980s. Both the Nature Conservancy Council for Great Britain (Nature Conservancy Council, 1984) and the Countryside Commission (Countryside Commission, 1982) had articulated the concept of partnership as an element underpinning their policies for the environment in the 1980s. This implied partnership with other interests in the public, private and voluntary sectors. It also meant exploring partnerships with local people and their communities.

In the case of the Countryside Commission these commitments were translated into a series of experimental projects to explore the implications of local environmental action based on a blend of community practice and environmental action (Bishop et al, 1991). The experimental projects supported the production of self-help guides, such as the TACTICS pack (Prior, 1988) as well as a range of local initiatives (see, for example, Roome, 1988 and 1990a). These sought to put environmental interests more firmly on the agenda of Rural Community Councils and other community and enterprise agencies; to use adult education as a spur to empowerment and action; and to explore the potential for environmentally centred community practice in specific areas or on specific themes.

The importance of this reshaping of agency agendas and the difficulties inherent in the shifts in agency cultures to accommodate those changes should not be underestimated. In the case of the Nature Conservancy Council, its work since the late 1940s had placed emphasis on the protection of nature through the designation of wildlife areas. In support of that approach it had appointed staff with scientific and land management expertise. The promotion of partnership work demanded different inter-organisational skills. The Countryside Commission was little different. Whilst it had a remit to promote landscape management and encourage informal recreation in the countryside, it had traditionally delivered this through the agency of local authorities. Policies were instrumental. Admittedly they were often set after consultation with a wide range of groups but, then, local authorities and voluntary bodies were the means of implementation. The possibility that local people might be empowered to shape local policy and action and that these organisations would then respond to locally set agendas, was a relatively alien concept to the mindset in these organisations.

However, there were organisations in the public and voluntary sectors with experience of community practice but for whom environmental concern had been a peripheral issue. These included the Rural Development Commission and the Rural Community Councils, National Council for Voluntary Organisations, the Association of Community Technical Aid Centres, local Architecture Workshops and the Community Projects Foundation. The twin notion of partnership and community environmental action offered a framework to develop links across environmental and community practice organisations; to blend skills and approaches and in that way to help reshape agency agendas (Nature Conservancy Council, 1989).

The experience of the Nature Conservancy Council's Partnership in Practice initiative and the Countryside Commission's community environmental action programme is that there is scope for developing more participative forms of environmental action based on community action and community practice. The most recent expression of this is to be found in the Rural Action leaflet which indicates co-operation between the Countryside Commission for England, the Rural Development Commission, English Nature and the voluntary sector to establish a Rural Action Unit (Rural Action Unit, 1992). The purpose of this unit is to facilitate the formation of local networks of organisations and interests which are committed to the support of environmental action at the community level. Part of that commitment involves the establishment of co-ordinated support for local communities.

In addition to this organisational framework there is a strong body of experience captured in reports on two seminars dealing with community environmental action (Warburton, 1988; Hashagen, 1991) which demonstrate that the links between environmental action and community practice are well understood and supported by committed practitioners.

This work articulates the contribution of community practice to the promotion of sustainable communities which are more in harmony with their environment. It is confirmed that this approach places demands on environmental agencies and interests to reach out and engage more constructively with local people and to listen to their concerns. It also requires community facilitators to acknowledge the potential of environmental action as a component of community practice. Warburton's and Hashagen's reports contain aspirations as well as realistic assessments of the capacity of organisations to respond to this challenge. A central role is given to the development of networks at national and more local level as a means to construct bridges and new relationships between community practice and environmental interests. However, these new networks should be seen to act in three directions.

First, they are important as a basis for sharing understanding between community and environmental interests. Secondly, they are important frameworks for the support of local environmental action through community practice. Thirdly, they provide mechanisms for mediating local concerns and bringing local agendas to the attention of other levels of the network and ultimately to national bodies and their forums.

The limiting factor, in establishing wider support for these ideas, appears to rest on the ability of organisations to understand how to blend the traditions of environmental policy and concern with that of community policy and practice; to avoid parochial disputes about the boundaries of policy; to link national policy for environmental change effectively with local action which shapes tomorrow's environment; and to accomplish the changes in organisational style that are necessary to avoid jeopardising the outcomes of community practice simply because organisations are not totally aligned to support them.

The conundrum for environmental organisations in Britain is that they have tended to be dominated by 'light green' ideologies, of the kind outlined in the first part of this chapter. Rather than taking the lead in promoting a form of social order and organisation which is consistent with devolution of power and the promotion of self-reliant communities, they have perpetuated social organisation which resists the sharing of power with communities. There are, however, encouraging changes glimpsed in the concerns of the new environmental agencies in Britain, which were restructured by the Environmental Protection Act 1990, to adopt a more community-focused approach to their policies. So too in urban areas there is an increasing commitment to a community-focused approach and to a developing environmental role. There are also a growing number of practitioners working in the field of environment action and community practice.

Future Prospects for Community Practice and Environmental Action

What, then, are the prospects for community practice and environmental action in Britain as we move towards the new millennium? In many senses that future is bound up with the environmental epigram 'think globally and act locally' which appears to capture the spirit of progress towards sustainable communities and a sustainable world. In the case of community environmental action the important issue, at the global scale, is the extent to which environmental imperatives provide sufficient impetus for social and political opinion to press for the reform of social thinking and organisation. If there is a progressive move towards medium and deep green ideologies at a global scale, then this will provide a critical context to support the communitarian perspective outlined in Chapter 1. This global context will support local initiatives and action. If, however, there is no further shift in ideology, it will be difficult for a communitarian approach to take root in environmental policy and practice.

Although the shape of the global context is critical, so too is the rate at which reform takes place. At present there appears to be a possibility of a social transition towards deeper green and more communitarian principles. Possibly we are undergoing a period of transition. But, as with all transition phases the use of terms and ideas is subject to abuse by those who do not understand their meaning or their implications. The currency of terms like 'partnership', 'community practice' and 'local environmental action' are potentially corruptible by those who use the ideas carelessly.

It is necessary therefore to progress local action with caution. By accepting a future vision of more environmentally sustainable communities we also accept that not every community will take the same route or proceed at the same pace. The nature of communitarian principles in practice is that communities move at the pace at which they can cope with change. But that needs to be supported by agencies and individuals who are able to conceive and articulate new visions. The problem is that a vision based on environmental sustainability and communitarian principles is abstract and potentially confusing. This adds to the potential for the vision to be subverted, particularly as it demands that agencies adopt an approach which cuts away at bureaucratic structures.

In particular, community environmental action does not fit neat institutional boundaries. Neither does it conform to convenient budget heads or timescales, as it is led by the priorities and pace of local people. It also involves communities asking agencies for resources which those communities believe they need. The result is that agencies are obliged to follow local agendas, not simply to operate to their own programmes. The need for more flexible working practices is therefore a condition for the promotion of community environmental action. The progress towards improved agency networking is an important step to achieving this flexibility.

There are also issues at the community level. For professionals in environmental fields, community environmental action is all the more difficult because the concern is often with achieving the ends of environmental change rather than with recognising the value of the process of community environmental action. This is not helped by the lack of techniques to evaluate the performance of projects in a way which gives as much attention to the importance of community processes as to the achievement of environmental products.

For individual workers in the community, community environmental action requires them to have multiple skills. These include an appreciation of environmental systems, sensitivity to the human condition and an ability to relate to different organisational cultures. It also requires a willingness to accept that environmental consciousness has a critical cultural (Black Environmental Network, 1991) and gender (Caldecott and Leland, 1983) dimension, which conditions perceptions and actions. Unless these issues are recognised environmental action will remain ghettoised and irrelevant to the needs of all communities. There are similar demands on community leaders and community activists to develop the multiskilling required to tackle their community and environmental issues. This in turn requires highly developed skills in listening and empowerment.

One tool to advance this approach is the use of soft systems thinking. This technique accepts that the way each individual imagines the world may be fundamentally different. Unless we are able to identify those images for ourselves, it is not possible to have constructive dialogue about the substantive issues we face and to agree suitable ways forward. The use of this approach helps to construct a basis for dialogue about the differences between the models of the world held within communities and the realities those communities face. However there has been little use of this type of approach in community practice. The substance of community environmental action is the application of tools such as parish maps (Common Ground, 1988) or ideas for local environmental auditing (Roome, 1990b). The problem with these tools is that they can become descriptive, instead of helping to shape local visions of future communities and environments. However, there have been some imaginative attempts to develop dialogues around environmental futures using pictorial images and role-play games (O'Riordan et al, 1992).

It is clear that the development of new tools to help discussion and choice about futures seems to be essential if communities are to take more control of the options for change. It is possible that current ideas about environmental mediation offer communities a means to resolve particular environmental disputes (Environment Council, 1991). One feature of these tools should be that they are non-prescriptive. They provide frameworks to enable local communities to make their own decisions and to resolve their own conflicts. Clearly not all those choices will be sustainable but at least the product of self-determination should be a diversity of action which will lend stability to local and global environmental and social systems.

The prospects for community environmental action are therefore linked to our ability to respond to challenges at different levels. Its progress will depend on developments in ideology, social organisation and our capacity to think more constructively and creatively about our actions and their consequences. To be effective that will demand the applications of new skills and practice. In particular there will be a critical need to direct community policy towards education, aimed at developing new forms of thought in the search for restructured relationships between communities and the environment. The prize, if we meet this challenge, is in the making of more habitable and sustainable communities and through that a more sustainable world community.

13 Community Policy, Citizenship and Democracy

Hugh Butcher and Maurice Mullard

Introduction

The dominance of Conservative governments within UK politics throughout the 1980s and into the 1990s has produced a series of community policies which have set boundaries on the meaning of democracy and on the constituent elements of citizenship. The denationalisation of public utilities and the transfer of assets to private-sector monopolies have decreased rather than increased the accountability of natural monopolies to the individual consumer. Equally, both the legal and financial constraints imposed on local authorities have accelerated the shift towards further centralism at the cost of democracy, diversity and plurality in the provision of local public services. Reforms of health and education and the move towards grant maintained schools, centralised funding councils, and decentralised budgets reflect attempts by the government to depoliticise major areas of public provision. Overall, therefore, the process of privatisation is increasingly leading towards individualism and quietism as the government seeks to continue to lower the expectations that individual citizens have of the state, while emphasising the importance of individual effort, the family, friendship networks and voluntary provision within the context of a centralist political environment.

Further, trade union reforms, the gradual phasing out of wages councils, and the recent break-up of the National Economic Development Council (NEDC), all reflect the government's strategy to break with a politics influenced by functional groups and social movements and to move towards a democracy predominantly understood as a relationship between the individual and the state. The Citizens Charter confirms the government's perception of the citizen as a consumer of public services rather than a 'participative' citizen who seeks full engagement with the policy process. Governments over the past decade have, in short, sought to define democracy and citizenship within a framework of individual self-interest and a centralist state.

A major theme of this chapter is to demonstrate that concepts of citizenship and democracy are 'contestable' concepts; that choices are, and have to be, made about preferred interpretations; and that the process of constructing such interpretations necessarily involves political choices. Of necessity, such choices entail different interpretations of 'community' and therefore different visions of the role of community policy in modern society.

The first part of the chapter seeks to show that political perspectives on citizenship are constructed from four broad 'ideal type' positions and these are discussed under the labels 'independent citizen', 'public citizen', 'entitled citizen' and 'dutiful citizen'. These four dimensions of citizenship are seen to draw, in differing measure, upon individualist and communitarian views of human nature and human society.

Competing models of democracy, it is similarly argued, are also rooted in different philosophical assumptions: liberal democracy is built on individualistic assumptions and embraces libertarian and pragmatic variants, whilst communitarian assumptions underpin what we call the radical and pluralist models of participatory democracy. It is our contention that most of such models of citizenship and democracy can 'do business' with community policies (and we illustrate this thesis as our argument unfolds), but it is our final conclusion that community policies can find their fullest expression only in and through *particular* visions of democratic citizenship and, indeed, that such visions *require* the further extension and development of such public policies for their optimum realisation.

Dimensions of Citizenship

Citizenship is one of those concepts, like 'democracy', 'freedom' and 'community', whose meaning is open to vigorous debate and interpretation; it is a 'contested' concept, the meaning of which, for the time being at least, it is fruitless to try to pin down in any once-and-for-all way. Nevertheless, as Ungerson (1992) states, one thing about the idea is clear – 'it is always concerned with the relationship between the individual and the state'. She puts the point thus:

> Of course, we can and we do argue about the nature of that relationship: whether, for example, it contains a notion of reciprocal rights and duties between state and citizen; whether citizens' rights are more important than citizens' obligations; whether there are different kinds of citizens' rights – such as legal, civil and social rights – and whether these can be placed in historical sequence, and/or normative hierarchies . . . But the one immovable feature of the idea of citizenship is that it is placed in the public domain: it is concerned with how the individual and the state relate to each other across public concerns, and how public institutions, such as the judiciary and the polity, mediate that relationship. (Ungerson, 1992, p. 143)

Contemporary citizenship is, we suggest, constructed from four elements, or dimensions. Each dimension has a history, emphasises distinctive values and beliefs, presupposes particular institutional structures, and entails the citizen acting in accordance with particular norms and roles. The four dimensions – we have characterised them above as 'public citizen', 'independent citizen', 'entitled citizen' and the 'dutiful citizen' – are to be thought of as the conceptual building-blocks from which 'actually existing' patterns of citizenship are constructed. In one sense they are 'ideal types', yet they are not intended to be taken as alternative, or wholly competing, models of citizenship. Western European societies have developed political systems that embrace all four elements, although particular configurations have in practice varied between states, and over time. Two points need to be stressed. First, there are tensions between the four elements – the fact that they embody an emphasis on different values ensures this – but there does, nevertheless, seem to be a practical limit to how far one dimension can 'crowd out' the others. The practical implications and consequences of this 'dynamic tension' between the competing dimensions of citizenship will become clear later in this chapter. Secondly, shifts in balance between the dimensions over time, while partly the result of ideological debate and struggle, have also been a response to widespread social changes within the world economy and the international political order, as well as a reaction to the continuing revolutions in technology and communications. Some of the key characteristics of each dimension of citizenship are illustrated in Table 13.1.

Table 13.1: Four Dimensions of Democratic Citizenship

	The public citizen	The independent citizen	The entitled citizen	The dutiful citizen
Key value:	Democracy	Liberty	Distributive justice	Order
Supportive values:	Deliberation Participation Rational judgement	Self direction Choice Toleration	Responsibility Reciprocity Fairness	Security Tradition and sentiment Organicism and hierarchy
Emphasis on:	Political rights and obligations	Civil and legal rights and obligations	Economic social, etc rights and obligations	Duties prescribed by status, in range of corporate bodies
Concern with proper functioning of:	Decision making in legislatures, parliaments, etc	Rule of law – judiciary Separation of powers	Effective admin., planning and resourcing of state activity	Intermediate structures, anchoring the individual in the community
State/civil society relationships	Democracy to permeate all society	Separation of state and civil society	State responsible for intervening/regulating many aspects of civil society	Society as organic, an interdependent whole, each part with role
Democratic processes viewed as:	End in itself – developmental	Means to an end – instrumental	Instrumental and developmental	Instrumentally necessary; potentially corrosive of social unity, atomising
View of liberty:	To be bound only by deliberative decisions, freely determined	Freedom from interference (by other citizens and by state)	Effective freedom secured via state intervention and regulation	Ordered society preserved through functional diversity
Ideal of justice entails:	The application of reason in pursuit of common good	Securing the individual's inalienable natural rights	Securing a fair distribution of life chances	A balance between elements that constitute state and society
Citizenship at risk from:	Privatism; intrusion of private interests in public affairs	Centralised and oppressive power, tyrannical majorities, interference in free market	Countervailing structures, patriarchy, racism and class	Abstract/formula and 'principled' planning and social organisation
Contemporary theorists:	Macpherson (1973) Pateman (1970) Arendt (1959)	Hayek (1960) Nozick (1974)	Rawls (1971) Titmuss (1968) Dahrendorf (1988)	Scruton (1984) Oakeshott (1962)

The Public Citizen

This is the 'active' dimension of citizenship, in which the individual enjoys a 'public' and political existence, forging, with others, the conditions of their common life. In its most elevated expression, this dimension of citizenship is celebrated as the highest role to which the individual can aspire – one in which the full nature of wo/man as 'zoon politikon' is properly realised. Great value is placed on public deliberation, direct political participation, and the exercise of rational judgement; emphasis is given to establishing structures in which individuals can actively share in a 'commitment to the resolution of problems of collective choice through public reasoning' (Cohen, 1990). Diversity and plurality of view are acknowledged, but the central belief is that citizens have a capacity for engaging in productive public debate and dialogue, for rationally deliberating on public issues and, through supporting the most cogently formulated argument, reach a rationally motivated consensus. There is an expectation, then, that reason (not power, or calculation of private interest) will settle the fate of political and policy proposals; the better argument, not the size of a majority, should determine the shape of the common good. It is the illegitimate intrusion of private interests into public decision making that, indeed, undermines the realisation of this ideal of public citizenship.

The Independent Citizen

This, on the other hand, represents the triumph of the private over the public realm. Human potential is realised not through engagement with others within the public domain, but through independent, self-directed, autonomous activity directed to individually determined projects pursued within 'civil society'. The only constraint – or 'interference' – warranted on the exercise of such freedom is that which is necessary to ensure that 'my' actions and choices do not diminish or undermine 'your' actions and choices. The rights and obligations that a political authority must be contracted to uphold are, then, of a legal and constitutional nature – its role is to 'hold the ring' in such a way that the diversity of freely chosen ends may be given the maximum opportunity to come to full fruition without outside interference. Individual citizens are, ultimately, the best judges of their own interests, and are conceived as free and equal beings with inalienable (natural) rights. A minimally regulated civil society – with free markets and private property, strong voluntary organisations within an autonomous intermediate sector, inviolable households and families – represents the institutional expression of liberty. A strong, but circumscribed, state (circumscribed ideally by a written constitution) acting as the protector of individual rights and freedoms represents the rational outcome of a free people who determine to associate together to pursue more effectively their personal aims within an agreed framework.

The Entitled Citizen

The third dimension of citizenship is underpinned by commitment to positive freedoms and a proactive, interventionist and regulatory state. The liberty of most citizens is imperilled not so much by interference with, or constraints upon, their individual choices, as by the lack of material and other necessary opportunities required to turn choices into realities. The citizen is entitled to enjoy a range of economic, social and other rights (including the right to education, health, welfare) that would ensure a fairer distribution in the enjoyment of life chances. This entails a citizenry that is prepared to embrace notions of distributive justice, and a state apparatus charged with implementing the conditions of the individual social development of its members. Liberty and free choice for the individual, along with a belief in representative democracy to authorise the nature and extent of collective provision, are important but justice also demands the development of an effective 'welfare' state, along with governmental responsibility to intervene in the economy. Counterveiling and untamed power structures – exemplified in inequalities of class, race, and gender – do, however, provide a continuing challenge to effective entitlement. This view of citizenship reached its fullest institutional expression in Britain during the quarter-century following the end of World War Two: Beveridge-inspired social welfare, Keynsian economic management for full employment, and commitment to a mixed economy with significant public ownership and direction of key industries constituted the main features of the post-war settlement (Mishra, 1984) and gave practical expression to the idea of the entitled citizen. Though the 'post-war consensus' that underpinned this model has disappeared there remain powerful lobbies in support of such institutions and social rights.

The Dutiful Citizen

This occupies a conceptual position that is in some respects the polar opposite to that of the 'independent' citizen. Here the individual is securely embedded within the range of groups and corporate bodies that comprise the total society. It is this totality, along with its constituent families, communities, classes, economic and political bodies, and voluntary organisations, that constitutes society. Society as 'organism', rather than as an aggregate of individuals that fulfil roles within the social order, is the important reality when considering citizenship. Citizenship signals 'membership' – of society and its constituent parts – and such membership provides identity, security, rootedness and social position.

In return, though not in any mechanistic or contractual sense, societal members act out the roles and duties prescribed by the corporate bodies of which they are a part. Like an idealised family, society, as 'nation', provides a history and a sense of belonging, a point of reference and an object of love.

Holistic rather than individualistic in orientation, this strand emphasises the *contribution* that the person can make to the overall functioning of the whole, thus a focus on duties rather than 'rights'. There is a wariness of democracy, and distrust of blueprint planning and social engineering.

Democracy encourages citizens to think in terms of claims, although it is recognized that democracy, like property, can provide a stake in society, thereby 'binding' the individual into the whole through a sense of membership, through shared activity and decision making, and through a shared understanding of the world; also, 'representative' democracy is preferred; it can be modelled to maintain an element of deferential passivity on the part of those who are natural 'followers'. Large-scale social engineering, on the other hand, has next to no saving graces; rationality can reek great mischief when misapplied to finely balanced organic systems.

The Process of Democracy

If the nature of citizenship is concerned with the relationship between the individual and the state then democracy, in its various guises, focuses on the process of regulating, developing, and rendering accountable those relationships as they relate to collective decision making about the public good. Accounts of democracy are located within two major paradigms – liberal and communitarian – each of which entails distinctive, even 'incommensurate', core assumptions and which lead to radically different interpretations of what the proper concerns and machinery of modern democracy should look like. For example, while advocates of liberal ('representative') democracy emphasise the ethic of negative freedom and value the democratic process for its protection of the individual from the coercive powers of the state, communitarian ('direct' or 'participative') democracy emphasises positive freedom and the potential for increasing the liberty of the individual through community. We will distinguish two models of democracy underpinned by liberal assumptions, and two that are founded on communitarian principles.

Liberal Democracy – the Ultra-minimalist Variant

As the label implies this view emphasises the limits of democracy; the boundaries of democratic government must be explicit, constrained, and legally upheld. Establishing and safeguarding the right to individual liberty comes before all else; liberty emancipates the subject, a subject historically treated by the monarch as a body to be disposed of without recourse to justice. Democracy is preferable to monarchy, autocracy or oligarchy, but it too is capable of 'taking liberties' away from the independent, sovereign, individual.

Thus ultra-minimalists argue for a constitutional form of government, one in which the obligations and limits of the legislature are set within a strict framework of law, and where an independent judiciary secures the rights of the individual, seeing that the process of government works within the framework of law. The constitution is there to establish the rights of the individual in such a way that changes in government do not lead to changes to these rights. Ultra-minimalists expect that individuals will wish to retreat from the public sphere because 'politics' is prone to be unpredictable, unstable and unjust. Their aim is to secure, expand and indeed celebrate 'private' life, where autonomous individuals can seek to realise their individual life projects.

Liberal Democracy – the Pragmatic Variant

In contrast to the ultra-minimalist vision of democracy, the pragmatist's view of liberal democracy sanctions proactive interventionism while nevertheless holding that the potential of democracy is limited and that voters should beware of harbouring expectations which democracy cannot deliver. Pragmatists accept that democracy can provide a vehicle for political choice, and political parties should have scope to compete for people's votes. The pragmatic tradition is, however, anti-foundational; in other words pragmatists inhabit a world of universal doubts, suspicious of those who appear to have ready-made explanations and once-for-all prescriptions. As a consequence pragmatists are suspicious of both libertarian and communitarian democracy with their belief, for example, that creating a more democratic culture is likely to lead to greater tolerance. There is no craving for absolutes; instead their concern is for knowledge which is deemed to be tentative, open to interpretation, and always subject to correction. The balance between liberty and equality, market and state action, political choice and professional expertise, and a host of other dualisms, can never be 'resolved'; they will remain the subject of continuous debate, with liberal democracy the best mechanism for reaching workable, day-to-day compromises. The threats to liberal democracy are posed by those who have fanatical visions for society and who have no tolerance for the visions of others; by those who take advantage of liberal institutions to pursue doctrine and turn democracy as a means to their ends.

Bernstein puts the matter succinctly:

> The type of pluralism that represents what is best in our pragmatic tradition is an engaged fallibilistic pluralism. Such a pluralistic ethos places new responsibilities upon each of us. For it means taking our fallibility seriously – resolving that however much we are committed to our styles of thinking we are willing to listen to others without denying or suppressing the otherness of the other. (Bernstein, 1986, p. 336)

Communitarian Democracy

Communitarians tend to focus on the normative analysis of democracy, to ask how democracies *ought* to work. Their models are characterised by an attempt to provide an agenda for democracy, showing how opportunities for participation may be enhanced. They point out that participation should not be confined to electoral democracy but that a democratic dynamic should actually be promoted throughout society:

> The problem of building a democratic society is thus one of a dynamic interaction of rules and actors with the actors rendering the rules more democratic, and the increasingly democratic rules rendering the actors more firmly committed

to skilled democratic participation and decision making. We term this process a democratic dynamic. (Bowles and Gintis, 1986, p. 186)

The communitarians point to the limits of liberal democracy, arguing that individuals cannot be perceived to exist in a vacuum or as 'unencumbered' selves. Individuals are an inherent part of their community and it is within communities that ethics of democracy and citizenship are created. It is community that creates opportunities and public spaces, that can generate options which guarantee diversity and pluralities of views and therefore a more discursive model of democracy. Freedom of the individual cannot be realised in a void but can only be understood within the wider social context – it is the community which therefore defines freedom.

Communitarian democracy therefore stresses the centrality of dialogue as an underlying ethic which guarantees contestation and which allows for the articulation of a plurality of demands and interests. Freedom and democracy do not depend on *a priori* agreed definitions but derive their meanings from within specific, evolving, social contexts.

According to this approach it is not sufficient simply to understand how democracy works at present; a culture of democracy for the future must be established. The ethics of participation in decision making should not be confined to the electoral process but should be extended to other aspects of our daily lives. This means the right to participate at our place of work, in our local communities, and to be involved in decisions on investment which are likely to affect our daily lives. And it entails a wider economic democracy which establishes consumer rights against monopoly suppliers. At present democracy is confined to the public sphere which mitigates against increased participation by women and many other groups. It also puts limits on the boundaries of what is perceived to be the public as opposed to the private sphere. The process of democracy seeks to turn the individual into a public citizen.

> [The individual] loses his [sic] personal identity and becomes a part of a purposive social unit. Here the group absorbs all his [sic] resources, emotional as well as physical . . . and this is the very essence of the psychological transformation of man [sic] into a citizen. (Shklar, 1985, p. 15)

There are two major variants within this model which need to be distinguished. These derive from the tension between those who argue for substantive democracy but still seek to preserve the homogeneity of community, and those who argue for a more heterogeneous approach to democracy and who seek to constitute community rather than assume that community actually exists.

Communitarian Democracy – the Radical Variant

Radical democrats embrace the general assumptions outlined above, holding that as direct democracy extends and deepens its permeation throughout society so common interests will be seen to supplant sectional interests, and rational deliberation and decision making will replace a politics predicated on sectional interests. Unitary in its conception of community, radical democrats believe that a common humanity and a universal community is ever more fully realised as the 'democratic dynamic' becomes more firmly embedded in the social institutions of society and the social psychology of its members. So-called 'structural' conflicts and sectional interests are dissolved in and through the advance of democratic participation. Democracy is inherently egalitarian. All 'votes' count equally and everyone is equally implicated in the social formation whose shape and development is determined through democratisation. The most complete statement of this approach comes from Heller and Fehrer (1988). They hold that to move from procedural democracy to direct democracy is to create a vastly enhanced public sphere, one which will involve widespread public debate, a more equal recognition of all needs, a collective conscience, a power structure that contributes to trade-offs and compromises in a way that prevents any particular group feeling maltreated or unjustly rolled over by other views.

Heller has written:

> There cannot be more freedom than the right and the possibility of equal participation in decision-making processes in terms of the democratic concept of freedom. In terms of the democratic concept of freedom the more everyone has the right and the possibility to participate the freer people are. Liberation can thus be conceived as a lengthy process in which everyone has the right and the very increasing possibility for participating. And that is what democratic freedom is about. (Heller and Fehrer, 1988, pp. 367–8)

Communitarian Democracy – the Pluralist Variant
Here the assumption of a unified public interest and a holistic community is deemed to be utopian. There is a realisation that people will always have a diversity of needs, interests and views. The emancipation of 'the working class', or any other social category, will not bring about an end to social divisions and conflicts. Like the liberal-pragmatic democrat, the communitarian pluralist does not have a predetermined view of the good society; the continuing existence of social diversity and competing interests are recognised as a continuing reality. The pluralist project becomes one of recognising the inevitable existence, and competing claims, of new social movements; of supporting a climate of toleration and of respect for diversity; and of ensuring that all voices are heard and, if necessary, committing resources so that their capacity to advocate their point of view is enhanced.

Synthesis

The previous sections have been concerned with identifying and describing the constituent elements from which modern democratic citizenship is constructed. We are now in a position to draw the strands together, to move from analysis to synthesis. In Figure 13.1 the four models of citizenship have been arrayed in schematic form, located along two key dimensions; these relate to whether the particular model rests primarily upon individualistic or communitarian assumptions about the nature of wo/man and society (vertical axis), and according to whether the civic virtues are appropriately exercised within the sphere of civil society or within the public domain. In similar fashion, Figure 13.2 locates the four models of democracy along the dimension of 'individualism and communitarianism' (vertical) and the dimension of 'pluralism to unitary' (horizontal). It becomes clear that there exists a kind of 'affinity' between the various dimensions of citizenship and democracy analysed in this chapter (see Figure 13.3). For example liberal-pragmatic democracy (rooted in individualism, yet founded on a belief in a unifying public interest and general will) has, historically, developed in parallel with the institutions of universal citizenship rights and the social security state (the entitled citizen). In similar vein, the policy thrusts of modern (new right) conservatism, outlined at the very beginning of this chapter draws sustenance from both the individualistic vision of the 'independent', privatised citizen and the 'ultra-minimalist' vision of liberal democracy.

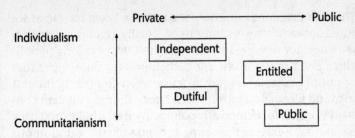

Figure 13.1: Dimensions of Citizenship

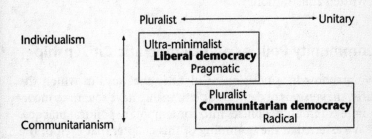

Figure 13.2: Processes of Democracy

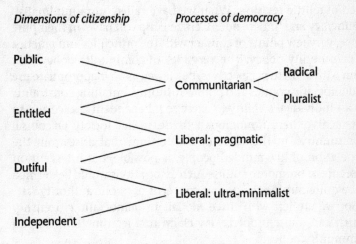

Figure 13.3: Democratic Citizenship

These connections must not, of course, be taken too far; as we pointed out earlier the institutions of actually existing citizenship and democracy develop in piecemeal fashion, over long periods of time, and display all the contradictions and ambiguities that arise out of historical compromises between competing interest groups and ideological movements. Thus, while the modern conservative project for democratic politics involves a bid to 'roll back the state' and extend the scope for individuals' autonomous choice within the free market, there exists a continuing, historically rooted suspicion of enshrining liberties and rights within a written constitution.

Community Policies and Democratic Citizenship

We are now in a position to identify the ways in which the different versions of democratic citizenship have sought to incorporate community policies into contemporary political practice.

We asserted at the beginning of this chapter that each of the models of citizenship and democracy identified can 'do business' with community policy, as it is understood in this book. It is now clear that this was a somewhat sweeping generalisation and is in need of a little revision. What we have called 'ultra-minimalist' democracy and 'independent' citizenship will have, in their pure sense, very few points of contact with the principles and practice of community policy. The very idea of community policy will, from within these perspectives, be viewed as an inappropriate use of democratic politics and public authority, entailing constraints on an individual's ability to exercise independent choice and to pursue his or her autonomous activities in civil society. Of course, 'community', in the sense of the feelings that arise from the association of like-minded people, is possible, but intervention to secure or promote or utilise such associations would be deemed to be quite outside the proper concerns of public authority.

So, we are left with three models of democratic citizenship which can, quite properly, lay claim to a legitimate interest in community policy.

It is to these claims that we now turn, identifying how, within each dimension, community policy is seen to offer a solution to pressing policy problems.

The Dutiful Citizen: Enhanced Opportunities for Community Service, Mutual Aid, and Voluntary Action

Interest in community policy (in terms of the idea of the 'dutiful' citizen) derives from two divergent analyses concerning the malaise of modern society. From the Conservative right, the 'problem' is that democratic citizenship has been progressively undermined and weakened during the course of the twentieth century as nannying bureaucracy, state welfareism and misplaced attempts at large-scale social engineering have undermined the impulse to altruistic civic action.

A return to 'Victorian' ideals of active citizenship has been canvassed. Douglas Hurd has argued that:

> We have to find, as the Victorians found, techniques and instruments which reach parts of our society which will always be beyond the scope of statutory schemes. I believe that the inspiring and enlisting of the active citizen in all walks of life is the key. (Hurd, quoted in Carvel, 1988)

In the same speech Hurd went on to talk positively about the role of housing associations, tenants' co-operatives and neighbourhood watch schemes as alternatives to state bureaucracies, alternatives which resonate with one-nation Conservative ideals and traditions of voluntary service, civic obligation and the diffusion of power in society.

From the democratic left the diagnosis is rather different; it is the widespread permeation of commercial values along with the celebration of possessive individualism in society at large that has undermined the civic virtues of co-operation, solidarity and fraternity – virtues that are deemed both to underpin and to draw strength from a caring social order founded on principles of fairness and social justice.

Earlier chapters in this book have identified a variety of community initiatives and policies predicated on a belief in people's commitment to voluntary service, mutual aid, and co-operative working practices. Community service schemes and community care, neighbourhood watch and community co-operatives may still not be 'mainstream' but they nevertheless offer signposts to forms of social organisation which emphasise values very different from those that sustain conventional commercial and bureaucratic modes of social organisation.

The Entitled Citizen – Promoting Social Justice through Community Approaches to Service Delivery

As noted, the social organisations (as well as the justifying ideas) of welfare statism are the subject of sustained criticism – for over-centralised decision making, paternalistic professionalism, and ineffective and wasteful bureaucracy. Defences can, and are, mounted against all of these charges and yet, as noted in Part One of the book, numbers of social and cultural changes have conspired to weaken the credibility of the organisational and service delivery assumptions of the Beveridge-inspired model of welfare stateism.

At the same time there also exists significant evidence of continuing public support for the idea of collectively organising to share risks and promote the common good, as well as support for the ideas of social rights and entitlements as important con-stitutive elements of modern citizenship (Rentoul, 1990).

It is through the attempt to resolve the apparent contradictions between these two aspirations – to maintain universal rights to welfare while avoiding the worst features of bureaucratic and paternalistic welfare organisation – that community initiatives and policies have assumed some importance. Their significance must not be overstated. Nevertheless, the overview of practice fields in Part Two of this book provides ample evidence of initiatives – in youth work, social care, arts provision, police work and economic development – directed to maintaining (and, at times, extending) citizen entitlements while at the same time developing anti-bureaucratic delivery systems that embrace the user as 'partner' (rather than client), and that can respond flexibly to local cir-cumstances, needs and aspirations, while also enjoying the capacity for innovation and self-renewal.

It is, then, no accident that writers like Donnison (1989) and Willmott (1989) can write of the proliferation of initiative and policies that embrace elements of the 'community practice approach to service delivery' (Butcher, 1986). Such initiatives represent positive attempts to keep faith with the ideal of the 'entitled citizen' while rethinking and modernising the institu-tional framework through which such ideals may be realised.

The Participative Citizen – from Involvement, via Empowerment, to Democratic Control

Throughout this book we have highlighted the idea of participatory democracy as integral to the concept of community policy.

Many of the examples explored underline the value of involving the citizen in exercising some influence, better still democratic control, over the initiative, project or service with which they are involved. It is seen as a legitimate right of the individual and as a significant contribution to effective decision making, to have tenants play their part in estate management, employees to become involved in workplace democracy, and service users to be heard in the policy forums of the agencies which serve them.

In Chapter 1 and then more fully in Chapter 10 the theme of neighbourhood and community democracy was explored. The fully 'participative' citizen required, it was argued, deeper and more extensive opportunities for playing a part in decision making and decision taking in matters that contribute to the conditions of their lives; a view that stems from a critique of existing democratic institutions as narrowly focused on the governmental, restricted to intermittent 'ballot-box' involvement, and inherently alienating (in that the citizen typically discharges democratic rights through his or her representative).

Conclusions – Democratic Citizenship and Community Policy

It is illuminating, we have argued, to see the development of community policy as an attempted solution to difficult problems confronting those wishing to make a reality of democratic citizenship in modern society. The argument has been multifaceted, partly because citizenship and democracy are themselves multidimensional and contested concepts, but also because in translating them into practice 'actually existing' democratic citizenship will be the outcome of complex, and at times contradictory, historical forces.

Community policy, we have suggested, is given a distinctive interpretation within each dimension of democratic citizenship and we have acknowledged that because these different interpretations exist side by side, tensions and ambiguities arise which are apt to tax those seeking clarity of purpose in day-to-day practice.

Throughout this discussion we have put questions of citizenship and democracy centre stage; we can conclude by reviewing matters the other way round, by making community policy itself the focus of attention. Figure 13.4 charts, in summary form, the three major and interconnected contributions that community policy makes to the realisation of democratic citizenship in modern society.

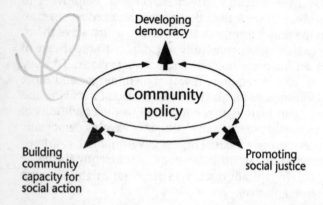

Figure 13.4: Community Policy – Contributions to Democratic Citizenship

'Thick Democracy'

First, by promoting democratic participation within decision-making processes, community policy helps to build the 'democratic dynamic' within society as a whole. Earlier chapters suggested that economic democracy is strengthened through the development of community enterprise, that community youth work can help young people to play an enlarged role in determining the shape of youth provision, that community groups and organisations can be assisted in exercising greater influence over the operations of influential agencies like local government departments and the police service. Strengthening democracy is not easy; it means inventing, and then putting into place, the institutional structures and processes through which ordinary citizens can gain a voice and exercise influence. It also entails, as Habeebullah and Slater argue in Chapter 9, significant changes in political culture. Earlier chapters suggest that here, too, community policy and practice have a vital role to play. Community development and community action, discussed in Chapter 2, through promoting and resourcing robust and effective grassroots community groups and voluntary organisations, ensure both that the channels for articulating and expressing interests and views are opened up, and that the art of democratic participation is 'learnt' experientially, as it were, in local and familiar surroundings.

Community policy and practice involve, then, to borrow Barber's (1984) terminology, a commitment to augmenting 'thin' representative democracy with 'thick' participative democracy – to building a society in which democratic principles permeate decision taking far beyond the established centres of parliament and city hall.

Promoting Social Justice

Contemporary discussions about citizenship have been overwhelmingly conducted within a framework of liberal–individualistic assumptions: they have been concerned with arguing the relative merits of what we have called the 'entitlement' and 'independent' strands of citizenship. Within both positions the individual is put centre stage – as a bearer of rights, or as an independent, self-actualising actor. Only rarely in such debates is the defining characteristic of citizenship viewed as the *relationship* between the individual (as citizen) and the wider political community. To de-centre the individual in this way (as in the notion of the 'public citizen' and the 'dutiful citizen') has far-reaching implications for how we regard community policy. There are examples in this book that presuppose just such a relationship. Lynn, in Chapter 7, stresses how community enterprise explicitly recognises and addresses community interests, interests that transcend the immediate concerns of employees, owners, and other individual 'stakeholders'. Again, Chapter 6 shows that community arts practice usually embraces objectives that go beyond the private edification of the artists and audiences directly involved in the creative act. We conclude that while 'community' policy can be (and often is) harnessed to a variety of political positions, such policy seems to achieve the best fit with, and be able to make the most effective contribution to, 'public' and 'dutiful' notions of citizenship.

Building Community Capacity

Finally, what of the proposition that 'developing community capacity' is the third key concern of community policy? In one sense, of course, developing community is almost by definition a central underpinning assumption of community policy. If, as we have argued, particular dimensions of citizenship are implied, rather more than others, in the theory and practice of community policy, then the enhancement of 'community' becomes a vital prerequisite. This is so at a number of levels: social-structural, organisational, and philosophical.

In *social-structural* terms, if 'attachment' community (as defined in Chapter 1) is to provide the foundation for collective action – whether based on territory, or on some other social base like common culture, or interest, or identity – then it has to be resourced and sustained. This was illustrated in the chapter on community care where it was shown that the community sector has much to contribute to realising a policy for social care, but only if underpinned by the resources of a community development worker.

Secondly, it implies that *agencies* committed to developing and delivering community policies must modify their organisational practice. Community policy requires new ways of relating to communities served (which will involve organisational change and possibly also changes in day-to-day practice, professional attitudes, budgetary priorities, and decision-making methods). Chapters in Part Two again provide illustrations. Community policing, for example, if it is to be more than merely cosmetic, entails modifications to the functions of patrol, reorganisation of aspects of command and control, and opportunities for the involvement of the community in new forms of open and consultative decision making about policy. Similar implications, for delivery and organisation, training and policy-making processes, hold for agencies moving to embrace a community approach to youth work, care work and local economic development.

Finally, the community approach involves a paradigm shift in some of the underlying assumptions of those concerned with designing and implementing public policies. 'Public citizenship', 'participatory democracy' and enhanced 'community capacity' are rooted in *philosophical* assumptions that offer a challenge to much conventional thinking. In Chapter 1 we noted that the values and beliefs of communitarianism provide the moral and philosophical underpinning for community policy. While progress towards implementing community policy and practice in a range of fields has been illustrated, the full benefits of the models of citizenship, democracy and community put forward in this chapter will be fully realised only with and through a fundamental change in our philosophical assumptions about wo/man, society and politics.

The three 'spokes' of the community policy 'wheel' can exist in their own right; acting together they can achieve more than the sum of their respective parts. Community policy, we argue, although only one weapon in the policy armoury available for achieving social change, is, nevertheless, a significant one. It offers members of modern society new opportunities to act together as a community in order to play a full part in realising the rights and duties of modern citizenship, while at the same time performing an enhanced role in democratically determining the future direction of social development and change. As such, the picture of democratic citizenship presented here represents a significantly richer and more coherent vision than the somewhat limited and attenuated reality overviewed at the very beginning of this chapter.

Part 4 Conclusions

In this final part we conclude our reflections on the interrelationships between community and public policy. First of all we seek to capture the key concepts of community policy and outline the case for it to become more central to the policy formulation processes of central and local government. We draw attention to some central themes which emerge from the previous chapters and which appear to us to be significant. We do this by identifying key findings, based mainly on the community practice examples in Part Two, and the central conceptual frameworks which derive principally from Parts One and Three. We then consider possible trends and developments in community policies.

14 Findings, Frameworks and Futures

Paul Henderson

Introduction

There is a paradox concerning the quality of life of the individuals, communities and networks about whom we write. On the one hand, commentators draw attention to the impoverishment and nascent violence of many urban areas, and this kind of portrayal is sometimes supported by the views of local people. On the other hand, it is upon the resilience and energy of people that community policies and practice depend. It is people in communities who take the risks and have the imagination to pursue projects which often cut across the professional and administrative barriers which constrain agencies and bureaucracies. David Donnison recognises the extent to which it has been the 'transforming experience' of these projects which has been important for community leaders:

> They have learnt capacities for leadership, gained the confidence to deal decisively with politicians, officials and professionals of all sorts, and demolished the myth of credentialism – the idea that you cannot do anything until you are labelled as officially qualified for the job. (Donnison, 1990b, p. 110)

A crucial lesson to be learnt from the struggles of urban and rural communities to survive and progress is that they cannot do this on their own. Nor must it be assumed that they should always be the target group of interventions. It is the connection *between* public policies and communities which is the critical factor. There has to be more than a bridge between community and public policy – the two have to be brought together in a fully

241

integrated partnership. We have tried to be precise about what such a partnership entails, have offered an account of the growing pressure to adopt such an approach, and distinguished the methods deployed by those seeking to realise this new policy framework. To summarise, community policy involves:

1. relating to 'communities of attachment' – in a social as well as a psychological sense
2. the realisation of community values of solidarity, participation and coherence
3. embracing 'active' community – non-paternalistic and participative ways of working with people
4. commitment to working with oppressed and disadvantaged people as a priority.

The analysis of community policy and practice by Hugh Butcher in Chapter 4 suggests that the explanation for the growth of community policies over the last 25 years can be made at three levels. These move from relatively superficial to progressively deeper levels:

Level 1   Community policies are adopted which offer a useful, pragmatic response to urgent problems facing the hard-pressed policy maker.
Level 2   Community policies tend to have been used as partial 'solutions' to different types of state crises that have confronted British governments.
Level 3   Community policies and practice can be interpreted as the outcome of a movement from 'Fordist'/modernist to 'post-Fordist'/post-modernist forms of society and social organisation.

In her chapter, Helen Meekosha similarly provides a number of examples to show how the state has responded to different crises:

*   the management of diversity through regulation
*   social justice programmes
*   creation of 'Units'
*   equal opportunities legislation
*   community strategies.

One effect of these initiatives, she argues, has been to empower elites within disadvantaged groups.

At the same time as community policies have been used to respond to a variety of social changes, the idea of 'community' in public policy has become more important. This, Jerry Smith suggests in Chapter 3, is because of growing awareness of the decline of 'natural' and self-organised communities. In a sense, policy makers have turned to community practice in order to fill a gap. There has been an awareness of the need to reconstruct 'community' on a top-down basis.

Finally in terms of methods, the community practice that we have described as emanating from community policies usually has the following characteristics:

- the sustained involvement of paid community workers and/or a range of professionals working with communities
- encouragement of self-managed community groups
- the restructuring of services, notably in terms of access by the public, and community involvement.

In Chapter 2 Andrew Glen shows how programmes and action resulting from community practice can broadly be placed in three categories: community development, community action and community services approaches. These can be seen as distinctive methodologies which guide the community practitioner. It is important to note the extent to which community participation is emphasised in all three categories.

As our arguments about community policies and practice have unfolded we have been aware of differing degrees of conviction or prescription. Some of the ideas rest on solid experiences, others do not, and the varying levels and kinds of analysis assume different emphasis in the four parts of the book. The remainder of this concluding chapter reflects this variation in that the discussion of futures is more speculative than that of the book's findings and frameworks.

1. Findings

What does community policy offer to the solutions of policy problems? What are the distinctive strengths of community policy in addressing service, governance, resource, economic and public order issues?

The following findings about community policy emerge from the preceding chapters.

Community policy encourages the capacity to develop, maintain and draw upon the particular strengths of 'active' communities.

Community policy works *across* a range of policy areas and, because its values and core principles are community based, it can make connections *between* policy areas. It can reduce the fragmentation which often exists between different agencies. An example is when a neighbourhood experiences high crime levels, yet major agencies – police, housing, economic development, social services – often fail to work together effectively.

Partnership approaches between communities and agencies are promoted by community policy. In reducing 'them and us' attitudes (from both sides), agencies become more approachable and user-friendly, and the creativity and energy of local networks are used to maximum advantage. Instances where this has occurred – such as some of those described in Part Two – give a hint of the real potential waiting to be harnessed through this approach.

Community policy speaks to the uniqueness of every community. Working on a partnership basis requires flexibility by all concerned. It puts a premium on delivering what it is that specific communities need at particular times. While this presents a major challenge to large, bureaucratically organised agencies, we have highlighted examples where specially designed services have been delivered to communities because of the particular circumstances and experiences they face. Community policy offers a framework for extending such practice.

Support for self-help and mutual aid groups, alliances, coalitions and the development of community capacity is central to community policy. Community policy and practice can be conceived of as the essential link between the formulation of national policies and their impact on communities. It promotes social justice and can contribute powerfully to the struggles for equal opportunities. As demonstrated by Helen Meekosha in Chapter 11, community practice can promote both neighbourhood action and identity politics.

Community policy promotes the restructuring of services. In several of the chapters in Part Two we detect a certain pessimism concerning possibilities for community practice to become part of agencies' mainstream work. This is apparent, for example, in Liz McShane's discussion of community care and community development and in Jenny Lynn's examination of community enterprise. However the implication of community policy is that services require restructuring.

Community policy and practice provide support for self-managed community groups. Within discussions of community groups and social movements in Parts Two and Three, we detect more optimism. Lola Clinton and Andrew Glen's study of community arts certainly illustrates this, and a similar vein is apparent in Helen Meekosha's examples of identity politics. Spontaneity and the welcoming of diversity are important in this dimension of community practice.

There is recognition that some practitioners are better placed than others to implement community policies and employ community practice approaches. This general statement derives particularly from the chapter on community policing by Mollie Weatheritt. She shows that the police lack widespread contact with community activity and have limited expectations about improving the situation. On the other hand, economic development staff are shown to have the potential to develop a significant community practice role; so too, to a lesser extent, do social workers and youth workers.

Within the development of community policy and practice there is a trend from organisation building in communities to personal growth and development of activists. This important theme is discussed by both Jerry Smith and Helen Meekosha in their respective chapters. It is evident too in some of the other contributions, notably those on community arts and community care. In the latter context, support to vulnerable individuals and groups, given the sectarian divide in Northern Ireland, is seen to be crucial. The theme links also to Hugh Butcher's third level of explanation referred to above – the post-Fordian world into which we are entering. These various authors are suggesting implicitly that, in the context of the goals of community policy and practice, we are in a transitory phase.

Yet if community policy offers so much, why has it not taken a greater hold on policy making? What are the forces which prevent it moving from being peripheral to becoming part of mainstream policy deliberation and formulation? We identify the following blocks.

Conflicting Values

Underneath much of contemporary writing on public policy there runs the theme of ideological struggle. It surfaces in public debate or in the run-up to the enactment of government policy. The struggle is about different values concerning the governance of society. This is apparent from Hugh Butcher and Maurice Mullard's analysis of democracy, citizenship and community in Chapter 13. We would agree with those who argue that it is a debate which goes far deeper than a simple left–right divide.

The effect of this struggle over contested values requires virtually every policy debate to come to terms with competing visions and ideas. The picture is one of a complex web of ideas and positions, to the extent that it is difficult to obtain clarity through the plethora of concepts and rhetoric.

Mohammed Habeebullah and Dave Slater's analysis of 'community' in local government illustrates the point starkly: all three main political parties make use of the concept, linking it back to their manifestos. Not surprisingly, it is possible to see how community values are used in a variety of ways, reflecting differing political positions.

The presence of ideological struggle should lead to an approach to public policy which embraces complexity rather than to a simplistic, packaged approach. Such a rigorous approach has often been lacking from political debate in recent years. Debate has been partisan in a fixed and sterile way, with individuals, interest groups and political parties adopting fixed positions and apparently content merely to restate their messages. This reminds us that community policy is not something easily incorporated into existing ideological and political positions and institutional frameworks. It requires a radical policy and political rethink.

Conflicting values which have the effect of holding back the development of community practice are evident too among professional practitioners and within social movements. A clear example of the former is Sarah Banks's discussion of community youth work (Chapter 5). She identifies key components of a community practice approach to youth work: values of solidarity, participation and coherence would mean the active involvement of young people in planning activities; and collective empowerment would lead to a 'social action' rather than a service delivery model of youth work. Yet these objectives are in tension with current trends in the youth service with its emphasis on targeting, providing services to contract, and more specialisation.

Conflicting values are apparent also in Liz McShane's discussion of the innovatory community care programme in Northern Ireland. Is mobilisation of informal networks and community resources, when resources from the state are clearly inadequate, compelling people to tolerate the intolerable?

An example of conflicting values within social movements is given by Nigel Roome (Chapter 12) when he makes a point about environmental concern: how we behave and the views we express are not always consistent – 'where as commuters, we expect new and improved roads and, as residents, we object to road building programmes'.

Differing Uses of 'Community'

The analysis and examples provided in this book aim to contribute to the process of understanding the multifaceted ways in which 'community' is used and applied, and the genuine dilemmas of choice that this presents both to professionals and local people. Hugh Butcher, in Chapter 1, suggests three distinctive aspects of the way that 'community' is used:

> It involves understanding, and relating to, the beneficiaries or recipients of the policy as members of a community (territorial or interest); it implies that the policy will embrace one or more distinctive community values (solidarity, participation, coherence); and it requires that policy implementation involves working in partnership with groups and organisations active at the community level.

It is inevitable, given the contrasting organisational contexts in which 'community' is used, that it will be given different meanings. We should not expect programmes, projects and services to meet the whole of the above definition. The crucial point is that the way in which the term is used should be made clear.

Several of the contributors demonstrate the varied use of 'community' in public policy. For example, in both Sarah Banks's and Mollie Weatheritt's chapters we can trace its links with social control policies, whereas in Lola Clinton and Andrew Glen's chapter we see how it has been a cornerstone of liberal community arts policies. In the community enterprise field Jenny Lynn charts its positive development but she also gives warning of the dangers inherent in overexposure of the concept, pointing to evidence of 'growing scepticism about what are perceived as alien regeneration initiatives offering little in the way of permanent solutions to poverty, unemployment or rising crime'. Liz McShane's chapter on community care demonstrates the degree to which local people and their organisations have been left on the sidelines in plans for care in the community.

Critics might argue that there is an accumulation of evidence that the term 'community', in addition to being exposed to contrasting uses, has been used inconsistently by policy makers. The book's contributions provide examples to show how, more often than not, there have been good reasons for this although on occasions it has been a matter of muddling through, of catching hold of an accessible portmanteau term and using it to buttress mainline public policies.

Lack of Coherence

The need for policy makers to draw together the different strands of community policy into a more coherent whole is very evident from the contributions. The functional divisions of public policies promote incoherence; community policy can overcome it.

The reasons for, and degree to which, community policies have permeated mainstream service provision are explored by Hugh Butcher in Chapter 4. It is noticeable how many of the examples and projects discussed in Part Two have taken place on the edges of mainstream provision. For example, local authorities committed to 'going local' policies remain in the minority, and the community-based community care schemes described by Liz McShane are all in the voluntary sector. In her chapter Jenny Lynn states that community enterprise is only now beginning to be incorporated into mainstream economic regeneration programmes after 20 years of being on the margins. A strategic approach to community policy and practice needs to ensure that questions of policy and organisational change are addressed; it must not be assumed that the focus is always on service delivery and community participation at a local level.

A similar case for coherence can be made from analysis of a series of small-scale local research studies undertaken by the editors during the preparation of this book. One of these was a survey of paid community practitioners in Bradford which was undertaken with the intention of 'mapping' the diversity of community practice in the area (see Glen, 1993). A total of 246 practitioners was identified, nearly half of whom were employed in the local voluntary sector. Most of the rest were employed either by the local authority or by national voluntary organisations. Between them they covered 14 policy areas. The types of community practice ranged from self-help and cultural activities to campaigning and advocacy, developing services and resources, training and research/information. While it is not possible to draw general conclusions from only one study area, the data obtained from the Bradford survey does reveal a surprising breadth and variety of community practice under a number of auspices. At the same time, the very diversity of the practice demonstrated by this particular survey raises the question of coherence: to what extent are the different sets of practitioners working on similar assumptions, and how much common thinking and co-ordination on the concept of community practice exists between the various employing bodies?

The other small-scale empirical studies included a review of the community policies of public agencies in West Yorkshire, and a survey of nationally advertised posts in community practice. Both of these indicate interesting trends: more extensive recruitment of community practitioners by statutory agencies and across a range of policy fields; positive advances in the employment of black community practitioners; and a more extensive range of support networks than had been anticipated. The findings suggest a continued commitment to employing community practitioners as a vehicle for the implementation of community policies, although further studies elsewhere will be needed to confirm this.

2. Frameworks

We hesitate to use the word 'crisis' to convey a broad-brush description of the condition of British society in the mid 1990s. It may suggest a too limited analysis, and imply that measures can be taken to avert it relatively easily. Yet the message throughout this book indicates quite the opposite: if there is a crisis it is both profound and complex, and is present in both the institutional and community contexts. Crisis can induce a state of paralysis, and in that sense it can be a barrier to understanding. However, it can also be a stimulus to debate, forcing an array of interest groups to listen to each other and to be willing to change.

Several chapters in the book reveal the extent to which the state has changed its policies significantly in response to circumstances and pressure, whether these arise from the international economic system, inner-city riots or the ideology of the ruling political party. *Local authorities* have, more often than not, been pawns in this wider struggle. Particularly since the early 1980s they have been forced to cut expenditure and turn towards a new 'enabling' role. As a result their confidence to pursue consistent, long-term policies has been eroded. The *private sector,* having been promised a new dawn of successful enterprise, has had the ground cut from under it by the long-running and deep recession of the early

1990s. Finally, growing numbers of *communities* have experienced worsening social and economic conditions. It is on 'labelled' council estates and in particular inner areas of Britain's cities that the contrast with the relative affluence of the rest of society is most stark. It is in such neighbourhoods that community policies and practice must prove their effectiveness; it is right that they should be underpinned by a bias towards the poor.

This book will have failed if its conclusions are seen as no more than pragmatically helpful guidelines for hard-pressed policy makers concerned to include the community dimension in their programmes. What we seek to do is to locate the strengths and advantages of community policy and practice in a framework containing fundamental social principles of democracy, equality, citizenship, ecological integrity and justice. Indeed, we wish to go further, and argue that community policy constitutes an essential contribution to reorganising the way in which citizens and policy makers alike seek to realise these principles and values. We consider that at the end of the twentieth century, societies need deeper and broader forms of democracy, new ways of ensuring that entitlements are taken up, better ways of promoting active citizenship through enhancing community capacity, and innovative ways of progressing equality. Community policy offers so much precisely because it draws from values which exist on a partial basis already but which will be fundamental to society in the twenty-first century.

Implicit in several of the contributions we see the search for alternative approaches for addressing key issues to those offered at present by most mainstream public and private agencies. On this basis, community policy can address major and controversial issues: alienation and poverty, inequality, individualism and failures of statism.

Community policy and practice hold the key to unlocking the route to a more optimistic future because of their reaffirmation of essential values and their encouragement of alternative ways of analysing and solving social problems. That is why analytical frameworks developed by the contributors are of direct relevance. The chapters in Part Three in particular help to refine community policies in relation to the central themes of citizenship, community and personal identity, and environmental globalism. It is vital for citizenship to be claimed back from the individualistic and consumerist meaning it has been given in recent years. The three dimensions of citizenship as discussed by Hugh Butcher and

Maurice Mullard are fundamental to collectivist democractic processes and therefore to community policy:

- promoting social justice
- building community capacity for social action
- developing democracy.

3. Futures

How do we envisage the development of community policy and practice over the next ten years? What kinds of development might indicate that society is moving in the direction of the new paradigm which we advocate? Inevitably the following ideas are speculative. They may, however, provide enough of a 'futures scenario' to give readers some pointers to ways forward.

1. A key question is how the state will handle the uncertainties and crises caused by institutional and policy changes. Will it continue with the minimalist stance articulated by recent governments, particularly in terms of urban policies? Or will the extent of disenchantment, frustration and anger of some communities force the state to adopt a more proactive strategy, in recognition of the vacuum its policies have created? Evidence of the need for new directions accumulates on two fronts: the increasing impoverishment of many urban areas, and the inability of new, enterprise-based agencies to provide a meaningful and sufficient response. Significant private-sector funding of community practice is unlikely to be achieved; there appears to be a trend for private-sector involvement to concentrate increasingly on sponsorship and community award schemes. The implication is that if partnerships between the different sectors are to be effective at community level, then state support will need to increase rather than decrease.

High levels of unemployment, poverty, and casualisation of the lower income end of the labour market will continue to exist for the foreseeable future. They will increasingly be subject to geographic concentration in small areas, although regional imbalances may become less marked. Schemes aimed at training and access to employment will focus on these areas, and the theme of 'community partnerships' between the statutory, voluntary and private sectors will remain dominant.

Our prognosis, therefore, is that government will return – willingly or not depending on the party in power – to critical policy issues, prompted largely by growing lawlessness and alienation and the continued trend towards a sizeable proportion of the population being excluded, because of unemployment and poverty, from mainstream society and hence having no reason to conform. The challenge this will present to community policy and practice can hardly be overstated.

2. We anticipate that at the same time as the state is forced to be more proactive it will be required to handle increasing tensions between nationalism, regionalism and internationalism. There will be renewed efforts to counteract tendencies towards fragmentation caused by religious, cultural and ethnic conflicts. And in addition to giving greater recognition to demands from Northern Ireland, Scotland and Wales, it will face demands from regions in England for devolved forms of government.

3. The extent to which the future of communities and regions is shaped by worldwide factors will become increasingly apparent. This is likely to be most evident in the environmental field, but the effects of civil wars and oppressive regimes in different parts of the world, with a consequent growth in the number of refugees, will also impact directly on communities.

4. At the same time, grassroot pressure for more enhanced democratic involvement will grow. Less deferential communities will help to ensure that the issue of democracy is not dominated by politicians and commentators.

5. The so-called enabling role of local authorities is likely to increase in importance. There is an irony in the use of the term enabling in the local government context, for the skills and methods of enabling lie at the heart of the community practice tradition. The more alert local authorities will begin to see the opportunity that is contained in the role and will make effective use of it, thereby perhaps regaining some of the influence and status that Conservative governments have sought to take away.

6. There will be a growth in contract work by community practitioners, in the sense that their support for community organisations will be based on time-limited if renewable agreements with those most involved. The role of specialist consultants and trainers, working alongside practitioners, in providing short-term inputs will grow in importance.

7. The contract culture will continue to impact more on the funding of community practice in the voluntary sector. Projects

will need to gather funding from a number of sources, with a large proportion of income dependent on fulfilling contracts with a range of agencies – local authorities, other public bodies and non-governmental organisations. Alongside this will go an increased stress on performance indicators and evaluation.

8. One can anticipate that training for community practice will be drawn into accreditation of voluntary and paid activity linked to non-vocational qualifications. At the same time, the principles and skills of community practice will be offered either as an integral part of professional training courses or as a course in its own right. Some employers, especially those in the economic development and housing sectors, will gradually become interested in acquiring staff who have the non-prescriptive skills – listening and empowerment – referred to by Nigel Roome.

The Wider Context

A future scenario for community policy and practice does not imply limited horizons. On the contrary, many of those involved at community level, professionals and local people, would reject any charges of parochialism. They are aware of the need to understand local issues and problems in the global context, and to forge links with like-minded people in other countries – the crossing of political and mental borders referred to by Helen Meekosha. They are committed to the politics of location, not of localism. They recognise the potential for choice, independence and mutual aid within and by communities. Solidarity is paramount.

We are aware of exciting links being made within Europe on the issue of poverty between practitioners and community groups. Global networking by non-governmental organisations and community groups on environmental questions is further evidence of the development of an internationalist perspective.

Citizenship has to go beyond relationships between people and systems, it has to be concerned with the question of who takes responsibility for control or management of the world's resources. As Nigel Roome shows in his chapter, the debate about the future of the planet is highly complex because the concerns 'embrace economic, political and cultural perspectives as well as involving scientific and social scientific explanations'. Yet it is precisely the complexities and difficulties of working with the total picture with which community policy and practice will have to engage.

The scenario of a world in which there will be an increasing awareness of limits to growth has far-reaching implications. These go far beyond encouraging people to change their individual lifestyles because limits to growth, when taken seriously, question how people survive together in a wide variety of communities. It is critical that, in addition to trying to understand the wider context, we search for the links with community policy and practice. The two are bound together. Local communities have the right to be in charge of their resources, and to help build a meaningful society.

In a similar vein, we re-emphasise that community policy has to form part of a wider debate on the principles and values under which citizens are governed. In other words, community policy will be nothing if it is perceived simply to be the preserve of a handful of individuals and organisations interested in how services are delivered and what the 'rules' should be that guide citizen participation. Community policy must be in the vanguard of the movement which challenges paternalistic or autocratic government, and which is prepared to identify the ideas which cross-cut conventional divides between left and right politics.

It is here that questions concerning the intersections of race, class and gender conflicts may lead to the formation of new coalitions united on principles of social justice and anti-oppressive practice. Community policy and practice is not just about making connections between national policies and local communities; it is also about campaigning by communities of identity which, at appropriate moments, become integral to the processes of political debate and social change.

We see the wider context, then, as a radically changed 'social landscape', one in which the credibility of the two existing orthodoxies – social democracy in a 'statist' mould and new right market individualism – has been seriously undermined. As a result the scope for a vision of society in which community policy and practice constitute key ingredients is considerable. We are aware, when making this statement, that it aspires to fundamental, long-term change. It may also appear to underestimate the power of the opposing forces to which many of the contributors allude.

A future scenario which does not contain community policies and practice will be flawed. This is because at root the option of continuing a society which is severely divided between the two-thirds affluent and one-third poor is ultimately unsustainable. Modern communication methods, and the interdependence of groups and interests in society, mean that it will become impossible for the state, local authorities, the private sector and others to ignore or marginalise communities. The challenge to community policy and practice, and the accompanying principles and methods, are very clear.

Bibliography

Abrams, P. and Brown, R. (1984) *UK Society: Work, Urbanisation and Inequality* London: Weidenfeld & Nicolson.

Adams, M. (1989) 'There is No Place Like Home: On the Place of Identity in Feminist Politics' *Feminist Review*, no. 31, spring.

Albemarle Report (1960) *The Youth Service in England and Wales* London: HMSO.

Albrecht, L. and Brewer, R. (1990) *Bridges of Power – Women's Multicultural Alliances* Philadelphia: New Society.

Alcoff, L. (1988) 'Cultural Feminism Versus Post-Structuralism: the Identity Crisis in Feminist Theory' *Signs*,13, 3.

Alderson, J. (1979) *Policing Freedom* Plymouth: Macdonald and Evans.

Alinsky, S. (1969) *Reveille for Radicals* New York: Random House.

Allison, L. (1986) 'Spirit of the Eighties' *New Society*, 25 April, p. 24.

Anarchy (1963) *Direct Action for Houses: The Story of the Squatters Anarchy*, January, pp. 9–15.

Anthias and Yuval-Davis (1992) *Racialized Boundaries: Race, Nation, Gender, Colour and Class and the Anti-racist Struggle* London: Routledge.

Ardill, S. and O'Sullivan, S. (1989) 'Sex in the Summer of '88' *Feminist Review*, 31, pp. 126–34.

Arendt, H. (1959) *The Human Condition* New York: Anchor.

Arts Council of Great Britain (ACGB) (1974) *Community Arts – the Report of the Community Arts Working Party* (Baldry Report) London: ACGB.

Arts Council of Great Britain (1984) *The Glory of the Garden: Strategy for a Decade* London: ACGB.

Arts Council of Great Britain (1989) *Urban Renaissance* London: ACGB.

Arts Council of Great Britain (1993) *A Creative Future: the way Forward for the Arts, Crafts and Media in England* London: HMSO.

Ascher, K. (1987) *The Politics of Privatisation* Basingstoke: Macmillan.

Association of British Credit Unions (1993) *Guide to Credit Unions, and Credit Union Training Pack* London: Association of British Credit Unions.

Association of Chief Police Officers (1990) *Strategic Policy Document. Setting the Standards for Policing: Meeting Community Expectations* London: ACPO.

Association of Metropolitan Authorities (AMA) (1989) *Community Development – the Local Authority Role* London: AMA.

Attenborough, R. (1985) *Arts and Disabled People* London: Bedford Square Press.

Aucoin, P. (1990) 'Administrative Reform in Public Management: Paradigms, Principles, Paradoxes and Pendulums' *Governance*, vol. 3, no. 2, pp. 115–37.

Audit Commission (1991) *Local Authorities, Entertainment and the Arts* London: HMSO.

Australia, Commonwealth of (1991a) *Towards a Fairer Australia, Social Justice under Labor* Canberra: Australian Government Publishing Service.

Australia, Commonwealth of (1991b) *Report of the Royal Commission into Aboriginal Deaths in Custody* Canberra: Australian Government Publishing Service.

Australia, Department of Finance and Department of Prime Minister and Cabinet (1989) *Towards a Fairer Australia, Social Justice and Program Management: A Guide* Canberra: Australian Government Publishing Service.

Baker, J. (1977) 'Applying Community Development Principles to Youth Work' *Community Development Journal*, vol. 12, no. 3, pp. 212–18.

Baldock, P. (1977) 'An Historical Review of Community Work, 1968–78' *Community Development Journal*, vol. 14, no. 3.

Baldock, P. (1981) 'Why Community Action? The Historical Origins of the Radical New Trend in British Community Work' in Henderson, P. and Thomas, D. (eds) *Readings in Community Work* London: Allen and Unwin.

Banks, S. (1990) 'Doubts, Dilemmas and Duties: Ethics and the Social Worker' in Carter, P. et al (eds) *Social Work and Social Welfare Yearbook* Milton Keynes: Open University Press.

Banks, S. and Noonan, F. (1990) *The Poll Tax and Community Work* London: ACW Talking Point no. 117.

Barber, B. (1984) *Strong Democracy* Berkeley: University of California Press.

Barr, A. (1987) 'Inside Practice – Researching Community Workers in Scotland' *Community Development Journal*, vol. 22, no. 1.

Barr, A. (1991) *Practising Community Development* London: Community Development Foundation:

Barrigan, S. and Manktelow, A. (1985) *Street Wise: Meadow Well Detached Project* Annual Report published by Meadow Well Detached Project, North Shields.

Batten, T. R. (1965) *The Human Factor in Community Work* Oxford: OUP.

Batten, T. R. (1967) *The Non-directive Approach in Group and Community Work* Oxford: OUP.

Bayley, J. E, Parnell, E. and Colley, N. (1991) *Yearbook of Co-operative Enterprise 1992* Oxford: Plunkett Foundation.

Beardon, S. (1993) *The Contract Culture: A View from West Yorkshire* Leeds: VA-L.

Bell, H. and Newby, C. (1971) *Community Studies* London: George Allen and Unwin.

Bennett, R. J. and Krebs, G. (1990) *Towards a Partnership Model of Local Economic Development Initiatives in Britain and Germany* London: Anglo German Foundation.

Bennett, T. and Lupton, R. (1992a) 'A National Activity Survey of Police Work' *Howard Journal*, 31, 3.

Bennett, T. and Lupton, R. (1992b) 'A Survey of the Allocation and Use of Community Constables in England and Wales' *British Journal of Criminology*, 32, 2.

Benyon, J. and Solomos, J. (eds) *The Roots of Urban Unrest* Oxford: Pergamon.

Bernstein, R. (1986) *Philosophical Profiles* Cambridge: Polity Press.

Biddle, W. W. and Biddle, L. J. (1968) *Encouraging Citizen Involvement* Holt Reinhart & Winston.

Bishop, J. et al (1991) *Countryside Community Action: an Appraisal* Countryside Commission, CCP 307.

Black Environmental Network (1991) *Black Environmental Network Report* London: Black Environmental Network.

Blunkett, D. and Jackson, K. (1987) *Democracy in Crisis: The Town Halls Respond* London: Hogarth Press.

Boaden, N., Goldsmith, M., Hampton, W. and Stringer, P. (1982) *Public Participation in Local Services* Harlow: Longman.

Bonner, A. (1961) *The History, Principles and Organisations of the British Cooperative Movement* Manchester: Cooperative Union.

Bornat, J. et al (1993) *Community Care: a Reader* Basingstoke: Macmillan.

Bottoms, A. E. (1989) 'Crime Prevention. Facing the 1990s' *Policing and Society*, 1, 1.

Bowles, S. and Gintis, H. (1986) *Democracy and Capitalism* London: Routledge and Kegan Paul.

Bradley, C. (1986) *Community Involvement in Greening Projects* Bolton: Groundwork Foundation.

Briscoe, C. (1977) 'Community Work and Social Work in the United Kingdom' in Specht, H. and Vickery, A. (eds) *Integrating Social Work Methods* London: Allen and Unwin.

Broady, M. (1979) *Tomorrow's Community* London: Bedford Square Press.

Broady, M. and Hedley, R. (1989) *Working Partnerships: Community Development in Local Authorities* London: Bedford Square Press.

Broom, D. (1991) *Damned If We Do: Contradictions in Women's Health Care* Sydney: Allen and Unwin.

Brown, D. and Iles, S. (1985) *Community Constables: a Study of a Policing Initiative* London: Home Office, Research and Planning Unit Paper 30.

Brundtland, G. (1987) *Our Common Future: Report of the World Commission on Environment and Development* Oxford: Oxford University Press.

Bryant, R. (1981) 'Community Action' in Henderson, P. and Thomas, D. N. (eds) *Readings in Community Work* London: Allen and Unwin.

Bryson, L. and Mowbray, M. (1981) '"Community": The Spray-on Solution' *Australian Journal of Social Issues*, 16:4, pp. 255–67.

Buckingham, G. and Martin, M. (1989) *Community Development, Harassment and Racism* London: ACW Talking Point no. 103.

Bulmer, M. (1987) *The Social Basis of Community Care* London: Unwin Hyman.

Bulmer, M. et al (eds) (1989) *The Goals of Social Policy* London: Unwin Hyman.

Burrows, J. (1989) 'Achieving "Value for Money" from Police Expenditure: the Contribution of Research' in Weatheritt, M. (ed.) *Police Research: Some Future Prospects* Aldershot: Avebury.

Butcher, H. et al (1980) *Community Groups in Action: Case Studies and Analysis* London: RKP.

Butcher, H. (1986) 'The Community Practice Approach to Local Public Service Provision' *Community Development Journal* 21, 2.

Butcher, H., Law, I. G., Leach, R. and Mullard, M. (1990) *Local Government and Thatcherism* London: Routledge.

Cain, H. and Yuval Davis, N. (1990) 'The Equal Opportunities Community and the Anti-racist Struggle' *Critical Social Policy*, 29, 10, 2, pp. 5–26.

Caldecott, L. and Leland, S. (1983) *Reclaim the Earth* London: The Women's Press.

Calouste Gulbenkian Foundation (1973) *Current Issues in Community Work* London: RKP.

Campbell, B. and Jacques, M. (1986) 'Goodbye to the GLC' *Marxism Today*, vol. 30, no. 4.

Caraway, N. (1991) 'The Challenge and Theory of Feminist Identity Politics: Working on Racism' *Frontiers: A Journal of Women's Studies*, XII, 2, pp. 109–29.

Carley, M. (1990) *Housing and Neighbourhood Renewal: Britain's New Urban Challenge* London: Policy Studies Institute.

Carson, R. (1962) *Silent Spring* Houghton Mifflin.

Carvel, J. (1988) 'Restrain Greed, Tories Urged by Hurd' Manchester: The *Guardian*, 6 February.

Central Council for Education and Training in Social Work (CCETSW) (1989) *Paper 30: Requirements and Regulations for the Diploma in Social Work* London: CCETSW.

Civic Trust (1989) *Regeneration: New Forms of Partnership* London: Civic Trust.

Clarke, R. V. G. and Mayhew, P. (1980) *Designing Out Crime* London: HMSO.

Clarke, M. and Huggins, D. (1982) 'The Scrap SUS Campaign' in Ohri, A. et al (eds) *Community Work and Racism* London: RKP.

Clarke, R. V. and Hough, M. (1984) *Crime and Police Effectiveness* London: HMSO, Home Office Research Study no. 79.

Cliffe, D. (1985) *Community Work in Leicester* University of Leicester.

Clinton, L. (1993) *Community Development and the Arts* London: Community Development Foundation.

Cochrane, A. (1991) 'The Changing State of Local Government: Restructuring for the 1990s' *Public Administration*, vol. 69, autumn, pp. 281–302.

Cockburn, C. (1977) *The Local State* London: Pluto.

Cockburn, C. (1991) *In the Way of Women – Men's Resistance to Sex Equality in Organisations* London: Macmillan.

Cohen, G. A. (1990) *Self Ownership, Communism and Equality*, proceedings of the Aristotelian Society supplementary vol. 64.

Colenutt, B. (1988) 'Local Democracy and Inner City Regenera-tion' *Local Economy*, vol. 3, no. 2, May.

Common Ground (1988) *The Parish Mapper* Common Ground.

Commoner, B. (1971) *The Closing Circle* London: Jonathan Cape.

Community and Youth Workers' Union (1992) *Youth Work and Community Work into the Twenty-First Century: Policy Statement* Birmingham: CYWU.

Community Development Foundation (CDF) (1992) *Mind the Gap: The Community in City Challenge*. London: CDF.

Community Development Foundation (CDF) (1992) *Arts and Communities: Report of the National Inquiry into Arts and the Community* London: CDF.

Community Projects Foundation (1986) *Leominster Marshes Project* Community Projects Foundation.

Connell, R. (1990) 'State, Gender and Sexual Politics' *Theory and Society*, 19:5, October, pp. 507–44.

Connolly, C. (1990a) 'Washing our Linen: One Year of Women Against Fundamentalism' *Feminist Review*, pp. 68–77.

Connolly, C. (1990b) 'Splintered Sisterhood: Anti-racism in a Young Women's Project' *Feminist Review*, 36, autumn, pp. 52–64.

Conway, E. (1992) 'Digging in to Disorder; Some Initial Reflec-tions on the Tyneside Riots' *Youth and Policy*, no. 37, pp. 4–14.

Cornforth, C., Thomas, A., Lewis, J. and Spear, R. (1988) *Developing Successful Worker Cooperatives* London: Sage Publications.

Costigan, S. (1991) 'The Teesdale Community Bus – Reaching Out in a Rural Area' *Youth and Policy*, 33, pp. 66–7.

Council for Education and Training in Youth and Community Work (CETYCW) (1989) *Guidelines for Endorsement* Leicester: CETYCW.

Countryside Commission (1982) *Countryside Issues and Action* Countryside Commission, CCP 15.

Craig, G. (1989) 'Community Work and the State' *Community Development Journal*, vol. 24, no. 1.

Craig, G. et al (1982) *Community Work and the State: Towards a Radical Practice* London: RKP.

Cross, C. (1977) 'Youth Clubs and Coloured Youths' *New Community*.

Curno, P. (ed) (1978) *Political Issues and Community Work* London: Routledge and Keegan Paul.

Dahrendorf, R. (1988) *The Modern Social Conflict* London: Weidenfeld and Nicolson.

Davidson, J. (1988) *Green is Your City* London: Bedford Square Press.

Davies, J. (1972) *The Evangelistic Bureaucrat* London: Tavistock.

Davis, M., Hiatt, S., Kennedy, M., Rudick, S. and Sprinker, M. (eds) (1990) *Fire in the Hearth: The Radical Politics of Place in America* London: Verso.

De Lauretis, T. (1986) *Feminist Studies/Critical Studies* London: Macmillan.

Department of the Environment (1988) *Creating Development Trusts: Good Practice Guide* London: HMSO.

Department of Health and Social Security NI (1990) *People First: Community Care in Northern Ireland* Belfast: HMSO.

Di Stefano, C. (1991) 'Who the Heck are We? Theoretical Turns Against Gender' *Frontiers: A Journal of Women's Studies*, XII, 2, pp. 86–108.

Dixon, G. et al (1982) 'Feminist Perspectives' in Craig, G. et al (eds) *Community Work and the State* London: RKP.

Dominelli, L. (1990) *Women and Community Action* Birmingham: Venture.

Donnison, D. (1988) 'Secrets of Success: What Makes Some Community Projects Work While Others Collapse?' *New Society*, 29 January.

Donnison, D. (1989) 'Social Policy: The Community-based Approach' in Bulmer, M. et al (eds) *The Goals of Social Policy* London: Unwin Hyman.

Donnison, D. (1990a) 'Social Policy: the Community Based Approach' in Bulmer, M. et al (eds) *Goals of Social Policy* London: Unwin Hyman.

Donnison, D. (1990b) *A Radical Agenda* London: Rivers Oram Press.

Dyen, M. (1989) 'Organize the Activists' *Social Policy*, spring, pp. 27–33.

Eisenstein, H. (1991) *Gender Shock – Practicing Feminism in Two Continents* Sydney: Allen and Unwin.

Eisenstein, H. and Jardine, A. (1980) (eds) *Future of Difference* New Brunswick: Rutgers University Press.

Ekblom, P. (1986) 'Community Policing: Obstacles and Issues' in Willmott, P. (ed.) *The Debate about Community: Papers from a Seminar on 'Community in Social Policy'* London: Policy Studies Institute.

Environment Council (1991) *Conference on the Environmental Challenge: Making the Solutions Work* London: RSA, October.

Eversley, D. (1974) 'Conservation for the Minority?' *Built Environment*, 3, 1, pp. 14–15.

Fabes, R. and Banks, S. (1991) 'Working with Young People in Rural Areas' *Youth and Policy*, no. 33, pp. 1–9.

Fabes, R. and Knowles, C. (1991) *Working with Young People in Rural Areas* Leicester: Youth and Community Section, Leicester Polytechnic Occasional Paper.

Fairbairn-Milson Report (1969) *Youth and Community Work in the Seventies: Proposals by the Youth Service Development Council* London: HMSO.

Federation of Community Work Training Groups (1990) *Annual Report* Sheffield: Federation of Community Work Training Groups.

Fielding, N., Kemp, C. and Norris, C. (1989) 'Constraints on the Practice of Community Policing' in Morgan, R. and Smith, D. J. (eds) *Coming to Terms with Policing: Perspectives on Policy* London: Routledge.

Findlay, J., Bright, J. and Gill, K. (1990) *Youth Crime Prevention: A Handbook of Good Practice* Swindon: Crime Concern.

Finnegan, G. (1985) *Marketing For Coops: A Practical Guide* London: ICOM Co-Publications.

Franklin, A. and Franklin, B. (1990) 'Age and Power' in Jeffs, T. and Smith, M. (eds) *Young People, Inequality and Youth Work* London: MacMillan, pp. 1–27.

Freeman, J. (1972) 'The Tyranny of Structurelessness' *Berkeley Journal of Sociology*, 17, pp. 151–64.

Galbraith, J. (1958) *The Affluent Society* Houghton Mifflin.

Gans, H. (1990) 'Deconstructing the Underclass: The Term's Dangers as A Planning Concept' *Journal of the American Planning Association*, summer 1990.

Gibson, T. (1986) *Us Plus Them* Town and Country Planning Association.

Glen, A. (1993) *Survey of Community Practitioners in Bradford* Bradford: Bradford and Ilkley Community College.

Goetschius, G. (1969) *Working with Community Groups* London: RKP.

Goetschius, G. and Tash, J. (1967) *Working with Unattached Youth* London: RKP.

Goldthorpe, J., Lockwood, D., Bechhofer, F. and Platt, J. (1968) *The Affluent Worker* Cambridge: CUP.

Goodman, P. (1972) *After the Planners* London: Penguin.

Gordon, L. (1991) 'On Difference' *Genders*, 10: 91.

Gordon, P. (1984) 'Community Policing: Towards the Local Police State', *Critical Social Policy*, no. 10, summer.

Gordon, S. (no date) *Balancing Acts* Leicester: NYB.

Griffiths, Sir R. (1988) *Community Care: Agenda for Action* London: HMSO.

Gurhah, A. (1984) 'The Politics of Racism Awareness Training' *Critical Social Policy*, 11, winter, pp. 6–20.

Gutch, R., Kunz, C. and Spencer, K. (1990) *Partners or Agents?* London: NCVO.

Gyford, J. (1985) *The Politics of Local Socialism* London: George Allen and Unwin.

Gyford, J. (1991) *Citizens, Consumers and Councils* Basingstoke: Macmillan.

Hain, P. (1975) *Radical Regeneration* London: Quartet.

Hall, S. and Jacques, M. (eds) (1989) *New Times* London: Lawrence and Wishart.

Hambleton, R. and Hoggett, P. (1990) 'Beyond Excellence: Quality Local Government in the 1990s' *Local Government Studies*, vol. 16, no. 2.

Harding, A. (1992) 'Urban Economic Development Programmes Under the Thatcher Governments 1979–87: An Analysis of Public Policy Making DPhil. (Oxon) thesis in politics, Oxford: Nuffield College.

Hashagen, S. (1991) *Sustainable Communities: the Community Development Approach and Environmental Issues* Edinburgh: SCVO.

Hausner, V. and Associates (1992) *City Challenge: Working Partnerships* advisory note for the Department of the Environment, London: HMSO, February.

Hayek, F. A. (1960) *The Constitution of Liberty* London: Routledge and Kegan Paul.

Heathfield, M. (1988) 'The Youth Work Response to Lesbian and Gay Youth' *Youth and Policy*, 23, pp. 16–21.

Heginbotham, C. (1990) *Return to Community: the Voluntary Ethic and Community Care* London: Bedford Square Press.

Heller, A. and Fehrer, F. (1988) *The Post-Modern Political Condition* Cambridge: Polity Press.

Henderson, P. and del Tufo, S. (1991) *Community Work and the Probation Service* London: HMSO.

Henderson, P. and Thomas, D. (1980) *Skills in Neighbourhood Work* London: Allen and Unwin.

Her Majesty's Inspectorate (HMI) (1991) *Youth Work with Young People with Disabilities* London: Department of Education and Science.

Hicks, C. (1987) *Who Cares: Looking After People at Home* London: Virago.

HMSO (1989) *Caring for People, Community Care in the Next Decade and Beyond* Cm 849, London: HMSO.

Hobbs, D. (1992) 'A White Riot or the Sound of breaking Glass? Meadow Well 1991' *Youth and Policy*, 37, pp. 2–3.

Hoggett, P. (1991) 'A New Management in the Public Sector?' *Policy and Politics*, vol. 19, no. 4, pp. 243–56.

Hoggett, P. and Hambleton, R. (1987) *Decentralisation and Democracy* Bristol: School of Advanced Urban Studies.

Home Office (1978) *Circular 211/1978. Juveniles. Cooperation between the Police and Other Agencies* London: Home Office.

Home Office (1982) *Circular 54/1982 Local Consultation Arrangements between the Community and the Police* London: Home Office.

Home Office (1983) *Circular No 114/1983. Manpower, Efficiency and Effectiveness in the Police Service* London: Home Office.

Home Office (1984) *Circular 8/1984. Crime Prevention*, issued jointly with Department of Education and Science, Department of Environment, Department of Health and Social Security and Welsh Office, London: Home Office.

Home Office (1985) *Circular 2/1985 Arrangements for Local Consultation Between the Community and the Police Outside London* London: Home Office.

Home Office (1989) *Circular 62/1989. Police/Community Consultation Arrangements under S.106 of the Police and Criminal Evidence Act 1984: Report of an Internal Home Office Review* London: Home Office.

Home Office (1990) *Partnership in Crime Prevention* London: Home Office.

Home Office (1991) *Safer Communities: the Local Delivery of Crime Prevention through the Partnership Approach* London: Home Office.

Hooks, B. (1991) *Yearning: Race, Gender and Cultural Politics* London: Turnaround.

Hope, P. (1985) *Young People and the Community: a Consultative Paper* Leicester, NYB.

Hull, G. T. et al (eds) (1982) *All the Women are White, All the Blacks are Men, But Some of Us are Brave* New York: Feminist Press.

Hunt Thompson Associates (1992) *Creating the New Heart of Hulme: A Report on the Community Planning Weekend, 19–23 November 1992* London: Hunt Thompson Associates.

Hutchison, R. and Feist, A. (1991) *Amateur Arts in the UK* London: PSI.

Hutchison, R. and Forrester, S. (1987) *Arts Centres in the United Kingdom* London: PSI.

Hutchison-Reis, M. (1989) 'And For Those Of Us Who Are Black?' *Radical Social Work Today* in Langam, M. and Lee, P. (eds) pp. 165–77.

Industrial Common Ownership Movement, *Various Model Rules for Worker Cooperatives, Community Cooperatives, Secondary Co-operatives etc* Leeds: ICOM (Vassalli House, 20 Central Road, Leeds, LS1 6DE).

IUCN (1991) *Caring for the Earth – A Strategy for Sustainable Living* Earthscan Publications Ltd.

Ivory, M. (1992) in *Community Care* 3 December.

Jackson, B. (1968) *Working Class Community* London: Routledge.

Jakubowicz, A. (1988) 'The Celebration of (Moderate) Diversity in a Racist Society: Multiculturalism and Education in Australia' *Discourse*, 8(2), pp. 37–75.

Jeffs, T. (1987) 'Youth and Community Work and the Community School' in Allen, G. et al (eds) *Community Education: An Agenda for Educational Reform* Milton Keynes: Open University Press, pp. 100–22.

Jeffs, T. and Smith, M. (1988) *Welfare and Youth Work Practice* London: MacMillan.

Johns, R. (1992) 'Partnerships: Dancing Together – Or Off On The Wrong Foot?' *New Sector*, no. 4, Leeds: ICOM, Oct/Nov.

Johnston, M. (1984) *The Welfare State in Transition* Brighton: Wheatsheaf Books.

Joint Consultative Committee (1990) *Operational Policing Review* Surbiton: Joint Consultative Committee.

Joint Working Party on the Future of Community Pharmacy (1992) *Pharmaceutical Care: The Future of Community Pharmacy* London: Royal Pharmaceutical Society.

Jones, C. (1983) 'Thatcherism and the Attack on Expectations' *Bulletin of Social Policy*, no. 14, autumn.

Jones, K. (1991) 'The Trouble with Authority' *Differences*, 3, 1, pp. 104–27.

Jordan, B. (1991) 'Competencies and Values' *Social Work Education*, vol. 10, no. 1.

Kelly, O. (1984) *Community Art and the State: Storming the Citadels* London: Comedia.

Kennedy, M., Gaston, M. and Tilly, C. et al (1990) 'Roxbury: Capital Investment or Community Development?' in Davis et al 1990.

Kent-Baguley, P. (1990) 'Sexuality and Youth Work Practice' in Jeffs, T. and Smith, M. (eds) *Young People, Inequality and Youth Work* London: MacMillan, pp. 99–119.

Khan, N. (1976) *The Arts Britain Ignores: the Arts of Ethnic Minorities in Britain* London: CRE.

Khan, U. (1989) 'Neighbourhood Forums: the Islington Experience' *Local Government Policy Making*, vol. 16, no. 2, September.

Killeen, D. (1992) 'Leaving Home: Housing and Income – Social Policy on Leaving Home' in Coleman, J. and Warren-Adamson, C. (eds) *Youth Policy in the 1990s: the Way Forward* London: Routledge, pp. 189–202.

King, A. and Clifford, S. (1987) *Holding Your Ground* (Second Edition) Aldershot: Wildwood House.

Kirk, D., Nelson, S., Sinfield, A. and D. (1991) *Excluding Youth: Poverty Among Young People Living Away from Home* Edinburgh: Bridges Project and Centre for Social Welfare Research.

Kotler, P. (1982) *Marketing for Non-profit Making Organisations* 2nd edition, New Jersey: Prentice Hall.

Kymlicka, W. (1990) *Contemporary Political Philosophy* Oxford: Clarendon Press.

Lacey, F. (1987) 'Youth Workers as Community Workers' in Jeffs, T. and Smith, M. (eds) *Youth Work* London: MacMillan, pp. 38–51.

Land and Urban Analysis Ltd (1990) *Community Businesses: Good Practice Guide* London: HMSO.

Landry, C., Morley, D., Southwood, R. and Wright, P. (1985) *What a Way to Run a Railroad: An Analysis of Radical Failure* London: Comedia.

Langam, M. and Lee, P. (1989) (eds) *Radical Social Work Today* London: Unwin Hyman.

Larkham, P. (1985) *Voluntary Amenity Societies and Conservation Planning* University of Birmingham. Geography Working Paper Series no. 30.

Lawless, P. (1979) *Urban Deprivation and Government Initiative* London: Faber & Faber.

Leadbeater, C. (1989) 'Power to the Person' in Hall, S. and Jacques, M. (eds).

Lee, Julian, 'Age-old Barter Systems Revived' in *The Times* 13 March 1993.

Lee, L. (1989) 'Tensions between Black Women and White Women: a Study' *Affilia*, 4, (2), pp. 31–45.

Leissner, A. (1975) 'Models for Community Workers and Community Youth Workers' *Social Work Today* , vol. 5, no. 22.

LETSLINK (1992) *The Lets Infopack* Warminster: LETSLINK.

Liberal Party (1982) 'Community Government' London: Liberal Party

Lightfoot, J. (1990) *Involving Young People in their Communities* London: Community Development Foundation.

Lilley, R. (1989) 'Gungarakayn Women Speak: Reproduction and the Transformation of Tradition' *Oceania*, 60, 2, December, pp. 81–98.

Loney, M. (1983) *Community against Government* London: Heinemann.

Lorde, A. (1981) 'The Master's Tools Will Never Dismantle the Master's House' in Moraga, C. and Anzaldua, G. (eds), pp. 98–101.

Lovelock, J. (1987) *Gaia* Oxford: Oxford University Press.

Lowe, P. and Goyder, J. (1983) *Environmental Groups in Politics* London: Allen and Unwin.

Mabey, R. (1973) *The Unofficial Countryside* London: Collins.

MacDonald, D. (1980) 'Detached Youth Work in the Late 1960s and the 1970s' in Booton, F. and Dearling, A. (eds) *The 1980s and Beyond* Leicester: NYB.

MacFarlane, R. (1988) *Communities in Business: The Process of Development* Liverpool: CDS Training for Enterprise.

MacFarlane, R. (1991) *Using Local Labour in Urban Regeneration* London: Business in the Community.

MacFarlane, R. and Mabbott, J. (1993) *City Challenge: Involving Local Communities* London: NCVO.

MacLennan, D., Gibb, K. and More, A. (1990) *Paying for Britain's Housing* York: Joseph Rowntree Foundation.

Macpherson, C. B. (1973) *Democratic Theory: Essays in Retrieval* Oxford: Oxford University Press.

Manchester City Council (1991) *Local Labour in Construction: Hulme City Challenge Action Plan* Manchester: Manchester City Council.

Mani, L. (1990) 'Multiple Mediations: Feminist Scholarship in the Age of Multinational Reception' *Feminist Review*, 135, pp. 24–41.

Marks, K. (1977) *Detached Youth Work Practice in the Mid-Seventies* Leicester: NYB.

Matthews, N. (1988) 'Surmounting a Legacy: Explanations of Racial Diversity in a Local Anti Rape Movement' *Gender and Society*, 3, 4, pp. 518–53.

Mayhew, P., Elliott, D. and Dowds, L. (1989) *The 1988 British Crime Survey*. London: HMSO, Home Office Research Study no. 111.

Mayo, M. (1982) 'Community Action Programmes in the Early 1980s. What Future' *Critical Social Policy*, spring.

McEnery, M. (1989) *Bootstrap: Ten Years of Enterprise Initiatives* London: Calouste Gulbenkian Foundation.

McMichael, P., Lynch, B. and Wight, D. (1990) *Building Bridges into Work: the Role of the Community Worker* Harlow: Longman.

McNaught, A. (1987) *Health Action and Ethnic Minorities* London: Bedford Square Press.

McShane, L. (1991) *The Community Support Programme Interim Report* Belfast: NI Voluntary Trust.

McShane, L. (1993) *Community Support: a Pilot Programme* Belfast: NI Voluntary Trust.

Meadows, D. et al (1974) *The Limits to Growth* London: Pan.

Meekosha, H. (Forthcoming) 'Anger and Angst' *Community Development Journal*.

Meekosha, H. and Pettman, J. (1991) 'Beyond Category Politics' *Hecate*, 17, 2, pp. 75–92.

Meekosha, H. et al (1987) *Equal Disappointment Opportunity: a Report to the Department of Community Services on Programs for Immigrants and their Children* Canberra: Department of Community/Services and Health.

Mellor, M., Hannah, J. and Stirling, J. (1988) *Worker Cooperatives in Theory and Practice* Milton Keynes: Open University Press.

Mercer, K. (1990) 'Welcome to the Jungle: Party and Diversity in Post-Modern Politics' in Rutherford, J. (ed) (1990) *Identity: Community, Culture, Difference* London: Lawrence and Wishart.

Miliband, R. (1982) 'A Case of De-subordination' *British Journal of Sociology*, vol. XI, no. 1.

Milson, F. (1974) *An Introduction to Community Work* London: RKP.

Minh-Ha, T. (1989) *Women, Native, Other: Writing, Post Colonialism, and Femininity* Bloomington: Indiana University Press.

Mishra, R. (1984) *The Welfare State in Crisis* Brighton: Wheatsheaf Books.

Mitton, R. and Morrison, E. (1972) *Community Project in Notting Dale* London: Allen Lane.

Moraga, C. and Anzaldua, G. (eds) (1981) *This Bridge Called My Back: Writings by Radical Women of Color* Watertown, Mass: Persephone Press.

Morgan, R. (1990) '"Policing by Consent": Legitimating the Doctrine' in Morgan, R. and Smith, D. J. (eds) *Coming to Terms with Policing: Perspectives on Policy* London: Routledge.

MORI (1987) *Women in London* London: LSPU.

Morris, J. (1991) '"Us and Them?" Feminist Research, Community Care and Disability' *Critical Social Policy*, 11, 3, 33, pp. 22–9.

Morris, J. (1992) *Pride Against Prejudice: Transforming Attitudes to Disability* London: Women's Press.

Morris, P. and Heal, K. (1981) *Crime Control and the Police*. London: HMSO, Home Office Research Study no. 67.

Moseley, M. (1985) *The Waveney Project* University of East Anglia.

Moss Side and Hulme Community Development Trust (1992) 'Mission Statement'.

Mowbray, M. (1984) 'Localism and Austerity – The Community Can Do It' *Journal of Australian Political Economy*, 16, March, pp. 3–14.

Mulgan, G. and Worple, K. (1986) *Saturday Night or Sunday Morning: from Arts to Industry – New Forms of Cultural Policy* London: Comedia.

Mundine, K. (1990) 'Women in this Land for Another 60,000 Years' in the National Women's Conference *Proceedings*, pp. 166–9.

Murgatroyd, N. and Smith, P. (1984) *The Third Sector Economy* Newcastle upon Tyne: Northern Regional Group of Councils for Voluntary Service.

Myerscough, J. (1982) *The Economic Importance of the Arts* London: PSI.

National Advisory Council for the Youth Service (1988a) *Participation, Parts A, B and C* London: Department of Education and Science and Welsh Office.

National Advisory Council for the Youth Service (1988b) *Youth Work in Rural Areas* London: DES and Welsh Office.

National Advisory Council for the Youth Service (1989) *Youth Work with Girls and Young Women* London: Department of Education and Science and Welsh Office.

National Arts and Media Strategy Monitoring Group (1992) *Towards a National Arts and Media Strategy* London: ACGB.

National Black Workers and Trainers (1990) *Conference Report on Core Curriculum for Community and Youth Work and Training from a Black Perspective* London: Goldsmiths College Research Resource Unit.

National Youth Agency (1991) *Towards the Third Ministerial Conference*, papers for the Consultation Seminars, Leicester: NYA.

National Youth Agency (1992a) *Youth Service Funding and Expenditure 1988–92* Leicester: National Youth Agency.

National Youth Agency (1992b) 'A Background to the Delivering Local Youth Services Project' in *National Youth Agency Policy Update*, March.

National Youth Agency (1992c) 'Resource Allocation and Management in the Youth Service' in *National Youth Agency Policy Update*, March.

National Youth Bureau (1983) *Looking Beyond Street Level – Detached Youth Work with Young Women* Leicester: NYB.

National Youth Bureau (1990) *Danger or Opportunity: Towards a Core Curriculum for the Youth Service* Leicester: NYB.

Nature Conservancy Council (1984) *Nature Conservation in Great Britain* London: Nature Conservancy Council.

Nature Conservancy Council (1989) *Partnership Review* Nature Conservancy Council.

Nava, M. (1984) 'Youth Service Provision, Social Order and the Question of Girls' in McRobbie, A. and Nava, M. (eds) *Gender and Generation* Basingstoke: Macmillan.

NCC (1988) *Measuring Up: Performance Indicators in Local Government* London: NCC.

Nelson, A. (1990) 'Equal Opportunities: Dilemmas, Contradictions, White Men and Class' *Critical Social Policy*, 10, 1, pp. 35–42.

Nicholson, L. (ed.) (1990) *Feminism/Post Modernism* New York: Routledge.

Nozick, R. (1974) *Anarchy, State and Utopia* New York: Basic Books.

O'Connor, J. (1976) *The Fiscal Crisis of the State* New York: St Martin's Press.

O'Donoghue, L. (1992) *Reconciliation, Social Justice and the Aboriginal and Torres Strait Islander Commission* Canberra: ATSIC.

O'Halloran, G. and Lisicki, B. (1988) *Segregation is Enforced: Autonomy you Choose* London: Inner London Education Authority.

O'Malley, J. (1977) *The Politics of Community Action* Nottingham: Spokesman.

O'Riordan, T. (1971) *Perspectives on Resource Management* Pion.

O'Riordan, T. (1991) 'The New Environmentalism and Sustainable Development' *The Science of the Total Environment*, 108, pp. 5–15.

O'Riordan, T. et al (1992) *Landscapes for Tomorrow: Interpreting Landscape Futures in the Yorkshire Dales National Parks* Technical Series Yorkshire Dales National Park.

Oakshott, M. (1962) *Rationalism in Politics* London: Methuen.

Office of Multicultural Affairs (1992) 'Managing Cultural Diversity: OMA's Strategy' *Focus: For a Multicultural Australia*, 6, May.

Oster, S. (1990) *Modern Competitive Analysis* New York: Oxford University Press.

Owusu, K. (1986) *The Struggle for Black Arts in Britain* London: Comedia.

Parker, K. (1984) *A Tale of Two Villages* Peak Park Joint Planning Board.

Parmar, P. (1990) 'Black Feminism: The Politics of Articulation' in Rutherford, J. (ed.), pp. 107–26.

Pateman, C. (1970) *Participation and Democratic Theory* Cambridge: Cambridge University Press.

Pearce, D. et al (1989) *Blueprint for a Green Economy* Earthscan Publications Ltd.

Peters, T. and Waterman, R. (1982) *In Search of Excellence* New York: Harper and Row.

Pettman, J. (1992) *Living in the Margins: Racism, Sexism and Feminism in Australia* Sydney: Allen and Unwin.

Phelan, S. (1991) 'Specificity: Beyond Equality and Difference' *Differences*, 3, 1, pp. 128–43.

Pinder, C. (1985) *Community Start Up* National Extension College/National Federation of Community Organisations.

Pitt, J. and Keane, M. (1984) *Community Organising? You've Never Really Tried It!* London: J & P Consultancy.

Pitts, J. (1992) 'Juvenile Justice Policy in England and Wales' in Coleman, J. and Warren-Adamson, C. (eds) *Youth Policy in the 1990s: The Way Forward* London: Routledge, pp. 172–88.

Piven, F. and Cloward, R. (1977) *Poor People's Movements: Why They Succeed, How They Fail*. New York: Pantheon.

Plant, R. (1974) *Community and Ideology* London: Routledge and Kegan Paul.

Popple, K. (1990) 'Youth Work and Race' in Jeffs, T. and Smith, M. (eds) *Young People Inequality and Youth Work* London: Macmillan, pp. 120–53.

Presley, F. (1985) *Women and the Community 1983–4: A Review and Bibliography*. London: CPF.

Prior, D. (1988) *Tactics for Local Environmental Action* TVS Community Unit.

Pusey, M. (1991) *Economic Rationalism in Canberra* Cambridge: Cambridge University Press.

Radford-Hill, S. (1986) 'Considering Feminism as a Model for Social Change' in De Lauretis, T. (ed.), pp. 157–72.

Raskall, P. (1992) 'The Widening Income Gap' *Modern Times*, 9 March.

Rawls, S. J. (1971) *A Theory of Justice* Oxford: Oxford University Press.

Reagon, B. J. (1983) 'Coalition Politics: Turning the Century' in Smith, B. (ed.) *Home Girls: a Black Feminist Anthology* New York: Kitchen Table.

Reid, W. J. (1969) 'Inter-organisational Co-ordination in Social Welfare: A Theoretical Approach to Analysis and Intervention' in Kramer, R. (ed) *Readings in Community Organisation Practice* New Jersey: Prentice Hall.

Reiner, R. (1985) *The Politics of the Police* Brighton: Wheatsheaf.

Reiner, R. (1991) *Chief Constables* Oxford: Oxford University Press.

Rentoul, J. (1990) 'Individualism' in Jowell, R. et al *British Social Attitudes, the Seventh Report*, Aldershot: Gower.

Report of the Committee on Local Authority and Allied Personal Social Services (Chairman Lord Seebohm) (1968) London: HMSO, cmnd. 3703.

Research Surveys of Great Britain (1991) *Report on a Survey of Arts and Cultural Activities in Great Britain* London: ACGB.

Richardson, A. (1984) *Participation* London: Routledge.

Ricketts, E. and Sawhill, I. (1988) 'Defining and Measuring the Underclass' *Journal of Policy Analysis and Management* vol. 7 no. 2.

Rigby, A. (1982) 'Managing Management: The Exploration of the "Nooks and Crannies" of Community Work' *Community Development Journal*, vol. 17, no. 1.

Ristock, J. (1990) 'Canadian Feminist Social Service Collectives' in Albrect, L. and Brewer, R. (eds).

Roberts, H. (1979) *Community Development: Learning and Action* Toronto: University of Toronto Press.

Robinson, F. and Shaw, K. (1991) 'Urban Regeneration and Community Involvement' *Local Economy*, vol. 6, no. 1, May.

Rogers, B. (1991) 'Equality – Now!' *Every Woman*, November, pp. 12–14.

Roome, N. (1986) 'New Directions in Rural Policy, Recent Administrative Changes in Response to Conflict between Rural Policies' *Town Planning Review*, 57, 3, pp. 253–64.

Roome, N. (1988) 'Take Care' *Landscape Design*, 174, pp. 56–8.

Roome, N. (1989) 'Planning for Rural Conservation and Development: Recent Changes in Policy and Future Needs in Planning Practice and Research' *Planning Practice and Research*, 4, 2, pp. 7–12.

Roome, N. (1990a) 'Community Action as a Mechanism for Rural Policy' in Buller, H. and Wright, S. (eds) *Rural Development: Problems and Practices* London: Avebury.

Roome, N. (1990b) *Local Environmental Auditing: a Feasibility Report for the Countryside Commission* Countryside Commission.

Roome, N. (1992) 'Developing Environmental Management Strategies' *Business Strategy and the Environment*, 1, pp. 11–24.

Rothman, J. (1987) 'Three Models of Community Organisation Practice' in Cox, F. M. et al (eds) *Strategies of Community Organisation* 4th edition, Itaska: Peacock.

Rothschild, M. A. (1979) 'White Women Volunteers in the Freedom Summers' *Feminist Studies*, 5, 3.

Rowse, T. (1991) 'ATSIC's Heritage: the Problems of Leadership and Unity in Aboriginal Political Culture' *Current Affairs Bulletin* 67, 8, January, pp. 4–12.

Rubinstein, P. (1993) 'A Common Culture for All – Arts Work with Young People after Willis' *Youth and Policy*, no. 39, December.

Rural Action Unit (1992) *Rural Action* Cirencester: Rural Action Unit.

Rutherford, J. (ed) (1990) *Identity: Community, Culture, Difference* London: Lawrence and Wishart.

Salmon, H. (1991) 'Policy Issues for Community Development in the 1990s' Conference Paper, West Midlands.

Sampson, A. and Farrell, G. (1990) *Victim Support and Crime Prevention in an Inner-city Setting* London: Home Office, Police Research Group, Crime Prevention Unit Series Paper no. 40.

Saulsbury, W. and Bowling, B. (1991) *The Multi-agency Approach in Practice: the North Plaistow Racial Harassment Project* London: Home Office, Research and Planning Unit Paper no. 70.

Sawbridge, M. and Spence, J. (1991) *The Dominance of the Male Agenda* Durham University Department of Adult and Continuing Education Occasional Paper.

Scarman, Lord (1981) *Report of an Inquiry into the Brixton Disorder, 10–12 April 1981* London: HMSO.

Schumacher, E. (1976) *Small is Beautiful* London: Sphere.

Scott, I. (1985) *On the Map: a Review of the Rural Communities Project* Avon Community Council.

Scott, J. (1988) 'Deconstructing Equality – Versus – Difference: Or, The Uses of Post Structuralist Theory for Feminism' *Feminist Studies*, 1, spring, pp. 33–50.

Scott, P. (1991) 'Community Development and HIV' *Community Work*, no. 144, ACW, September.

Scruton, R. (1984) *The Meaning of Conservatism* London: Macmillan.

Seabrook, J. (1984) *The Idea of Neighbourhood: What Local Politics Should Be About* London: Pluto.

Segal, L. (1987) *Is the Future Female?* London: Virago.

Self, P. (1975) *Econocrats and the Policy Process* London: Macmillan.

Shklar, J. (1985) *Men and Citizens* Cambridge: Cambridge University Press.

Simonside Lodge Report (1990) South Shields: unpublished report, 8 November.

Simpson, R. (1981) *Working with Volunteers in the Countryside and Urban Fringe* Peak National Park Study Centre.

Skeffington, A. M. (1969) *People and Planning: Report of the Committee on Public Participation in Planning* London: HMSO.

Skogan, W. G. (1990) *The Police and the Public in England and Wales: A British Crime Survey Report* London: HMSO, Home Office Research Study no. 117.

Smith, A. (1981) *The Ethnic Revival* Cambridge: Cambridge University Press.

Smith, D. (1989) *Taking Shape: Developments in Youth Service Policy and Provision* Leicester: NYB.

Smith, L. (1981) 'A Model for the Development of Public Participation in Local Authority Decision Making' in Smith, L. and Jones, D. (eds) *Deprivation, Participation and Community Action* London: Routledge.

Smith, M. (1988) *Developing Youth Work* Milton Keynes: Open University Press.

Smith, M. (1991) 'Trends in Youth Work Practice' in Smith, M. (ed) *The Challenge for Voluntary Youth Organisations* London: YMCA National College, pp. 13–21.

Social Trends 20 (1990) London: HMSO.

Social Trends 21 (1991) London: HMSO.

Sones, D. (1993) 'A Question of Distribution – Getting Community Arts Out of the Closet' *Mailout: Artswork with People*, April/May.

Spelman, E. (1988) *Inessential Woman* Massachusetts: Beacon.

Spence, J. (1990) 'Youth Work and Gender' in Jeffs, T. and Smith, M. (eds) *Young People, Inequality and Youth Work* London: Macmillan, pp. 69–98.

Standing Conference on Community Development (1991) *SCCD Charter A Working Statement on Community Development* Sheffield: SCCD.

Standing Conference on Crime Prevention (1991) *Safer Communities. The local delivery of Crime Prevention through the Partnership Approach* London: Home Office.

Stevenson, D. (1972) *50 Million Volunteers: a Report on the Role of Voluntary Organisations and Youth in the Environment* London: HMSO.

Stewart, J. (1983) *Local Government: The Conditions of Local Choice* London: George Allen and Unwin.

Stoker, G. (1989) 'Creating a Local Government for a Post-Fordist Society: the Thatcherite Project?' in Stewart, J. and Stoker, G. (eds) *The Future of Local Government* Basingstoke: Macmillan.

Stratta, E. (1990) 'A Lack of Consultation?' *Policing*, 6, 3.

Teasdale, J. and Powell, N. (1987) 'Youth Workers and Juvenile Justice' in Jeffs, T. and Smith, M. (eds) *Youth Work* London: Macmillan, pp. 82–98.

Thomas, A. and Thornley, J. (1989) *Coops to the Rescue* London: ICOM Co-Publications.

Thomas, C. (1992) 'Issues for Aboriginal Women' address to *Rolling Back the Tide* Discussion Forum for Women, Sydney: Glebe. 24 May.

Thomas, D. (1983) *The Making of Community Work* London: Allen and Unwin.

Thompson Report (1982) *Experience and Participation: Report of the Review Group on the Youth Service in England* London: HMSO.

Thornley, J. (1981) *Workers' Cooperatives: Jobs and Dreams* London: Heinemann.

Titmuss, R. (1968) *Commitment to Welfare* London: Allen and Unwin.

Ungerson, C. (1992) 'Caring and Citizenship: a Complex Relationship', in Bornat, J. et al *Community Care – A Reader* Basingstoke: Macmillan Press.

Vickers, G. (1971) *Freedom in a Rocking Boat* London: Penguin.

Waddington, P. (1979) 'Looking Ahead – Community Work into the 1980s' *Community Development Journal*, vol. 14, no. 3.

Walker, A. (1982) *Community Care* Oxford: Basil Blackwell.

Warburton, D. et al (1988) *Making Community Action Work in the Environment* Losehill Hall/Shell.

Ward, D. and Mullender, A. (1991) 'Empowerment and Oppression: An Indissoluble Pairing for Contemporary Social Work' *Critical Social Policy*, 32, 11: 2, pp. 21–30.

Warren, A. and Goldsmith, F. (1983) *Conservation in Perspective* London: John Wiley.

Watney, S. (1990) 'Practices of Freedom: "Citizenship" and the Politics of Identity in the Age of AIDS' in Rutherford, J. (ed.).

Weatheritt, M. (1987) 'Community Policing' in Willmott, P. (ed.) *Policing and the Community* London: Policy Studies Institute.

Webb, A. and Wistow, G. (1982) *Whither State Welfare?* London: Royal Institute of Public Administration.

Wheelright, T. (1990) 'Are the Rich Getting Richer and the Poor Poorer? If So, Why?' in Gollan, A. (ed.) *Questions for the Nineties* Sydney: Left Book Club.

Williams, F. (1989) *Social Policy: A Critical Introduction* Cambridge: Cambridge University Press.

Williams, L. (1989) 'Black Youth Clubs and Black Workers' in Carter, P. et al (eds) *Social Work and Social Welfare Yearbook* Milton Keynes: Open University Press, pp. 129–42.

Willmott, P. (1989) *Community Initiatives, Patterns and Prospects* London: Policy Studies Institute.

Wilson, D. (1984) *Pressure: The A–Z of Campaigning* London: Heinemann.

Woolf, H. and Tumim, S. (1991) *Prison Disturbances April 1991* Cm 1456, London: HMSO.

'Work with Young Lesbians' (1992) *Leaving Home Newsletter*, no. 3, p. 5.

Wright, S. (1990) 'Theory and Community Development Practice' in Buller, H. and Wright, S. (eds) *Rural Development: Problems and Practices* Avebury.

WWFUK et al (1984) *The Conservation and Development Programme for the UK* London: Kogan Page.

Yeatman, A. (1990) *Bureaucrats, Technocrats, Femocrats* Sydney: Allen and Unwin.

Young, M. and Wilmott, P. (1957) *Family and Kinship in East London*. London: Routledge and Kegan Paul.

Yusuf, P. and Kettleborough, H. (1990) 'Starting to Give Black Women a Voice in Council Services' *CDJ*, vol. 25, no. 2.

Zavella, P. (1991) 'Reflections on Diversity among Chicanas' *Frontiers: A Journal of Women's Studies*, XII, 2, pp. 73–85.

Index